Praise for *The Scattered Tribe*

"Ben Frank's guides transcend the genre of travel books that crowd bookcases with facts and figures . . . his books have emerged as deep insights into places, cultures, histories through the voices of those who live there—stewards of tradition, caretakers of the present and the future. His interviews weave Jewish communities—who share concerns and joys common to many of us into the global community thus shrinking the distance among all travelers . . ."

> —Maria Lisella, author of *Amore on Hope Street* and *Two Naked Feet,*
> contributor to FOXNews.com and other travel outlets

"Ben Frank provides a fascinating, varied account of modern Jewish life across the globe. I learned something new on every page, and enjoyed the book immensely."

> —Martin Fletcher, former NBC News Middle East correspondent
> and Tel Aviv Bureau chief, is the author of *Walking Israel:*
> *A Personal Search for the Soul of a Nation, Breaking News,* and *The List.*

"Whenever Ben Frank writes a new book on the pulsating and multi-dimensional Jewish world, it's cause for celebration. *The Scattered Tribe* proves the point yet again. Bravo!"

> —David Harris, Executive Director of the American Jewish Committee

"A fascinating ode to a resilient people. Ben Frank reveals the road less traveled, following members of "the tribe" who have made lives for themselves in some of the most surprising and far-flung places around the globe."

> —Pat Farnack, WCBS Radio

SCATTERED

TRIBE

Traveling the Diaspora from Cuba to India to Tahiti & Beyond

BEN G. FRANK

Guilford, Connecticut

Text design by Sheryl P. Kober

All photos courtesy of Ben G. Frank and Riva Frank unless otherwise noted.

Library of Congress Cataloging-in-Publication Data

Frank, Ben G.
  The scattered tribe : traveling the Diaspora from Cuba to India to Tahiti & beyond / Ben G. Frank.
     p. cm.
  Includes index.
  ISBN 978-0-7627-7033-5
  1. Jewish diaspora—Miscellanea. 2. Frank, Ben G.—Travel. 3. Jews—Travel—Guidebooks. 4. Tourism—Religious aspects—Judaism. I. Title.
  DS134.F73 2012
  305.892'4—dc23

                                    2011028780

Printed in the United States of America

10 9 8 7 6 5 4 3 2 1

To my lovely wife Riva

And to our children and grandchildren

Contents

CONTENTS

THE WISE JEWISH TRAVELER

It was the Biblical Abraham, the ancestor of the Jewish people, who set a precedent and pattern for his descendants as the first monotheist to believe in one universal God. Abraham understood that he could travel anywhere, for his God would always be with him. Those who believed in local gods feared to travel outside the jurisdiction of those deities. Hence, Jews, the descendants of Abraham, became great travelers.

Travel books make for great reading, and there are wonderful collections of pioneering Jewish travelers' tales in both Hebrew and English. The wise Jewish traveler was indeed universal in outlook, and accurately reported in detail about the particular region visited, adding descriptions of Jewish sites, Jewish community, and the Jewish situation in that area.

Among Jewish travelers, we may include those who collected funds for Jewish schools and the Jewish poor living in the homeland, Israel, along with those who sailed as far away as Australia, leaving behind valuable diaries.

Sir Marc Aurel Stein pioneered the exploration, history and archaeology of the Silk Road in the 1900s and found the oldest Hebrew manuscript on paper in Dandan-Uiliq, near the Chinese-Tibetan border. He wrote many precious volumes that continue to inspire readers.

Benjamin of Tudela, who lived in the twelfth century, is perhaps the most famous and best-known among the Jewish travelers and even today is widely read and quoted.

Sir Matthew Nathan, distinguished Jewish governor of Hong Kong during the early 1900s, delivered a magnificent lecture on the history of Jewish travel. Elkan Nathan Adler (1861–1946) collected many diaries and reports which were published under the title, *Jewish Travellers*. Pedro Teixeira, a *marrano* (secret Jew), was the first to circumnavigate the globe, and left us a valuable record of his journey. He returned to his ancestral faith when he finally reached safety.

Another probable *marrano* was Fernão Mendes Pinto, the first to describe the unique ceremonies of Japan in the 1500s. We even have the fascinating and magnificent diary of Jacob d'Ancona, who visited China before Marco Polo, but alas, it is a forgery. And recently, Raphael Patai published a most informative and enlightening book called *The Children of Noah: Jewish Seafaring in Ancient Times.*

We must now add the current volume, *The Scattered Tribe: Traveling the Diaspora from Cuba to India to Tahiti & Beyond,* to the impressive list of Jewish travelers' accounts.

The reader will be fascinated by reports of a Yiddish-speaking Jewish region of Siberia, where the sign at the Trans-Siberian Railway station is written in Yiddish, and even today, all signs on government buildings are in Yiddish. Who would believe there was a Jewish king of a principality in India where the original copper plates, etched in Tamil, can still be found in a historic synagogue? And who could imagine that Jews lived in the interior of India—without contact with other Jews—for about two thousand years, and survived successfully?

We all owe a great debt to Ben G. Frank for adding the Eastern world to our Jewish itinerary and agenda. He walks in the footsteps of the many great Jewish travelers before him, recording his travels with a keen eye and an inquisitive mind. Each country, city, and community he describes will open your eyes to the previously unknown Jewish experience in the Eastern world.

Your mind and your eye will enjoy reading this volume!

Rabbi Marvin Tokayer
Great Neck, New York
July 2011

Acknowledgments

In every journey, no matter how curious and how adventurous journalists or travel writers might be, they need a road map, a signpost, good guides as well as people on the ground who are knowledgeable, trustworthy and informative. I have had those kind, patient and helpful souls.

Five dear friends and colleagues, make up the core of my experts for *The Scattered Tribe: Traveling the Diaspora from Cuba to India to Tahiti & Beyond,* who advised, consented, and were not afraid to criticize and get me back on the path when I willingly or innocently strayed off course. Rabbi Marvin Tokayer, scholar, author of *The Fugu Plan: The Untold Story of the Japanese and the Jews During World War Two,* and former Rabbi of the Jewish Community of Japan who advised me on India, Vietnam and Myanmar; Robert Leiter, literary editor of the *Jewish Exponent,* Philadelphia; Raphael Rothstein, National Public Relations Director of Israel Bonds; Amir Shaviv, JDC's assistant executive vice president for special operations; and Ruth Rich, travel consultant, New York City.

I also was able to move freely about the countries of the diaspora and interview many informative, knowledgeable men and women in each nation because of the following people, both in the U.S. and abroad, who helped me paint an accurate portrait of these exotic Jewish communities.

Russia, including **Siberia:** Shauli Dritter, JDC Director of Field Operations, Jerusalem, Israel, and his wonderful, dedicated staff in St. Petersburg, Moscow, Odessa, Irkutsk, Birobidzhan and Vladivostok; Amos Lev-Ran, JDC regional specialist for the Former Soviet Union; Dr. Sam Kliger, Director, Russian Affairs, The American Jewish Committee: Scott Richman, Regional Director, American Jewish Committee, Westchester County, NY; and Alla Markova, representative of Zekher Avoteinu, Jewish Tourist Agency.

Tahiti: Dr. Yonah Poul, Dr. and Mrs. Joseph Sebbag, of Papeete, Tahiti, French Polynesia.

Vietnam: Michael Kong, director of Lotus Tours, New York City, Nguyen Trung Thanh, (Thanh) travel executive and guide of Far East Tourist Company, Ltd., Ho Chi Minh City, Vietnam; Cathay Pacific Airways.

Myanmar: Sammy Samuels, and his father, Moses Samuels, of Myanmar Shalom Travels & Tours Co. Ltd, Yangon, Myanmar and New York City; Michael Kong, director of Lotus Tours, New York City.

India: Antony Korenstein, JDC Country Director; Elijah Jacob, JDC Country Manager, Ezekiel Malekar, honorary secretary of Judah Hyam Synagogue, Delhi; Norman Elijah, president of the Reform Jewish Movement in India, known as the JRU, of Mumbai; P. Gopal, guide, Kochi, India; Narendra Kothiyal of India Tourism, New York.

Morocco: Serge Berdugo, ambassador at large to the Kingdom of Morocco, general secretary of the Council of Jewish Communities of Morocco, and his assistant Leah Benhamou; Jacky Kadoch, president of The Jewish community of Marrakech and Essaouira; and Heritage Tours Private Travel, New York City.

Cuba: Dr. William Recant, JDC's assistant executive vice president and Julian Voloj, JDC's regional specialist for Europe and Latin America; Rabbi Shmuel Szteinhendler of Santiago, Chile; and Ellen Lavin, Esq., Sunny Isles Beach, FL.

Israel: Rabbi Jonathan D. Porath, author, lecturer, former JDC executive in Russia, now of Jerusalem, Israel; Kalman Goldner, tourist guide, Givatayim, Israel; El Al Israel Airlines.

With great fear of omitting some of the numerous people who helped me along the way, I should like especially to mention Allan "Geli" Gelfond, Regional Director, American Technion Society, of Farmington Hills, MI; Marcia Smithen Cohen, Esq., Jerry Goodman, founding executive director of the National Conference on Soviet Jewry, of New York City; Steve Lipman, staff writer at *The Jewish Week,* New York City; and Mauricio Escobar, computer specialist.

This book would not have been possible except for my wonderful and very competent editor, Amy Lyons, Editorial Director, Travel, of Globe Pequot Press who from the very beginning believed in this project. Thank you also to Project Editor, Tracee Williams, who skillfully shepherded the production of *The Scattered Tribe* to fruition.

Of considerable assistance to me was the information and articles I wrote previously for the following publications, excerpts of which are included in this book, *Hadassah Magazine, Reform Judaism Magazine, Jewish*

Exponent, and *Inside Magazine* Philadelphia, PA; *Jewish Forward,* New York City, *Jewish Frontier, Jewish Advocate,* Boston, MA; Jewish Telegraphic Agency; and *Inside Chappaqua Magazine,* NY.

Last, first and always, my lovely wife, Riva, who took many of the photos for *The Scattered Tribe,* an indefatigable traveler who kept me going to complete this work and inspired me when I faltered; as well as all my family, Martin, Jodi, Randy and Julia; and Monte, Leah, Rebecca and Sarah who were always in my thoughts whether I found myself in Cuba, India, Tahiti and beyond.

Introduction

The *madrileños* may have been taking their *paseo* on the wide boulevard in Madrid as I hurried to the synagogue and community center back in the 1960s, but I had no time to dillydally if I wanted to be punctual for my meeting with Jewish community leaders. So, when I arrived, I bounded up the steps to the second-floor office. I was convinced that the dreaded *Guardia Civil* (the Spanish *gendarmerie,* in their *tricorne* hats and dark uniforms) I had just passed on the street below were nipping at my heels. In the Spanish dictatorship of the 1960s, you never knew who might be following you.

I entered. I was shocked. Staring at me was the picture of the brutal dictator, Generalissimo Francisco Franco. Certainly not what I had expected, even if he was known to have saved Jewish lives during the Holocaust, when nonbelligerent Spain—closely tied to Nazi Germany—had allowed thousands of Jews to cross their border and receive safe passage. The fascist leader, whatever his motives, was certainly no hero to Jews and men and women of goodwill. So, their putting up the photo did not make any sense to me, for I never saw his picture anywhere else I went. Yet, maybe the community felt "obligated" to display the dictator's portrait.

After Franco's death, a free life began for all Spaniards, including Jews.

Years later, this experience in Spain made me wonder what surprises might await me in far more distant lands in the pages of *The Scattered Tribe: Traveling the Diaspora from Cuba to India to Tahiti & Beyond*. Travel is full of contradictions and unusual experiences, and my journey to find the scattered tribe would be filled with such incongruities, according to my world view.

There was the time north of Moscow, in the dead of winter, when our nature-loving guide unexpectedly roused us from a late-evening party in the hotel lobby. A few shots of vodka had not alleviated the cold, but in Russia, the guides rule. I soon found myself hiking down a riverbank, crossing a frozen river, and finally climbing up the bank on the other side. The guide led his charges to a small service being held in a Russian Orthodox Church, where a young priest and a group of worshippers were chanting somber prayers. In that one winter's moment, I entered the soul of Russia. I realized this was the environment that had surrounded Jewish people here for centuries.

Or take the time in 2009 that I was in Rangoon (now called Yangon) in Burma (now called Myanmar), where eight Jews resided, and where the synagogue was open. I sat in a restaurant in Yangon, gazing out at the alluring golden beams from the shimmering bells of the Sule and Shwedagon pagodas, which constantly reminded me I was touring a mystifying land. At that moment I noticed a table in the corner of the room around which sat six middle-aged Burmese women. They were charming and rather attractive, like "The Lady," Aung San Suu Kyi, the pro-democracy leader who was placed under house arrest twenty years ago, and released in 2010. Each woman was chewing a wad of betel in her mouth. Betel chewing originated in India, and this addictive habit stands out as the Asian parallel to tobacco chewing. This accounts for their teeth being purple, and yellow, too—that is, whatever teeth they have remaining.

Russian, Tahitian, Burmese, Indian, Moroccan, and Cuban Jews, and yes, even those who live in distant Siberia, as well as those American Jewish expats currently residing in Vietnam—they all maintain their Jewish identity.

We travel to observe, to experience, to have adventures. Many Jewish travelers seek out their brothers and sisters in far-flung Jewish communities, or comb far-off lands in search of the last fragments of the scattered tribe. It is a fine tradition that extends back to Spanish Jew Benjamin ben Jonah of Tudela, the twelfth-century rabbi who traveled the then-known Jewish world and recorded what he saw: how Jews lived and got along with their neighbors and rulers; how they survived under oppressive conditions; and how they were influenced by their environment. He also included strange tales, such as when he was in Istanbul, "where no Jew [was] allowed to ride on horseback."

Today, in the twenty-first century, little-known Jewish enclaves in the most unusual places call out to the traveler, who will discover them here in *The Scattered Tribe*. Jewish life exists in these exotic lands which today are popular tourist destinations. Across the vast expanse of Russia, for instance, Jews once again are working, studying, and leading Jewish lives. On the island of Tahiti, the synagogue known as Ahava v'Ahava *(Love and Friendship)* is maintained by about 250 Jews, most of them from France, but originally from Algeria in the Maghreb, with its *casbahs* and *mellahs,* whose history remains part of the Jewish mosaic of North Africa.

Included in this book are chapters on Russia, Siberia, Tahiti, Vietnam, Burma, India, Morocco, Cuba, and Israel. These nations contain ghosts of the past and pioneers of the present. Some are new, some ancient; they are all waiting for visitors to inhale their wonders, although globalization and tourism may soon crowd them. Each has a rich history filled with the contributions the Jewish community has made to their lands.

The countries in *The Scattered Tribe* are a proud part of the Jewish diaspora, while Israel remains the eternal homeland of the Jewish people. In Israel, one may meet newfound friends from Russia, Morocco, and India (just to mention a few) who have come home as part of the "Ingathering of the Exiles." Many of these Jews talk about their two lives—the former in the diaspora, and the present in Zion Restored. The Bene Israel of India who came from Maharashtra state where Mumbai is located, even though they now speak Hebrew, felt a need also to revive and communicate in Marathi, the language spoken in Maharashtra.

Nations and people may change, but the Jewish people live on. A common bond of faith, tradition and unity bind them into one people. Beauty and spirituality remain in the monuments and houses of worship located throughout this ever-shrinking globe. They influence us. Travel is knowledge, discovery, and enlightenment; the more we explore our world, the more we realize how much there is still to learn.

The scattered tribe awaits you!

Ben G. Frank
October 2011
Palm Beach County, Florida

Russia is in My Blood

Walking with Ghosts in St. Petersburg, Moscow, and Odessa

> *"Wretched and abundant,*
> *Oppressed and powerful,*
> *Weak and mighty,*
> *Mother Russia!"*
> —*Nikolai Nekrasov,* Who Is Happy in Russia?

Russia is in my blood, and its ghosts have haunted me for decades.

Somewhere in Odessa by the Black Sea, my mother, Sonya, went to a Russian school and learned folk songs from her father, a cantor in that port city until he left for America to make money and bring over the rest of the family. She taught me her songs.

Somewhere in that frozen land, I have a dead uncle who disappeared in the abyss of the 1917 Russian Revolution. He ran away and joined the army. He never came back.

Somewhere along the 6,000-mile Trans-Siberian Railway, my Aunt Clara—traveling alone at the age of seventeen through the total chaos and death of the 1917 revolution—fled eastward across *taiga* and *tundra* to reach Manchuria and Japan. She then sailed the Pacific for America to find her father, my grandfather.

Russia is in my blood. I have often awoken to the thought that one day I would go there, despite the fact that I knew the czars, including Stalin, did bad things to good people. I learned three key words growing up: *pogrom, gulag,* and *KGB. I* met, talked to, and socialized with Russian Jews, but always outside the Soviet Union. Although I worked during the Cold

War for Radio Liberty, which broadcasts to Russia, I never chanced a visit there for fear of being picked up by the police. I knew that if I contacted Soviet Jews within the border, as certainly I would and must to travel there, I might endanger them, too.

Years passed. Nobody ever dreamed that the "Communist god" would fail. Nobody, that is, but the ghosts. At a séance in Moscow in the 1980s, it is said that a group of young people sat around a table and in the eerie quiet of the room asked: "Will this regime ever end?" When the ghost answered "Yes," the whole room erupted in laughter. *Must be a joke,* they thought.

Wrong!

In 1991, the Great Soviet Socialist Revolution and its child, the USSR, imploded. In 1994, I finally had the long-awaited opportunity to see for myself the nation that had so infatuated me and filled me with both love and hate.

So, sixty years after my mother had taught me those Russian folk songs, fifty years after celebrating the defeat of the Germans and Japanese in World War II, forty years after the height of the saber-rattling Cold War, thirty years after participating in the Struggle for Soviet Jewry, twenty years after the wars in Vietnam, and ten years after watching from afar Gorbachev's *glasnost and perestroika,* I, Ben G. Frank, for the first time, touched down on Russian soil. Bolshevik Russia had self-destructed. I, along with other former "Soviet" Jews, now had nothing to fear.

I was off to St. Petersburg, mother of two Russian revolutions in 1917; the city on the Neva, the Venice of the North, the city that changes its name as the political winds blow—from St. Petersburg to Petrograd, to Leningrad and from Leningrad to St. Petersburg once again.

Not many cities can claim the titles of "beautiful" or "architectural gem," but St. Petersburg, with its sweep and artistry, can. The city's palaces and buildings exude "an almost mystical enchantment," especially during the white nights of early summer, "which change the classical architecture into an atmosphere of fantasy." Perhaps that's why Nicholas I, a cruel czar, noted correctly, "Petersburg is Russian, but it is not Russia." Wherever I went, the greats of the Russian arts were with me: Pushkin, Chekhov, Babel, Bely,

Brodsky, Dostoevsky, Gogol, Tolstoy, Chagall, Prokofiev, Shostakovich, Mussorgsky, Tchaikovsky, Glinka, Nijinsky, Nureyev, Baryshnikov, and Pavlova.

I walked the streets that Anna Karenina and her lover, Vronsky, must have traversed in their *droshky;* I searched for Raskolnikov of the famous nineteenth-century novel, *Crime and Punishment,* near author Dostoevsky's home, which is now a museum at 5/2 Kuznechny Pereulok. I gazed at the Winter Palace and climbed the steps that the Bolsheviks charged up at 2:00 a.m. in their coup of October 26–27, 1917, which hijacked the Revolution and overthrew the provisional government established after the first Russian Revolution that February of 1917. I relived history, including the city's very beginnings.

By choosing the mouth of the Neva River for his new capital in 1703, Peter the Great built his "window to the West," and, explains Nicholas V. Riasanovsky in his *A History of Russia,* "brought Russia forcefully into the community of European nations as a major power." Most Russians never looked back.

That day, standing alongside one of the most outstanding monuments in the world, the huge equestrian statue of Peter the Great, *The Bronze Horseman,* in Decembrists' Square, St. Petersburg, I was overwhelmed. Aleksandr Pushkin, father of Russian literature and modern Russian literary language, came to mind. From his poem of the same name as the statue:

> *By nature we are fated*
> *To cut a window through to Europe,*
> *To stand with a firm foothold on the sea.*
> *Ships of every flag, on waves unknown*
> *To them, will come to visit us, and we*
> *Shall revel in the open sea.*

Peter the Great has come under scrutiny recently. According to historians, he may not have been such a great leader, after all. As I stood next to the massive and magnificent statue, I remembered reading that while he has been revered and eulogized, and was certainly responsible for great reforms, he was also challenging, demanding, deliberately outrageous, and full of contradictions.

His idea of establishing a new city—the future capital of the Russian empire, St. Petersburg—appeared to be the whim of an incredibly rich, reckless, and lucky gambler. "Peter wanted to astonish Russia and the entire civilized world, and he succeeded," writes Solomon Volkov in *St. Petersburg: A Cultural History.*

I felt dwarfed standing next to this very impressive monument, commissioned by Catherine the Great and created by French sculptor Étienne-Maurice Falconet. A brief inscription was all that was needed: PETER THE FIRST, CATHERINE THE SECOND. The huge granite block that forms the pedestal is in the shape of a cliff, 46 feet long, 19.5 feet wide, and 16.6 feet tall. The statue itself is about 25 feet high, and portrays Peter the Great sitting heroically on the horse, his outstretched arm pointing toward the Neva River in the west. Peter's mount is trampling a snake which represents treason.

While there may be debate about the philosophical symbols of the statue, the conflict between czar and citizen, or empire and informed individual certainly remains a key theme in the poem and, indeed, in Russian history. But the young wedding couple I saw posing before *The Bronze Horseman* didn't seem to be overly concerned about it.

I would meet up with Pushkin again when I visited Odessa. Meanwhile, I continued pounding the pavement of the famous Boulevard Nevsky, agreeing with Nikolai Gogol that "there is nothing finer than Nevsky Prospekt; not in St. Petersburg, any rate, for in St. Petersburg, it is everything . . ."

"My, what a town it is! I mean, who on earth dreamed it up?" declared a character in Dostoevsky's *Crime and Punishment.* He raved about the theater, the fun, the plays, and the concerts. The merriment would have to be postponed for me, however—at least during that first visit to Russia in the 1990s. I wanted to find my people, so I made my way to the American Jewish Joint Distribution Committee (JDC) Hesed Welfare Center. In those early post-Gorbachev days, the first and largest welfare center in the former Soviet Union was located in a small apartment inside a typical Russian courtyard on Bolshoy Sampsonievsky Avenue.

At Hesed, I attended an educational program for Russian women who in their senior years were once again learning a few prayers and how to light the Sabbath candles, rituals which they had forgotten or not known during the Communist era. As often happens in life, you sometimes observe a person whom you mistakenly believe is a former friend, relative, or, even in some cases, a former lover. The woman I spotted that day in the JDC's Hesed reminded me of my maternal grandmother. She had a round face with rouge-powdered cheeks, a long, straight, Semitic nose, and white, braided hair parted in the middle.

My grandmother, whose name in Russia was Zlota Rasputnis, was known as Jennie Winerman in the U.S. She was cut off from her husband (my grandfather, the cantor), for seven years. He made it to Canada just before World War I broke out and took a new family name, Winerman, a name given to him by relatives.

The only problem was that the rest of the family, including my mother, were literally trapped in Odessa for the duration of the war. So during World War I, alone and penniless, my grandmother nurtured five children during the time period that history would record the entire First World War, the Russian revolutions, and the Russian Civil War. Who gave her money? Who supported her? As the only member of my family to visit Odessa, I wondered how, with four daughters and a son, she was able to endure poverty, famine, and brutality.

I imagine it was this fortitude that helped Jennie and her children to survive. Later, when she arrived in Canada in 1921, she was reunited with her husband Gershon. The couple had a son Jack, the author's Uncle Jack, who was born in 1922 in Winnipeg. The next year my grandparents moved to Pittsburgh. Three years later my grandfather died. After his death in 1926, Jennie ran a grocery store in a tough neighborhood in that city's Hill District. She would marry two more times. Her second husband, Joseph Rudolph, ran a bar, aptly called Rudolph's, in East Liverpool, Ohio. Frequent visitors to "Liverpool," as they called it, my cousins and I slept upstairs above the bar in the residential quarters, a sleep often interrupted by jukebox tunes wafting up from below, especially the words to "Beer Barrel Polka." *Roll out the barrel, we'll have a barrel of fun.*

As the years went by, the Winermans would always be happy they underwent a "name change."

In Russia, the family name, Rasputnis, was too close for comfort to the name of the debauched religious charlatan and "mad monk," Grigori

Rasputin (1869–1916), who was a confidant of Tsar Nicholas II and his wife, Tsarina Alexandra, as well as healer to their only son, Tsarevich Alexei, who suffered from hemophilia. Rasputin's undue political influence at court discredited the tsarist government and led to the downfall of the Romanovs.

On my trip, I would discover the mystery of our original family name: The suffix -*nis* (in the name Rasput*nis*) is usually attached to Lithuanian names. This means my grandfather could have hailed from Lithuania and migrated south, first to Zhitomir in the Ukraine—which I know to be true—and then further south to the big city of Odessa.

After the Hesed program, we all enjoyed refreshments together. The message from the women was clear: "If only we had been allowed to practice our religion in peace." I left, looking back at the woman who reminded me so much of my own grandmother.

⌒

Over the years, I always returned to the Nevsky to discover remarkable changes. Subsequent visits revealed that the drab sadness of Old Russia had disappeared; no longer did people wear dull clothes and hover in the shadows of musty, gray buildings.

Today, many Russians even smile. During a summer visit in 2006, when it was extremely hot for this arctic land, women's belly buttons showed, just like their counterparts' on Broadway. Their long-reaching shopping hands fondled blouses and dresses on the racks in the recently opened boutiques of fashionable Italian designers in the Gostiny Dvor department store. Chatting male colleagues walked down the sidewalk with computer notebooks slung over their shoulders. They beamed with pride in their city, which has been given a facelift, with repaved downtown streets and upgraded hotels. Mingling with and watching the under-thirty crowd, I noticed their ears on cell phones, their eyes straight ahead. They seemed to be aware that they had a brighter future, a better life than their parents and grandparents had had—especially since Russia is awash with oil.

After the hammer-and-sickle had slid down the flagpole of the Kremlin in 1991, Judaism fast-forwarded in the new Russia. I wasn't there very long in 1994 before I realized a miracle had occurred here: Despite the loss of two generations, several million Jews had been saved spiritually. A people that had suffered state-sponsored and unofficial anti-Semitism had survived. For those approximate million Jews who remained in Russia and the Ukraine, Jewish life, meager as it was at this point, had entered their lives again. In the words of the chief rabbi of Russia, Berel Lazar, "Nowhere in the world have we ever seen a Jewish community of this size reviving from essentially nothing."

Call it a "Jewish renaissance."

As an aside, the fall of Communism benefited not only the Jewish communities throughout the USSR, but also in one of the Soviet Union's clients, Fidel Castro's Red Cuba, which now, bereft of its benefactor, was forced to open up to the West. This meant that Cuba agreed to allow freedom of religion, which included Cuban Jewry (more on this in chapter 8).

Nearly two decades after Russia awoke from the deep sleep of Communism, I taxied over to YESOD, (the Hebrew word for "foundation"), the St. Petersburg Jewish Community Home. Amazing! This new state-of-the-art, twenty-first-century, four-story, 75,000-square-foot, $11 million building—replete with meeting rooms, offices, classrooms, and a blast-resistant security wall—stands as one of the largest Jewish buildings in the country. What a difference from the crowded quarters of the Hesed Avraham Welfare Center in Bolshoy Sampsonievsky, where, during the terrible economic crisis of the 1990s, Hesed-JDC saved lives with welfare programs, including meals-on-wheels.

Slowly, Russia was developing an emerging middle class, and Jews were part of it. Jewish leaders wanted to offer a comfortable, modern facility, a Jewish Community Center (JCC) that also would involve middle-class Jews. The JDC sponsored and organized the capital for the project, involving partners and foundations who also contributed to the building. The St. Petersburg Jewish Community Home has since won prizes for its architecture, including one from the World Club of Petersburgers, whose award to the JCC cited its "modern architecture in the context of historic city environment."

While there, I observed an Israeli dance class that was joined by visiting American Jews who linked arms and joyfully moved their feet with their fellow participants in an atrium made bright by the summer sun. The ghosts of the past frolicked in the clouds above, while down below humans danced, played, and planned for a future in this remarkable city on the Neva River.

Even the names of post-Communist Jewish institutions carry symbols of the Jewish renaissance. Today, JDC's Hesed-Avraham is housed in YESOD. JDC sponsored EVA (Eve in English; *Hava* in Hebrew for the first woman) serves as a second Hesed. EVA was established in 1989 by Polina Mendelevich who named it after her mother. YESOD also houses the "Granatik (little pomegranate) Kindergarten," as well as Hillel and other groups. The pomegranate is one of the seven species of foods native to Biblical Israel and a key element of the Jewish New Year. Another JCC, "Adain Lo," ("not yet") on Mokhovaya Street serves many active groups in the city. The name, *"Adain Lo,"* has various interpretations. One is that the name is attributed to the early twentieth century German Jewish theologian and philosopher, Franz Rozensweig, and refers to Jews who are in the process of reclaiming and regaining their lost traditions, culture, and knowledge—with the emphasis on "the process." Certainly true of Russian Jewry today.

In 2006, the Chabad–Lubavitch movement renovated a four-story former school building in Vyborgskaya Storona (Novolitovskaya Street, 7a) and opened a community center containing a synagogue, a preschool, and a day school. The JCC located in this Chabad facility conducts language activities and programs, offers computer courses, and hosts a club for Israelis and Hebrew speakers.

Here in St. Petersburg, as we shall see throughout Russia, Chabad pursues its goal of bringing Judaism to Russian Jews. Considered a dynamic force in Jewish life, Chabad defines itself as "a philosophy, a movement, and an organization." It also engages in social, humanitarian, and educational activities. And it is very active in the Former Soviet Union, (FSU), to the extent that it is represented by 350 rabbis in 400 cities and communities and in each there is a *shul* and in many cases a school, according to Rabbi Yaakov Klein of Chabad. The Orthodox organization sponsors a van that circulates throughout this city and Moscow as well. Chabad representatives pass out literature to Jewish men and call on them to put on *tefillin*. At

Hanukkah, Chabad lights a huge menorah in Sennaya Ploshchad in front of the busy shopping mall.

~

St. Petersburg, Europe's third-largest city after Moscow and London, boasted a 2010 population of 4.8 million residents, 100,000 of them Jews. Historically, until the 1917 Russian Revolution, Jews frequently were banned from St. Petersburg. But by 1910, 35,000 Jews resided in the city, where they made up less than 2 percent of the population. According to author Solomon Volkov, many of them were educated, affluent, and influential, including prominent bankers, accomplished musicians, and leading journalists.

The Grand Choral Synagogue, which in 2000 was refurbished and remodeled through the donation of the Safra family, is also known as The Edmond J. Safra Grand Choral Synagogue. This house of worship stands as one of the most beautiful, ornate, and well-preserved synagogues in Europe. Located on Lermontovsky Avenue No. 2, the building seats 1,200 people and features a whitish-blue dome. This is the second-largest synagogue in Europe, after the Dohány Street Synagogue in Budapest. The St. Petersburg structure stands as an eclectic blend of neo-Byzantine and Moorish revival styles with Arabesque motifs. Some observers believe that it is modeled in part after Berlin's Oranienburger Strasse Synagogue.

The recently restored synagogue displays an interior that is a fine example of the Moorish style that can be seen in synagogues across Eastern Europe, with Arabesque moldings and murals, as well as large white columns. A second tier features the women's gallery that surrounds the sanctuary on three sides. The outside of this house of worship is painted with a rust color that blends in with a lighter brown. A tall, thick brown door leads one into the main hall of the building. At the top of the door, a large Magen David is displayed and above that, a spectacular arch, obviously reminding one of Spain.

The Grand Choral Synagogue of St. Petersburg is a registered landmark and an architectural monument cited by the Federal Government. Recently, the Choral Synagogue officially opened a new Sephardic Georgian Synagogue, Ohel Moshe, at Dekabristov Prospekt 42. This new synagogue is located on the grounds of the Choral Synagogue and can be accessed through the courtyard.

Chabad rabbi Menachem Mendel Pewzner, formerly of Crown Heights, Brooklyn, has served as the spiritual leader of Choral Synagogue since 1992, one year after the fall of the Soviet Union. He is proud of the community's achievements, and during my interview with him in 2011, he noted that 1,200 persons had attended various Passover seders that year. Most Russian Jews do not routinely attend religious services, but Rabbi Pewzner told me that attendance at educational and holiday programs, lectures, and gatherings had increased. Chabad now sponsors four schools and four new small synagogues in other sections of St. Petersburg, which are geared to accommodate a *minyan* (a minimum of ten male worshippers required for an Orthodox service). A kosher restaurant on the synagogue premises welcomes tourists to the heart of Jewish religious life in the city.

In a photographic study titled *St. Petersburg,* published in 1994, Rabbi Pewzner told Steven Raymer, author and photographer, "Now that Jews and others can freely worship in Russia, Jews need to learn their history, their language, to be proud of their tradition. . . . It will take time, but my goal is to teach and live an Orthodox life."

Nearly two decades after he arrived in the former Soviet Union, Rabbi Pewzner reaffirmed those words. Many would agree that he is succeeding.

I stared at the words of Olga Berggolts on the wall of the Piskariovskoye Memorial Cemetery in St. Petersburg, words that are now immortal: *No one is forgotten, nothing is forgotten.* It is impossible to visit Russia and not feel the effects of the Great Patriotic War that took place nearly seventy years ago. Even today the bloodletting in that war, as well as the nation's proud victory, brings both sorrow and joy into every Russian's mind and heart.

At times, that war's ghosts descend and hover and haunt this beautiful yet tragic city. Hard to believe that here in Russia's second-largest city, a million people perished during the 900 days of the Siege of Leningrad in World War II, most of them from starvation.

The blockade, a two-and-a-half-year stretch that virtually isolated the city from the rest of the country, was the longest siege a great city had undergone since biblical times. "Woe to those trapped in a city under siege," goes an ancient saying.

I was told about Dora, a blockade survivor, who lived in the city in a sparsely furnished fifth-floor walkup apartment. She was twelve years old when the Germans began the siege on September 8, 1941. "My parents died of starvation," she told me. "My brother was only nineteen, and he went to the front and was killed. I was alone during that first winter of constant bombing and no food."

In July 1942, Dora was housed in a building with other orphans and evacuated during that winter along the famous "Road of Life," a narrow passageway across the frozen Lake Ladoga, which remained unoccupied by the enemy. After the war, Dora returned to Leningrad. With only five years of education, she supported herself by working in manufacturing plants, attending night school and then later, an engineering college. She got married and worked as an engineer, retiring in 1984. Dora and her husband, who died in 1994, did not have any children.

"This is my home," she said, proudly displaying her medals and membership in the organization of Jewish Veterans of World War II and the Blockade. "Where can I go?"

One always meets "ghosts of the past" in Russia. Cruising the Baltic on the cruise ship SS *Voyager* we docked in St. Petersburg. During dinner on the ship, I talked with a young Swedish officer who was the captain of the crew. He told me that if I really wanted to see a Russian skeleton, I would have to look out my cabin's porthole about an hour or so after departing the city.

Coming in view that evening was a battered harbor with rusting ships: the Kronstadt Naval Base, a fortified city, an abandoned base that flowered with huge silent cranes, rusting ship hulks, disheveled strips of armor, unused dry docks, and downed wires. Located on Kotlin Island in the Gulf of Finland, about 20 miles west of St. Petersburg, the port was constructed by Peter the Great, who designed it to protect his new Russian capital on the Neva from an attack from the open sea.

In 1917, Kronstadt was a hotbed of radicalism as tough sailors of the Baltic Fleet helped the Bolsheviks seize power. Sixty thousand sailors formed units of Revolutionary shock troops. Their job: to keep power and spread Soviet domination throughout Russia. They were the "torchbearers of revolutionary militancy."

By 1921, many of these same Kronstadt sailors, the "pride and glory of the Russian Revolution," would rise in revolt against the Bolshevik government which they themselves had helped bring into power. Disillusioned with the Communists, they accused the Red regime of betraying the peasants, and demanded new elections by secret ballot, seeking freedom of speech and the press.

For Lenin and company, the rebels had to be crushed and Bolshevism restored—whatever the cost. The Communist leadership ordered more than 25,000 handpicked troops to cross the ice and quell the Kronstadt Rebellion, which it did in March of 1921 as food, fuel, and ammunition ran out. Thousands on both sides died, but the base survived.

The massacre showed that the Reds would stop at nothing to destroy those who challenged their authority. Following this first revolt against Communism would come the liquidation of the *kulaks,* the suppression of religion, the Great Purge, the Nazi-Soviet pact which helped doom Europe and its Jews, Khrushchev's denunciation of Stalin, the Hungarian Revolution, the Prague Spring—until the mighty Soviet Union crumbled, leaving dead souls behind.

Seventy years later the end came not in St. Petersburg, where it had all started, but in the new capital, Moscow, which would never live up to its promise, according to an old saying, "Come the Revolution we'll all eat strawberries." Like the French Revolution, the Bolsheviks would devour their children.

～

"Don't go to Russia in the summer," a psychiatrist who had traveled the world once advised me. "Go in winter. You'll understand Russia better." I listened, and went in early March 1995, still part of the heartless Russian winter. The doc was right. One evening, a few weeks into my very first trip to the largest country in the world, we found ourselves trekking down the icy embankment of a frozen river and up the bank on the other side. Light, flaky snow began to fall. Our guide took us to a Russian Orthodox Church in Suzdal near Moscow. The service was conducted by a young priest with a salt-and-pepper beard, a thin, dour face, and long, flowing black robes that caressed the stone floor. Two old women, garbed in black, often fell to their knees in prayer as they chanted. The enveloping incense reminded us of the country's mystic and often-Eastern-influenced past. In that one winter moment, I entered the soul of Russia, especially in Moscow where church and state ruled millions for hundreds of years.

According to an old Russian expression, "All things roll down to Moscow." By the time I arrived in this regal capital, I had consumed four decades' worth of reading about the 850-year-old city of czars and Communism.

But unlike the "old days," Moscow today, with its glass high-rises, glitzy shopping malls loaded with designer boutiques, and expensive five-star hotels, is unrecognizable from what it was in the 1990s. Then, it still resembled the dour Cold War–era town of Stalin, Brezhnev, Gorbachev, and company, a city in the 1990s that saw frequent runs on its banks.

My, how things have changed. Today, Moscow, the biggest city in Europe, is all about money. The vast majority of the country's wealth is here, along with almost all of its billionaires, reportedly over fifty of them.

Speaking of money, from 2006 to 2008, Moscow held the title of the "World's Most Expensive City," but by 2011, it dropped off the list of 10 most expensive. Still, it flaunts its wealth with its new high rises, malls, swanky avenues, and the fact that it is the financial center of Russia. Despite the recent recession, unemployment in the city is low.

Though driven by money, Russians still love ballet, opera, theater, and art, along with sporting events and visiting their *dachas*.

It was my first night in Moscow in 1994 and I was on my way to a theater near the Kremlin. As I approached our destination, the vehicle I was riding in was suddenly waved over to the curb by a traffic cop brandishing a baton and wearing a sidearm. Here in the U.S. most of us, swearing under our breath, will roll down the window on the driver's side and ask—politely, of course—why we have been pulled over.

Not my driver. He literally leapt out of the car, stood at attention as if he were in front of a marine drill sergeant, and showed his license. I'd never seen anything like it. Of course, I realized bribing the police was common in Russia and thought this was the reason the officer had stopped us—because he wanted a handout. But it didn't happen this time; the cop just wanted to check our documents. The fear of the State lives on in Russia—perhaps less so in the new Russia, but it's still inbred in a country with a very strong central government.

We were soon on our way again, and as we passed the Kremlin, I couldn't help but reflect on the fact that four decades earlier, Stalin was about to deport Soviet Jews to Siberia. The boxcars, we were told, were already in place at train stations throughout Western Russia.

Ironically, the dictator died in 1953 after suffering a stroke and falling to the floor. None of his comrades dared to pick him up or summon a doctor. They wanted him to perish. It is said that he lingered for five days, silent, but still able to hear.

So I wondered, hypothetically, of course: What if he had fallen during the night of a Jewish concert or Israeli dance festival, routine today in the Russian capital? Jews singing and clapping their hands, and joining in the songs of their people. What would Comrade Stalin have said? No matter; the struggle for Russian Jewry and the Cold War are over. Jews are free at last, I said to myself as I imagined such a concert, just like the one I attended where we all stood and sang *"Hatikvah."*

Or take, for example, the 2010 appearance of the Israeli Army Band, marching in Red Square alongside the Kremlin, the ancient fortress that has been the touchstone of Russian history for more than 400 years. Along with a sense of history, the emotion you feel is unbelievable, especially when you see the huge flag of Israel flying alongside that of the Russian Federation, on a wall directly across from the Kremlin viewing stand. Imagine, again, Stalin standing on the platform and taking a salute from the young Jewish men and women in the Israeli Army Band. Another exciting moment to imagine indeed.

Speaking of Red Square, our guide said that the bus driver had a treat for us after we'd finished watching an evening of Russian folk dances. It was March, cold, with a full moon in the sky as we drove to Red Square, the number-one tourist site. Every visitor can see why: This is the source of Russian power. The May Day parade; the massive Red Army parades on the anniversary of the Bolshevik Revolution; the podium where the Bolshevik masters waved to the world; Lenin's Mausoleum; St. Basil's Cathedral and its golden-dome complex of buildings. As I walked the cobblestone square that frigid March night, I thought of all that Red might and how it had all crumbled when the USSR legally ceased to exist on December 31, 1991.

My reading stood me in good stead. I knew that here, on November 7, 1941, the anniversary of the Bolshevik Revolution, Stalin had exhorted his troops to save the Motherland. Heavy snowflakes were falling as the troops massed in Red Square, dressed in their battle gear, including fur-lined army hats with the embedded, immortal Red Star. The Germans were at the gates of Moscow, but unlike what had happened in 1812, the city was not to be abandoned. With shouts of *Hurrah!* echoing in Red Square, Soviet troops marched and tanks rolled straight off to the front lines. Once again the Allies waited on the Russians. A relatively unknown general rushed to defend the capital of Mother Russia and led a counteroffensive. Moscow was saved—a major turning point in the war. That general was Marshal Georgi Konstantinovich Zhukov, who became supreme commander of the Soviet armed forces. His statue stands in Manezh Square, near the huge mall and just outside the archway to Red Square.

I stared at the shining Red Star atop the Kremlin. In Communist days it was everywhere. Red was socialist red—the red lapels and banners displayed in the first Revolution and carried over to the Bolshevik coup in 1917. The red star was then sewn on the Communist Red Guard uniforms in time for the bloody Russian Civil War that followed. Even a few years after the downfall of Communism in 1991, the massive red six-pointer remained fastened tightly atop the Kremlin roof, illuminated in the dark night. No budget to remove the Bolshevik icon.

Here, within sight of the huge, rose-colored walls of the Kremlin, we could imagine the hidden mysteries of the building with its Byzantine architecture, its houses, palaces, government offices, churches—an entire inner city.

We tipped the driver for giving us *Podmoskovnye Vechera* ("Moscow nights"), but before we got back on the bus, we glanced again across the square, "to the world's most famous mummy," that of Vladimir Ilyich Uly-anov, whom the world knows by his revolutionary pseudonym, Lenin. His grandfather, incidentally, was Jewish. Vladimir Ilyich lives in Lenin's Tomb, embalmed for everyone to see—a relic, but no longer an icon. People are curious and want to look at a dead man who led an evil revolution.

Russia is great on monuments. Memory must be kept alive for those who remain in power. Others, out of favor, simply evaporate.

I remember driving past an open dirt field in Moscow in 1994 and strewn about like broken pencils tossed on a floor were the huge bronze statues of the former Communist leaders who had oppressed their people and ruined the country. Yakov Sverdlov, Bolshevik leader and chairman of the Russian Communist Party, was one. Today a section of the Fallen Monument Park in Muzeon Park contains statues of other fallen Bolshevik leaders.

~

"You must go out to Poklonnaya Gora, the Memorial Hill Park Complex," said Michael Steiner, then the energetic and charismatic Moscow director of the Joint Distribution Committee. It was a cold November night in Moscow. Outside, the crisp air bit into our faces as we looked up at the falling snow, accompanied by a freezing wind coming off the steppes, heralding the crushing Russian winter. Steiner, an Israeli, took a deep breath and exhaled. "You can almost smell Russian history here," he said, mentioning, for instance, Field Marshal Mikhail Kutuzov, who had defeated Napoleon.

Michael continued to tell me about Poklonnaya Gora, which is dedicated to the Soviet victory in the Great Patriotic War. I had taken his advice and was on my way. Fitting that this huge museum be in Moscow, for here, during the winter of 1941–42, was fought the most important battle of that conflict—a battle that for the first time stopped the then-invincible German army. How close was it? Well, the Germans had reached a point 22 miles from the city, a mere half-hour's drive from the Kremlin. A monument now marks the spot.

To this day, Russians take such great pride in the tremendous effort that went into hurling back the German invaders all the way to Berlin, a city the Soviets leveled to the ground.

About 30 million Russians perished in that conflict. Jews were part of the war effort, though never acknowledged by the Communists. Jewish losses totaled approximately 1.5 million, proportionately four times higher than those of the population as a whole. Two hundred thousand Jews serving in the Soviet military were killed.

At Poklonnaya Gora stand three houses of worship—a Russian Orthodox Church, a mosque, and a synagogue. After the demise of Communism, religion once again came into its own here. On this huge campus stands the Holocaust Memorial Synagogue and Museum, in memory of Jews who perished in 1941–45. This 32,275-square-foot, three-story, pyramidal building was dedicated in 1998, and displays photographs and objects related to the Holocaust.

In the early days of the new Russian Federation, one could certainly see the revival of Jewish life in the capital, Moskva (Moscow), the twelfth-century Byzantine heart of the Russian Empire, the City of the Czars where the gold church spires and onion domes glisten.

The Moscow Choral Synagogue, the oldest Jewish institutional building in Moscow, is located at Spasoglinishchevsky Pereulok (Archipova Street). Considered one of the most beautiful synagogues in the world, it is a monument to Jewish resistance against Communist oppression.

During the early 1970s, thousands of Soviet Jews gathered outside the Moscow Choral Synagogue on High Holidays and Simchat Torah. Natan Sharansky, symbol of Jews' refusal to be denied their religion, first met his wife, Avital, outside the synagogue during a demonstration.

Ah, those demonstrations! As a public relations person, I know demonstrations. Days and nights, winter months and summer months, I helped by alerting the media to cover vigils to "Save Soviet Jewry"; to photograph picket lines around the Russian consulate in New York City; to televise marches past the UN—always uttering the same battle cry as our brothers and sisters in the USSR: "Let my people go!"

Here in the Choral Synagogue, I recalled, history was made. Golda Meir, Israel's prime minister from 1969 to 1974, was appointed Israel's first diplomatic representative to Moscow just after the establishment of Israel in 1948, a post she held until April 1949. Golda (as she was affectionately called) was a native of Kiev who emigrated with her family to the U.S.

when she was eight years old. She arrived at the synagogue on the High Holidays, and thousands of Moscow's Jews came out to greet her. To say that her appearance caused great excitement among Soviet Jews was an understatement. They literally mobbed her.

But already in 1948, the Kremlin, which had recognized the State of Israel, unleashed "nightmarish days filled with fear [that] overtook Soviet Jewry," notes *Encyclopaedia Judaica*. Let us remember the twenty-five leaders of the Jewish Anti-Fascist Committee, including some of the greatest Russian Jewish writers, who were murdered by Stalin. Then the infamous, so-called Doctors' Plot burst upon the scene of Stalin's megalomania against the Jewish people. A group of prominent doctors, the majority of them Jews, were arrested in January 1953, accused of "deliberately killing government leaders." Two months later Stalin died and the doctors were free; however, despite the fact that new leaders took over, Soviet Jews would not be free until 1991.

A few years later in 1994 with my feet firmly planted in the Moscow synagogue, I could hear my people's chant, *Am Yisrael Chai* ("The people of Israel live"), echoing through the building. Jews had survived the tsars, the Cossacks, the Whites, Reds, Stalin, police harassment, purges, and plots. A dream come true.

Stalin is gone and Jews are here, in Moscow, near the Kremlin and beyond. They have repaired their houses of worship, such as the Choral Synagogue, which was founded the same year that the municipality had wanted to expel the Jews, in 1887. In this house of worship, the "choral" part of the synagogue's name refers to the fact that it incorporates several different areas set aside for use by Armenian, Georgian, or Bukharian Jews visiting Moscow. Another explanation for the Moscow synagogue is that the choir that sang in the synagogue was superb. (Finally, for the St. Petersburg congregation one reason given for the name, Choral, is that there are two sections in that Orthodox synagogue, one in the main downstairs prayer hall for male worshippers and an upstairs section for female worshippers.) The exterior of the Choral Synagogue in Moscow features a large silver dome, yellow-and-white walls, and a neoclassic facade. Across the street from the entrance is a modern sculpture centered on a golden hand. In the last few years, the synagogue has been renovated and a magnificent new dome erected.

The *shamash* (sexton) showed me the Torah scrolls, some of which were saved from cities that the Germans occupied. He asked for a donation, and I gladly gave one. We talked about the old days. He reminded me about the spies—Jewish informers who during the Cold War would tell the secret police about Jewish or non-Jewish Westerners who came to this house of prayer, as well as who talked to whom.

As I left this monument to survival, this Choral Synagogue that played such a role in the history of the Jewish people, in this capital of the czars and now in the new Russia, I felt I was missing something. Photos of the time do not do a building justice. So when the *shamash* showed me some paintings on display for purchase, I bought a small one entitled, in Russian, *Moscow Synagogue*. To this day, it stands proudly on my bookcase shelf.

⌒

Before the first Revolution in 1917, most Jews were not permitted to live in Moscow. Today about 200,000 Jews reside in the capital, out of a total population of approximately 10.5 million.

Three million Russian Jews survived World War II. With the fall of Communism, 1 million settled in Israel, a million emigrated to the U.S. and Germany, and approximately a million remain today in the former Soviet Union, 400,000 of which reside in Ukraine.

In 1991, Russian Jews overcame their fear of being Jewish. They had taken an arduous journey through years of being denied basic human and religious rights. The spark that energized them probably occurred just after the 1967 Six-Day War, when the pent-up emotion of this suppressed group erupted into strong Jewish pride and a wish to emigrate to the Jewish homeland. The Kremlin, which did not allow its citizens to leave, turned on the spigot a tiny bit, then shut it down in the 1970s. Then they opened the doors again under Gorbachev in the late 1980s. After the Soviet Union disintegrated, the mass immigration of Jews to Israel began, infusing the young nation with a new energy that would help pole-vault the Jewish state into the twenty-first century.

Today, Russian Jews have options; they can attend events at JCCs, as mentioned above, or belong to synagogues, clubs, and organizations. The buildings are there, and Jewish leaders know they have to be filled. But neither the JDC, Chabad, or The Jewish Agency for Israel—or the Russian Jewish leaders themselves—have an easy task. Eighty percent of Russian Jews are intermarried, and 90 percent of the Jewish population is secular. But unlike those Israelis, who are secular and observe holidays and know what it is to be Jewish, Russian Jews have very little background when it comes to Judaism.

Unlike in the U.S., no real Russian Jewish community, strengthened with federations and community councils, exists. Here people belong and/ or go to JCC, Hesed, Hillel, or Chabad. The challenge remains to work with and educate the young people. According to Shauli Dritter, JDC director of field operations, more and more young people are coming to JCCs. He is very optimistic about the future of Russian Jewish youth regarding Judaism. Approximately eight Jewish schools are located in Moscow, along with five Jewish community centers, five JDC welfare centers, a Sunday school with ten branches, a Hillel student center, and a Jewish cultural center.

I visited Jewish day schools, met with college students, and recorded the rising of new Jewish community and cultural centers. One such place is the Jewish Cultural Center on Bolshaya Nikitskaya Street, established by JDC in downtown Moscow to attract unaffiliated Jews to Jewish life and to act as an incubator for the development of Russian Jewish culture.

The multimillion-dollar, seven-story Marina Roscha Jewish Community Center, with its new large prayer hall, two *mikvehs* (ritual baths), a hall for large gatherings and weddings, a restaurant, an Internet café, two kosher butcher shops, an auditorium, and sports facilities including a gym and training rooms, is a prime example of Chabad initiative, just as is JDC's YESOD building in St. Petersburg. Once, a secret synagogue stood here. The original building, founded in 1926, was an underground synagogue, a symbol of resistance to Soviet repression of Judaism. Located at Marina Roscha JCC is the International Jewish Community of Moscow, headed by Rabbi Yaakov Klein, who has organized a group of expats. The group has a membership of about 300 Americans, British, and other nationalities. They meet at the JDC-sponsored JCC on Bolshaya Nikitskaya Street.

Another active Chabad synagogue is located at Bolshoy Bronnaya Synagogue, Bolshaya Bronnaya Street 6, which maintains a synagogue, a pizza parlor, a butcher shop, and a kindergarten.

In Moscow, Chabad sponsors a religious boys' school, a religious girls' school, a kindergarten, and a local Russian school. The organization supports hundreds of rabbis whose network is spread out through the entire former Soviet Union. Generally, these rabbis stay put in a community as they establish synagogues, yeshivas, schools, and study groups.

Many organizations aid and help Russian Jewry in Moscow and beyond.

The American Jewish Joint Distribution Committee, affectionately called the "Joint," supplies personnel and educational tools, and contributes thousands of dollars to education and welfare needs, not only in Moscow but throughout the former Soviet Union. In Moscow, JDC sponsors several JCCs and establishments of the Hesed Welfare Network, Hillel, young leadership projects, and a school for NGO Management and Leadership in the Jewish community.

The Reform Movement of Judaism started and maintains fledgling congregations in major cities.

The Jewish Agency for Israel provides educational services and Hebrew courses. *Aliyah* (individual or wave of immigration to Israel) is its main goal, and the organization sponsors activities that educate, instruct, and demonstrate to Russian Jews how to live a meaningful life in Israel.

Two decades into the history of post-Communism, it is clear that the image of this vast land as a forbidding and oppressive place for Jews and Jewish life has radically changed.

Some observers opine that the voice of Russian Jewry has yet to speak up as to what their community, its organization, its beliefs, and its educational process, will look like in the future. After all, modern Russian Jewry is only two decades old, and what is twenty years in history—especially in the long history of the Jewish people?

Chabad Chief Rabbi Lazar believes that Russia will eventually be one of the strongest Jewish communities in the world.

While the big cities are historic and touristy, my roots are in the south, so I headed to the birthplace of my "Odessa Mama."

I guess I fell in love with Odessa, especially since I feel at home in cities by the sea. You may love it or dislike it, but no other city in Russia resembles Odessa in the Ukraine.

Isaac Babel, native son and the city's most famous writer, called it "the most charming city of the Russian Empire." He claimed that it is a city in which an individual can "live free and easy," because of the Jews who make up nearly half the population. In Babel's words, the town was "The Star of Exile."

Jews do well in port cities—at least they did in Odessa, where they lived without the constraints and limitations put forth by the anti-Semitic Russian Empire.

And so, to really feel the charm of Odessa, I walked the city and admired the buildings designed in neoclassic architectural style, including the still-standing attractive yellow-and-white local mansions, many of which display a Mediterranean style.

⌒

I began walking in the footsteps of my family. My mother was born in Odessa. One of the few memories that she passed on to me dealt with war, a condition the city has known throughout its existence, including the Russian Civil War. She said that she and her mother and her two sisters, Lillian and Ann, hid in the cellar from the Bolsheviks and ate garlic and onion on black bread during that war, a war which, by the way, saw at least half a dozen different armies occupy the city, including Reds, Whites, Greens, Germans, and the French.

In Odessa, I sought out an archivist to learn more about my maternal grandfather, Gershon. If ever there was a city that could be called a cantor's city, it's Odessa, famous for producing musical geniuses, including cantors who were so outstanding that they sang in the city's famous opera house, with its rounded facade and tall white pillars. I noticed that this building was literally sinking into the earth and had to be propped up. Repairs were being made when I first observed it in 2001.

Like thousands of immigrants, Grandfather made his mark as a cantor in North America, but no mention of my grandfather as a cantor existed in synagogue records, according to the archivist. Maybe Grandfather was just a *baal korei* (a reader) in a small congregation, a prayer house. At one time, there were seventy-eight functioning synagogues in town. Another estimate indicates that in 1900, seven main synagogues and forty prayer houses functioned.

As noted, upon arriving in North America, Grandfather and the family took on the name Winerman, a name given to him by relatives in Canada. I have the honor of carrying one of his names, as do several of my cousins. My middle name is Gerald (*Gershon* in Hebrew).

But who was this man, Gershon Rasputnis Winerman? I never knew him, as he died in his early forties before I was born. Since I never saw him, I could only imagine him and report some of the facts of his life, a life devoted to his family and to music. Arriving in Canada in 1914, he obtained a cantorial position in the growing Jewish community of Winnipeg, Canada. This city in Manitoba does not have the perfect climate, to say the least. Freezing-cold winds and biting snow lash the locals in winter in this city on the prairie, which, as it would turn out, would contain at one time one of the best Jewish communities in North America.

Grandfather obtained a new cantorial position in 1923 in Pittsburgh, Pennsylvania. His business card read: "Rev. G. Winerman, Cantor of Washington Street Synagogue, *Beth Hamedrash Hagadol,* Specialist Mohel [one who performs the ritual of circumcision]. Marriages performed at my residence or anywhere else. 1400 Colwell Street, Apartment 6, Pittsburgh, PA. Phone: Grant 7295-R."

Gershon and Jennie's only male child in Russia was Mischa, who was one year younger than Clara, the oldest. Clara was seventeen when she left Odessa in 1917. Mischa disappeared shortly after Clara began her journey. The story goes that he ran away and joined the Russian Army out of pique after Clara was chosen to go to Canada to find their father, Gershon. Family tales disclose that the army offered Mischa a pair of boots if he signed up, which he did.

After arriving in America, Grandmother spent years trying to find Mischa, putting ads in newspapers and writing letters, but to no avail. Rumors also spread that after the Civil War, he came back a general and rode into town on a white horse. After a while, the family stopped talking about him.

"I had a brother who died in the war," was all my mother would say, even as much as forty years after his disappearance. They never found him, and he never came back.

I headed to the Odessa Steps, also called the Potemkin Steps. I walked along Primorsky Boulevard, also known as Nikolaevsky Boulevard, to inhale the "spicy aroma of acacias" hanging over the busy Black Sea harbor as well as the famous 240 Odessa Steps. Incidentally, the number of steps has been reduced to 192, and a street now separates them from the port. In the port there is now a skyscraper hotel, which unfortunately robs the city of a magnificent view, at least partially.

The effect and mystery of the staircase lives on. If you look at the stairs from the bottom, you will only see the steps, and they resemble a pyramid. However, if you look down from the top, you will see just the stretched flights of steps.

I imagine that Aunt Clara, about to leave Odessa for her long journey in 1917, probably went to this most famous site in the city. Maybe she went with Mischa to have what would turn out to be that final talk, for little did they know (or perhaps they did) that they would never see each other again. What did they talk about, I wondered as I walked up the steps. I saw young couples holding hands and looking into each other's eyes; older couples, silent, perhaps worried about the future; singles, perhaps planning their career in the new Russia. All of us were looking up . . . up . . . up.

At the top of the steps stands the statue of the Duc de Richelieu clad in a Roman toga. He is the French émigré who two hundred years ago served as governor of Odessa. Now the "stone duke" points at all those arriving to his beloved city.

Finally I was at the top, and I could feel the fast beat of Old Odessa's pulse as I strolled along the wonderful byways, those arteries that feed the heart of the port city: frantic Deribasovskaya Street, full of pedestrians; majestic and sleepy Pushkin Street, whose yellow-and-white stately homes were occupied by grain traders; pretentious Catherine Street, with its old-fashioned houses. In Catherine Square the city has erected the towering statue of Catherine the Great, where once stood the Soviet-style monument to the sailors of the *Potemkin*. The gold-trimmed Odessa Opera and Ballet Theater and the green parks still remain.

⁓

Russians often laugh about Odessa, this port on the northwestern shore of the Black Sea, founded on the site of a fifteenth-century Tartar settlement. "It's the way they speak the language," say the critics, always with their Jewish intonation and funny stories.

Laugh all they want, but as my mother used to say, Odessa was truly special. That's not to say that Jews didn't have trouble there from time to time. Generally, Odesseans got along with each other, but not always. Living with Albanians, Greeks, and Bulgarians had its challenges, especially when they inflicted *pogroms* on Jews in 1821, 1859, 1871, 1881, and 1905.

In 1905, a wave of strikes broke out throughout Russia, including the "Bloody Sunday" massacre of January 22 when Cossacks and police fired on a huge peaceful demonstration of 100,000 led by Father Georgy Gapon in St. Petersburg. The group had only desired to petition the czar to address their grievances. Gunned down by czarist troops, about 130 died and several hundred were wounded.

"The massacre led to a great outburst of indignation in the country and gave another boost to the revolutionary movement," wrote Nicholas V. Riasanovsky in his *A History of Russia*. The murder of innocent citizens touched off a massive strike in Odessa. On June 14, the police, supplying vodka to Cossacks and the anti-Semitic gangs of the Black Hundreds, joined in the massacre of Jews. In this outbreak, about 500 Jews were killed, thousands of families injured, and hundreds of businesses destroyed.

On June 15, officials put the city under martial law. Meanwhile, that same day, the battleship *Potemkin,* the pride of the *Black Sea Fleet,* sailed into Odessa with the Red flag flying. Throwing some of the officers overboard and locking the rest in the brig, the crew mutinied. Huge crowds gathered near the waterfront. The leader of the rebellion, Grigory Vakulinchuk, had been shot in the struggle, and his body was laid at the foot of the grand Odessa Steps. As fighting continued on land, about 2,000 persons were killed by police. The sailors bombarded the city, but the range-finding was inaccurate. The sailors gave up and steamed back to sea, eventually scuttling the battleship in Constanta, Romania, according to Brian Moynahan in *The Russian Century.*

The incident was made famous by the 1925 silent film, *The Battleship Potemkin,* directed by Sergei Eisenstein, whose German Jewish family had baptized him so a path of success would be open to him. This extremely influential propaganda film was named the greatest film of all time at the Brussels World's Fair in 1958. The most celebrated part of *The Battleship Potemkin* is the massacre of civilians on the Odessa Steps. Cossacks are seen marching down the steps, firing volleys into the crowd. Commentators have said that the massacre on the steps never happened, and was inserted for dramatic effect by Eisenstein, considered one of the best Russian film directors. Especially poignant are the scenes of the baby in the carriage tumbling down the steps and the woman whose pince-nez is shattered.

And then there stands the statue of Aleksandr Pushkin (1799–1837) on Pushkin Street.

In 2001, I had checked in at *the Krasnaya* (The Red) Hotel, an architectural monument to the nineteenth century, which featured—what else?—a redbrick facade. Since the hotel is located on Pushkin Street, I had a chance to see Pushkin's statue every day—like seeing the man in person. By the way, after I left in 2001, the Krasnaya Hotel transformed itself into the Bristol, a refurbished, luxury, five-star facility.

"And so, I lived a while in Odessa," wrote Pushkin, considered Russia's greatest poet—"one of the greatest Russian prose writers, master of the lyric, the epic, and the dramatic forms," and "even . . . a literary critic, publicist, and something of a historian and ethnographer," according to Nicholas V. Riasanovsky in *A History of Russia.*

Several monuments to the great Pushkin appear in Odessa. One is a bronze bust of Pushkin on Primorsky Boulevard in front of the Duma. I prefer to see this genius of Russian literature as he stands near my hotel, with top hat and cane right smack on the sidewalk of Pushkin Street.

I picked Odessa more so than St. Petersburg to reflect on the man and his writings because a writer, it seems to me, would feel more at home in this seaside city. While the great master only lived here for a short time, the city reveres him as much as St. Petersburg, where he lived much of a very short life.

Indeed, Pushkin wrote several chapters of his classic verse novel, *Eugene Onegin,* as well as the concluding lines of *The Fountain of Bakhchisarai,* right here in this city of writers.

In 1823, Pushkin moved to Odessa where he again clashed with the government, which then sent him into exile at his mother's rural estate in Mikhailovskoe, near Pskov, from 1824 to 1826. In 1837, besides falling into debt, Pushkin picked up rumors that his wife was having an affair. He challenged her alleged lover, his brother-in-law, Georges d'Anthes, to a duel that left both men injured, Pushkin mortally. He was thirty-seven years old.

Over the next decade and a half after the 1905 Revolution, the Jews of Odessa—indeed, the Jews of the Russian Empire—faced four choices: emigrate to the West; join the Zionists who were rebuilding the Jewish state in Palestine; stay in Russia and maintain Jewish social, religious, and cultural institutions; or "throw their lot in with the Bolsheviks."

History records that only a small minority of Jews joined up with the Bolsheviks, and those that did, only with the very top leadership. The masses refrained. And although Lenin and the early Communist comrades were not "overtly anti-Semitic," Jewish merchants and businessmen would be targeted later as scapegoats of the new regime, just as they had been in the old one.

During the Civil War, however, the Jews were caught in the middle. The Whites inflicted and tolerated pogroms and excluded Jews from their administration, although there were Jews in the White Army. The Red Army would include Jewish officers and commissars, although individual Red units also killed Jewish civilians. After White atrocities in the Ukraine, many Jews, for their own preservation, would gradually side with the Communist regime—that is, until it was too late. Stalin and the Party would soon close down the fading world of Russian Jewry.

After the October Revolution, the Russian Civil War, and the Red victory, Hebrew writers and Zionist activists scattered in every direction.

The third *aliyah* (wave of immigration) began and groups of pioneers left for Palestine while others headed to Berlin, Lausanne, and New York.

If you walk to 17 Rishelyevskaya Street in Odessa, you can see a memorial tablet on the facade of a private house, not open to the public. The plaque honors Isaac Babel (1894–1940), one of the greatest prose writers in the first decades of the Soviet Union, and indeed, of the twentieth century. Babel has the distinction of being the first Jewish writer to enter Russian literature as a Russian writer.

His collection of short stories, *Red Calvary,* which describes his 1920 ride in the ranks of the Cossack horsemen on the side of the Bolsheviks, is a must-read if you want to understand Russia in those terrible civil war years of 1918–22. He put to paper his experiences with General Semyon Budyonny in *Red Calvary,* noted Grace Paley who commented that the book "is about men and what they expect of one another in the way of honor, physical courage, love of horses, abuse of women and Jews."

A son of the ghetto, Babel became a literary success upon the publication of his *Odessa Stories,* tales set in the Moldavanka neighborhood, "crowded with suckling babies, drying rags, and conjugal nights filled with big-city chic and soldierly tirelessness," according to a passage in *The Complete Works of Isaac Babel,* edited by his daughter, Nathalie Babel. At their core, these stories describe the life of Jewish gangsters, especially mob boss Benya Krik. "Babel zealously attached himself to the Bolshevik cause," wrote Cynthia Ozick in her introduction to *The Complete Works of Isaac Babel.* But riding with the Red Calvary, "he fell into disenchantment."

Babel had a chance to defect during several trips to Western Europe, but as Cynthia Ozick reminds us, he "clung to Moscow, hotly wed to his truest bride, the Russian tongue. . . ."

Falling victim to the purges, and later arrested on May 15, his sentence was handed down on January 26, 1940. He was shot the next day, at the age of forty-five.

"Babel was murdered by the criminal agency of a cynically criminal government. His name and work was erased; he never lived," pointed out Cynthia Ozick. One of the foremost writers of his time, Babel became a non-person. In 1954, however, during the post-Stalin thaw, the great writer was, in Soviet terminology, rehabilitated with these words: *"The sentence of the Military College, dated 26 January, 1940, concerning Babel I. E. is revoked on the basis of newly discovered circumstances and the case against him is terminated in the absence of elements of a crime."*

Perhaps the most famous Odessa native who later made Tel Aviv his home was Chaim Nachman Bialik. He settled in Israel in 1924 and is considered the most influential Hebrew poet of modern times.

Bialik lived at 9 Malaya Arnautskaya Street. Like many other Jewish writers, his house today is occupied, but he is honored with a memorial tablet on the exterior of the building.

Bialik was part of the group from Odessa who arrived in Tel Aviv in the first several decades of the twentieth century, bringing culture, the arts, and entertainment to the then-small suburb of Jaffa, which we know today as Tel Aviv. In what was to be a harbinger of the future, they set up the first dance hall in the city, now renowned for its nightlife.

From his desk in Odessa, Bialik wrote in 1903, *"In the City of Slaughter,"* a poem wherein he depicted the horrors of the Kishinev pogrom in that year, but also expressed shame that the Jews had not resisted their attackers. The powerful poem had a tremendous influence on Russian Jewish youth and inspired young people to form self-defense groups.

I later passed by the apartment building of Zionist leader and author Zev Vladimir Jabotinsky, the founder of the Revisionist Movement and mentor of the late Israeli prime minister, Menachem Begin.

Jabotinsky was born at 33 Bazarnaya Street and lived also at 91 Novoselsky Street. A memorial plaque adorns one of his residences at 1 Yevreyskaya Street. I looked up, searching for his apartment, the one where he wrote probably his most famous novel, *The Five.* Jabotinsky wrote

I'll probably never get to see Odessa again. It's a pity, because I love the place. I was indifferent to Russia even in my youth. I recall that I always

got pleasantly agitated when leaving for Europe and would return only reluctantly. But Odessa—that's another matter; arriving at the Razdel-naya Station, I would already begin to be joyfully excited. If I arrived nowadays, my hands would probably tremble. I'm not indifferent only to Russia; in general I'm not really attached to any country; at one time I was in love with Rome, and it lasted a long time, but even that passed. Odessa's a different matter: it hasn't ever passed, and it won't.

Odessa is a city of the enlightenment and a Zionist city; in fact, it was one of the largest centers of the Zionist movement, and I think that's why I was happy here. As I breathed the air of Odessa, I realized that many great Jewish authors—more than I have mentioned in this book, and whose works of art have become classics of Jewish literature—have walked these very streets and avenues.

I was fascinated to learn that a hundred years ago, Jews from this very same port made their way to Palestine as Odessa became known as the Gate of Zion, a city from which thousands of Jews from all over Europe began their journey to the Land of Israel. Even David Ben-Gurion, the first prime minister of Israel, sailed from Odessa to *Eretz Yisra'el*.

At the end of the nineteenth century and the beginning of the twentieth century, Odessa also became a major center of enlightenment and secular Jewish life, and drew many who wanted to express themselves in Yiddish, Hebrew, and Russian.

Russian Jewry stood in awe of Odessa. People were lured here because they wanted to flee the stifling Pale of Settlement, that region of Imperial Russia were Jews were forced to reside. But they could "live like God in Odessa." And the czarist government encouraged their settlement in order to populate the town. From the 1880s to the 1920s, the Odessa Jewish community, about 140,000 souls, was the second largest in all of the Russian Empire, next to Warsaw.

Today, Odessa—which before the fall of Communism contained 70,000 Jews—now reports only about 30,000 Jews out of a million residents, approximately 3 percent.

I felt that I had been in Odessa long before this day. I fantasized that like my grandfather, I'd meet, nod to, or converse with some of the outstanding Jewish writers, Zionist thinkers, and leaders of the last century. Their memories are part of my education and knowledge.

Personally, their names remind me of my teenage years. As a member of Habonim (the Labor Zionist Youth Movement), we studied their works and I became an ardent Zionist, and I've never wavered. I accepted the ideal that Israel is the center of Jewish life. I even "almost" settled there. Contradiction possibly, but I also believed in the "sanctity of the diaspora," and that we are tied together as one people. "All Jews are brothers," an Iraqi Jew in Israel told me a long time ago; the story of how I met him will be explained in chapter 9.

Many of the great Jewish thinkers were from Odessa and other towns in the Ukraine. I am proud to say I knew most of their names and remembered them even into adulthood: the Yiddish giants, Mendele Mokher Seforim and Sholom Aleichem; and Ahad Ha'am, Menachem Mendel Ussishkin, Leon Pinsker, Meir Dizengoff, Saul Tchernichowsky, Joseph Trumpeldor, David Frischmann, and Simon Frug.

As I sauntered along the passageways of Odessa where Pushkin lived and worked, I realized that much of what Russian Jewish authors wrote yesterday was suppressed for a long time in the former Soviet Union.

⌒

I only knew the name of the street—Proharovskaya—where my Rasputnis family had lived in the traditional Moldavanka neighborhood, which occupies the area from Proharovskaya Square to Balkovskaya Street and makes for fascinating urban exploration. Proharovskaya is a main artery that runs down to the harbor area, so my guide Natalia Chernaya accompanied me to a typical courtyard on Proharovskaya. Two-story wooden apartments are built around the courtyard, with two stairways featuring wrought-iron banisters leading to the first and second floors. Each apartment has tall picture windows, and clothes hang from the laundry lines. Children scamper up and down, babies cry, and dogs howl. It is spring—Passover! Even in Russia, "And the voice of the turtle was heard in our land." *Song of Solomon, 2:12*

⌒

A World War II monument is located in a quiet park in Odessa. One day I stumbled onto a ceremony where I recalled the Great Patriotic War. I observed stout, gray-haired Red Army veterans marching and carrying their unit banners and flags along a well-paved path. I couldn't pass up an opportunity to shake hands with a few, and I told them I was American. We smiled at each other. Maybe they, too, recalled the meeting with my countrymen at the Elbe River in Germany, a half-century before—April 25, 1945, to be exact—when hundreds of Russian soldiers coming from the east crossed that river at Torgau and met GIs from the First Army pouring in from the west. Perhaps these very Russians exchanged greetings with my cousin, Manny, Aunt Clara's older son. His artillery unit was in the Elbe River area also. The two armies shook hands and partied the night away, celebrating the imminent end of the war. Little did they know that a Cold War would settle in for the next fifty years.

⁓

The past always haunts the Jewish people. Nearly 100,000 Odessa Jews were slaughtered by Germans and Romanians during the Great War. In one instance, 19,000 Jews were herded into a square where they were doused with gasoline, ignited, and burned to death.

How can people in Odessa exist with such scars and memories? While I felt good about Jewish life surviving despite everything, I faced reality as I recalled the words of Babel: "Odessa had its moment in the sun, but now it is fading, a poetic, slow, lighthearted, helpless fading."

In the Russia of 2011, most Jews are staying put, although a small number of Jews throughout Russia are still leaving for the Land of Israel.

In 2009, 16,244 Jews immigrated to Israel from throughout the world, the highest jump in ten years. "The largest number of new immigrants came from the former Soviet Union, where the numbers increased by 21 percent, from 5,867, to 7,120, many from small towns. At the same time, small numbers of Russian Jews who cannot adjust to Israel return to their former homeland, more in the past than currently. At any given point, 10,000 to 30,000 Israelis (many former Russian citizens) are visiting, working, and doing business in Russia."

Some Russian Jews are reconsidering their future here, for the economic downturn certainly hit Russia harder than it did Israel, which actually is doing very well economically, with a 5 percent GDP estimated for 2011.

Meanwhile, the Jewish community today is active and proud of the new JCC that opened in 2008, known as Beit Grand JCC. The three-story building was officially dedicated in 2010 by JDC and the Odessa Jewish Community. Here is housed Hesed, a kindergarten, ANAVIM, and Odessa Hillel, as well as an extensive library and community gym.

Today, the Migdal Center operates over a hundred programs in various areas of Jewish life, including the first Jewish library to open in Ukraine since the fall of the USSR, with a collection of over 10,000 books. JDC is Migdal's primary sponsor.

Across the street stands the Museum of History of Odessa Jews, "Migdal Shorashim," opened in 2002, and on its premises are displays of the history of Odessa Jews, museum clubs as well as the Holocaust Center, "Zakhor." Until then, the history of Odessa's Jewry was not exhibited or displayed in any other museum around the city.

Even with the reduced population, three religious communities function in Odessa. Chabad rabbi Avraham Wolff is the spiritual leader of Chabad's Synagogue, Central Synagogue of Odessa. Once, three synagogues stood on Osipov Street; now, only the Chabad synagogue is there, fully restored. During Soviet times, the synagogue was used as a warehouse by the KGB, but it was returned to the community after the fall of Communism.

On Shabbat, I prayed in the now fully renovated former Great Synagogue of Odessa, now called the Main Synagogue of Odessa, where Rabbi Shlomo Baksht serves as spiritual leader. The building was turned over to the Jewish community after the fall of Communism. Located on Yevreyskaya Street (which means "Jewish Street"), during Soviet times this house of worship was converted into a sports facility. As I recited the prayers with local Odesseans, tourists, and students from abroad, we all knew we were part of a history that survives, especially looking down at our shoes and noticing that we were standing on the floor of a synagogue where you could still make out the lines of a former Soviet basketball court.

Each of the above synagogues maintains religious Jewish schools, while World ORT sponsors a secular Jewish school. A Reform Movement of

Judaism group functions in Odessa. They rent space for their activities and programs, guided by spiritual leader Vladimir Torchinsky.

I believe the future of Jews in Russia, with its long history of anti-Semitism, is tied up with the course the new Russia pursues. So far, Judaism is being practiced very openly. Jews are a long way from the days when holidays were barely marked, if at all, or celebrated in whispers behind double-thick doors in gray apartment blocks. Russia in 2011, it seems, is stable, "with hardly any official manifestation of anti-Semitism at least on the governmental level" according to Dr. Sam Kliger, Director, Russian Affairs of the American Jewish Committee.

True, more could be done, and has to be done. Better Jewish education and Jewish schools, and more participation of American and European Jews in enhancing Jewish life in Russia—all of these are a must. In many cases, American Jewry has forgotten that there are active Jewish communities throughout this vast land. True, the Federation of Jewish Communities, headed by Chief Rabbi Lazar of Chabad, has cultivated close ties with the Russian government. How long those ties will last, however, no one would venture to guess—although as history has taught us, one is never sure of how long you might stay in favor with the Kremlin.

One aspect of the Jewish situation in Russia that will probably hold true for many years to come is that Jews now have an *accessible* address: Israel. Unlike just a few decades ago, Russian Jews have the right and freedom to emigrate and join a million Russian Jews who live in the Jewish state. Actually, neither Russians nor Israelis need visas for entry into each other's lands. Constant travel back and forth is a reality between the two states. Russian tourism to Israel is increasing. Those tourists will feel at home in an Israel where public and store notices in many cities are in Russian, and the language is frequently heard in street conversations and public places. Trade between the two nations flourishes, and cultural and religious exchanges occur frequently. It's quite unlikely that Russian Jews will ever be isolated again.

I also witnessed "middle-class" growth in Russia. The Jews are part of this relatively new venture in a country that has known a thousand years of autocracy and seventy years of Communism, and nothing else. There are even signs that middle-class elements are taking on some responsibility for supporting Jewish community centers and institutions.

The Jews that stay will be a part of Russia. They will walk arm in arm just as Russians do during any moment of national pride. The Jews will move along with the whole country of 142 million, just as they do along the canals of St. Petersburg during the long white nights in June; just as they do on the Nevsky Prospekt in the city Peter the Great built; just as they do on the cobblestones of Red Square before the red-stoned Kremlin; just as they do in the large waiting hall in the Moskovskaya Conservatory in Moscow during the intermission of their glorious ballet company; just as they do walking up and down the massive Odessa steps. Arm in arm.

Don't mess with Russians is the vernacular of the future, even though theirs is a sad, often badly ruled, often corrupt country. Russia will always rise again, and again. Ask the French, the Pole, the Turk, the Finn, the Swede, and the Hun.

⌒

To really understand Jewish survival, you have to head east to Siberia, the "Sleeping Land," where Jews have lived since the seventeenth century.

Before my journey is completed, I will pass through nine time zones.

Sibir, the Sleeping Land

Riding the Trans-Siberian Railway and Visiting Irkutsk, Birobidzhan, and Vladivostok

"You're from Russia?"
"Yes, from Russia."
"I've never been there at all."
— *Anton Chekhov, "Across Siberia"*

As the plane touched down in Irkutsk, in Siberia, the early-morning light illuminated the city's chimneys over a plain of shuttered wooden houses with tarpaper roofs.

I was told that Irkutsk—a six-hour flight from Moscow, and located halfway between the Urals and the Sea of Japan—was one of the stops my Aunt Clara made during her journey to find my grandfather, Cantor Gershon Rasputnis. To this day, Irkutsk remains a main rail hub and stop on the Trans-Siberian Railway.

I've often wondered about her journey—how this seventeen-year-old felt, finding herself in the midst of the Russian Revolution and the Russian Civil War of 1918–1922, which began the night the Bolsheviks seized the Winter Palace in 1917. The courage and sense of purpose that my aunt displayed provide a wonderful lesson for all who seek encouragement to face life's daunting tasks. So compelled was I to write her story that I traveled to Russia and Siberia to trace her journey through this vast land, including Manchuria and Japan.

Although Clara appeared resolute and in many ways fearless, she must have been bewildered and terrified, for just as she arrived in Irkutsk in the summer of 1918, the brutal, chaotic Russian Civil War flared up. The death and horror of that war in this frozen land "were unlike any previously seen," wrote Ian Frazier in *Travels in Siberia*. To this day, no accurate statistics exist, but estimates indicate that 25 to 30 million persons perished in the Civil War. This conflagration, however, did not just pit soldier against soldier; it also mushroomed into a class struggle, with workers against managers, peasants against landowners, and poor against rich.

The problem for my aunt was that the conflict between the Reds and the Whites in the eastern part of Russia would take place on or near the Trans-Siberian Railway. Although she joined up with a family later in her journey, she still would have to be cautious and keep her wits about her. Indeed, family lore has it that on one occasion, when Cossacks stormed through the train car she was riding in, looking for young Jewish girls, Clara hid under the skirts of a rather—how shall we put it—stout woman.

Visitors to Irkutsk during that time were told not to wander onto side streets. According to one story, *varnaki* lurked in the shadows—murderers who strangled their victims without blinking an eye. Roaming the streets, the killers would approach their victims from behind and throw a loop with grappling hooks attached to a sack over the person's head, cutting off all air. One quick jerk and the unfortunate wayfarer would be hurled backward, gasping for breath; his or her neck broken. The *varnaki* then emptied the pockets of the deceased, leaving the victim dead, sprawled out on the street.

Walking along some of the main city streets was also not a good idea in those days, as the town was full of anti-Bolshevik forces. Cossacks set up independent fiefdoms, and Whites—and, for a while, their allies, the Czechs—controlled the Trans-Siberian Railway, the Volga region, the Urals, and Siberia. But it would only be a matter of time for the White armies. Eventually, the Czechs would desert the White forces led by Admiral Aleksandr Kolchak. The Reds would counterattack and eventually defeat the Whites.

How dangerous was it to travel during the Russian Civil War?

Well, author Ian Frazier reported that an American Communist who was in Russia at the time said that a representative from the YMCA told him he had seen a sign that said, TOVARISCH SOLDIERS: PLEASE DO NOT THROW PASSENGERS OUT OF THE WINDOW AFTER THE TRAIN IS IN MOTION.

Travelers on the Trans-Siberian Railway, including my Aunt Clara, would also have had to avoid a certain ataman (general) of the Siberian Cossacks, Grigori Semenov, a terrorist who, with Japanese aid, robbed passing trains, murdered hundreds of passengers, and burned whole villages. He killed at will, especially Jews. Semenov was not alone, however. He had a comrade, Baron von Ungern-Sternberg, who had become a Buddhist and wanted to create an empire for himself out of Mongolia, Manchuria, and Transbaikal. His ambition was to lead his Central-Asiatic Empire against Europe, as Genghis Khan had done. Ungern-Sternberg was known for his extreme cruelty and mass killings that included many Jews.

Nearly a century later, I walked the very same streets that my aunt had walked. I did not know all the places in Irkutsk that Clara visited that summer of 1918, but I was sure she must have stopped at the main synagogue, which had topped my must-see list of sites in Irkutsk. I was shown buildings near the synagogue, with Stars of David emblazoned on their walls, and while no longer owned or occupied by Jews, word has it that if it contains the Jewish star, it is considered a Jewish site. A city-center drugstore or a government building that once housed a Jewish school—all are considered Jewish points of interest.

It was snowing in Irkutsk. No, not icy white flakes, but the silver fuzz from poplar trees that coats cars, buses, streets, and the tracks of the world's longest railroad line, the Trans-Siberian Railway. And along its route, at least ten new or renovated synagogues and Jewish community centers have sprung up in the last decade beginning in 2000.

Summer in Irkutsk, and believe it or not, the heat gets to you. There is very little air-conditioning. No wonder Russians call it the "sun-hole of Siberia," with an average of three hundred days of sunshine annually—more than any other city in Russia. But don't get me wrong; the mean temperature in Irkutsk in January is 6 degrees below zero, and winter temperatures can easily drop to 40 degrees below zero.

⌒

Because of the heat during this summertime visit, we guzzled down a cold drink at the city's classic railway station, which features a cupola. Located across the Angara River from Irkutsk's historical center, and 3,222 miles from Moscow, this station played a major role in Russian history; it is, after all, one of the largest in eastern Siberia. Czarist prisoners in chains passed through this station en route to prison compounds; Red and White troops, in their armored railcars during the Civil War; and condemned Communists on their way to the *gulag*.

In 1941, white-clad Red Army ski divisions filled with many native Siberian regiments traveled west through here on their way to battle the Germans and save Moscow.

Irkutsk made the history books when near the end of the Civil War, the Reds caught up with the leader of the White forces, Admiral Aleksandr Kolchak, and on February 7, 1920, executed him and his prime minister, Viktor Pepelyayev. They pushed the bodies down a hole in the ice on the Angara River.

⌒

Conventional wisdom has it that if you can afford only one stop on the Trans-Siberian, make it Irkutsk, which stands on the banks of the Angara River. Located at the mouth of the Irkut River, the city is named after that tributary, which means "rapid stream"; hence, Irkutsk, the "city near the rapid stream which flows into the Angara River."

A charming, relaxed city filled with art museums and restaurants and cafes. Irkutsk lies only 47 miles from the icy blue waters of Lake Baikal, the world's deepest lake. The city boasts that it remains the world headquarters of the Trans-Siberian Railway.

Founded in 1661 as a Cossack garrison to rule over the indigenous Buryats—and to collect a fur tax from them—Irkutsk became the springboard to and capital of eastern Siberia. Eighty years before, in 1581, a

Cossack hetman (military commander), Yermak Timofeyevich, invaded the political entity known as the Siberian Khanate, conquered its capital, and enabled Muscovy to annex western Siberia. This municipality ranks as the largest and most substantial metro area of Siberia. All meet in this city of "gold and sable"—the steppes and the desert, the mountains and the seas, the tilled lands and the tundra. "Our Irkutsk, a splendid city, indeed a gift of God," says a much touted 1846 couplet discussing this Siberian municipality.

Today, Irkutsk, with approximately 700,000 residents, flaunts its title as the "Paris of Siberia." Others like to call it the academic, cultural, and business center, and the capital of Siberia—even of Northern Asia. Even though the 2008 world economic crisis also hit this city, by 2011, unemployment had receded. The large aviation, aluminum, and cable factories located here keep most people working.

Irkutsk meets its obligation as an integral part of Siberia, the largest region of the world's largest nation, with 5.1 million square miles of marshy plains, vast forests, desolate plateaus, and rugged mountains—an area that could encompass all of the U.S., including Alaska, as well as all of Western Europe, and still have hundreds of thousands of square miles to spare. Frazier points out that Siberia makes up three-quarters of Russia today. Across the middle of Siberia, its latitude covers 3,600 miles and runs directly through the Russian taiga, the largest forest in the world. Siberia stretches across eight time zones, running from the Ural Mountains to the Pacific Ocean, bordered by Mongolia and China to the south and the Arctic Circle to the north.

Figures are hard to come by, but about 30,000 Jews reside in Siberia, whose population is approximately 40 million. About 3,000 Jews call Irkutsk home, down from previous years due to the large migration of Russian Jews to Israel in the 1990s.

And who are the Jews of Siberia?

According to the *Encyclopaedia Judaica*'s definition of a mid-nineteenth-century Siberian Jew, he "is similar in dress and language" to his Russian neighbor, not too well versed in Jewish learning, and doesn't follow too well the *mitzvoth;* he "nevertheless possesses warm Jewish sentiments and is attached to the Jewish people and religion." This could still define the Jews of Siberia today.

Yet Jewish life has changed. Whereas over a hundred years ago, Jews in the area were involved in the fur trade and gold mining, today, in Russia's "free market" economy, they are professionals, businesspeople, and entrepreneurs. They live alongside ethnic minorities such as Tartars, Chuvash people, and Buryats.

Jewish exiles and former prisoners settled in Irkutsk at the start of the nineteenth century. Jewish soldiers, discharged from the armies of the czar, came to Irkutsk and built wooden homes like their neighbors, some with hand-carved decorations that survive today. Those veterans were called *cantonists.* Some of them had been snatched up and hauled off to the army by decree of the czar when they were less than ten years old. They had to serve for twenty-five years. The army forced many of them to convert, and made them eat pork. No wonder the Irkutsk synagogue is known as the former "Soldiers Synagogue."

Indeed, in a country that proudly honors its veterans, the Jewish community in 2010 commemorated the sixty-fifth anniversary of the end of World War II. One of the most inspiring sights for this writer was to see men in their eighties wearing their medals on their jackets, these seniors who had fought at the Battle of Kursk in the Russian Southwest, who had crossed the Elbe River where they met American GIs coming from the West, and went on to conquer Berlin. Such is the custom in the former Soviet Union. So at the anniversary celebration, the synagogue hall at the JCC was filled with veterans who had served on the battlefront and on the home front in World War II, a conflict which took about 30 million Russian lives.

⁓

Siberian Jewish life revolves around one of the oldest houses of worship in Siberia—a three-story concrete building on Karl Liebknecht Street, 23. Street names mirror history—in this case, Stalinist history. Karl Liebknecht was the Jewish founder of the radical left-wing Spartacus Union in Germany. He and Jewish comrade Rosa Luxemburg were murdered by the German army in 1918, the year when the Communists thought they could export revolution and the world would become a workers' paradise.

Traveling through Siberia, one recalls that Jews were exiled to this vast land from Lithuanian towns captured by the Russians as far back as the

Russo-Polish War of 1632–34. By the beginning of the nineteenth century, Jews were still among the convicts and political prisoners sent to Siberia for settlement or hard labor. They helped found the first Jewish communities of Omsk, Tomsk, Tobolsk, and Kuibyshev. By the end of that century, further Jewish immigrants were banned from settling in Siberia, although they already had formed an active intelligentsia.

At the beginning of the twentieth century, Jews resided in many Siberian towns, with strong Jewish communities, and each with its own synagogue. The 1917 Bolshevik Revolution would soon put an end to all Jewish communal, cultural, and national institutions, however, as well as religious life. As we shall see, the region's population swelled with the creation of the "Jewish Autonomous Region" in Birobidzhan, along the Chinese border. Another wave of Jews arrived during World War II when the Soviet Union evacuated and moved major factories eastward of the German invasion. These Jews were followed by a steady stream of internal exiles sent by the Communists to the gulag.

Like most of the synagogues outside of Moscow, St. Petersburg, and Kiev, a few Siberian synagogues were kept open by the Kremlin as showcases for Western visitors. Irkutsk's synagogue was shut down in 1934 by the Soviet regime as part of an effort to snuff out Jewish religious life. First it served as a student hostel, and later, a military hospital. Luckily, in the early years of World War II, Stalin eased his crackdown on religious observance in hopes that the masses would more passionately resist the Nazi invaders. A few Jewish houses of worship, Irkutsk among them, were allowed to reopen, as were various cathedrals.

During my visit in 2004—a decade after the fall of the USSR—the Russian government declared the Irkutsk synagogue a historical and cultural monument. Good decision, as the building was nearing collapse, with the foundation sinking and floors caving in. I was told to walk carefully.

In Russia, perhaps more than other countries, tragic events have a way of making life even harder. In mid-2004, a middle-of-the-night electrical fire nearly destroyed the entire synagogue, including the loss of valuable records. Shocked, but far from beaten, the community began to renovate the synagogue. After all, this house of worship had outlasted czars, revolutions, wars, and the Soviet Union.

After a five-year struggle with renovation, the structure's rich facade, the decorative interior with elegant shining chandeliers, and the prayer hall with the Holy Ark were put in place. "The synagogue is a new building inside old walls," said a member of the congregation.

Historically, special permission had to be obtained to erect a synagogue for the fledgling community, which dates back to the 1860s. Approval was finally given in 1878, and the first service held in 1879, although another monstrous fire in the city also destroyed that building in 1882, and a new one had to be built that year.

One hundred and thirty years later from the first service, on March 24, 2009, an anniversary celebration took place at the synagogue, in the presence of the chief rabbi of Russia, Berel Lazar, who declared that "the synagogue renovation in Irkutsk is an unconditional confirmation of the fact that Jews feel comfortable here and feel respect for their religion, it was reported.

Chief Rabbi of Irkutsk Aaron Wagner pointed out that the new three-story concrete building contains the Jewish Community Center, a prayer hall, a meat kitchen, a *mikveh,* meeting rooms for the community—including one for the chess club, a very popular pastime in Russia—as well as rooms for groups and organizations, such as a sewing club, computer rooms, a preschool, and a library.

JDC's Hesed welfare network, which opened in 1990, is housed in a separate building at 5 Army Street. Olga, who works for JDC, explains that the organization provides food packages, medicine, meals-on-wheels, soup kitchens, medical equipment, and home care.

In the second decade of the twenty-first century, Jewish life coalesces around the synagogue. Olga shows me the *matzah* machine, noting how the congregation is proud of how it symbolizes the fight against repression, because it made this dietary staple even in the worst of Communist times. People had the courage to come to the building and pick up their *matzah,* the symbol of hope and freedom. Irkutsk has yet to establish a kosher restaurant.

The community is tight-knit. According to JDC's Olga, the vast majority of Jewish residents are recorded in a computer database. She adds that a large organization of volunteers is key when it comes to keeping their community cohesive. On High Holidays, about a thousand people attend services.

Leaving the synagogue, I walked around the neighborhood and passed a building which was once a Jewish school. At a nearby corner, I gazed at the early-twentieth-century structure, the Moise Feinberg building, part of which serves as a state library of rare books. Right at the top of the front facade, I saw a Star of David. As in other parts of Russia, Jewish destiny is constantly changing, and the Feinberg building, located in the center of the city and near the synagogue, eventually was returned to the community. Part of the building will house the first Jewish kindergarten in Irkutsk.

Symbolic, indeed—a former Jewish building coming back to the community in terms of offering Jewish education in a school where the curriculum will include learning about Jewish holidays and concepts. Thus are Russian children often educated in the former Soviet Union.

Rabbi Wagner explains that in the "initial stage, three classes will be set up, adding that the fees paid by parents will be minimal and purely symbolic." As of now, no Jewish school functions in Irkutsk, although a Sunday school with several dozen students meets at the synagogue.

It's clear that Russians and Russian Jews alike certainly believe in symbolism. The dedication ribbon at the kindergarten's entrance was cut by the oldest member of the Irkutsk Jewish community, Boris Gornykh, who had just celebrated his hundredth birthday. A three-year-old girl handed him the scissors for the ceremony. "We are certain that teaching Jewish values and ideals will help maintain a strong connection between the generations," said Rabbi Wagner, according to news reports.

Since the downfall of Communism in 1991, more symbolism—some of it small by certain standards—is added to the Jewish scene: In 2010, the Irkutsk city authorities announced that drivers will be prohibited from parking automobiles near the synagogue on Shabbat. Car owners who live near the synagogue were approached and agreed in advance to this act of respect toward the Jewish community, according to Rabbi Wagner. Unheard of twenty years ago.

Out again, and once more walking along Karl Liebknecht Street, I passed a number of old, wooden houses with fancy hand-carved wooden window frames. Easy to understand why Irkutsk's reputation rests on its log houses. In earlier days, homeowners decorated facades of their houses with beautiful, elaborately carved woodwork, known as the "wooden lace" of Irkutsk.

In the nineteenth century, many young, idealistic army officers and civilians were exiled from western Russia to Irkutsk for taking part in the Decembrist revolt against the Russian czar in 1825. They had been exposed to democracy during the Napoleonic wars. Even their wives came out here with them. Actually, these revolutionaries turned the city into the intellectual and cultural capital of Siberia. One of the exiles living in Irkutsk was Fyodor Dostoevsky, who has been described as one of the greatest, if not *the* greatest, of novelists. Dostoevsky had been sentenced to death for anti-czarist activities but was spared at the last moment and sent to serve a term of hard labor in Siberia.

One of the most famous sights of the city is the "Monument to Russian Pioneers of Siberia." Whose statue is on the top? you may ask. None other than Czar Alexander III. Although he gave the go-ahead for the construction of the Trans-Siberian Railway, he remained a notorious anti-Semite. Alexander III vented his wrath on the Jews and sparked the issuance of *numerus clauses,* which limited the number of Jews entering university, as well as the land exclusion law; both kept Jews from advancing.

An interesting structure that is sure to please the eye is the former Governor's House, locally called the White House even though it's actually painted yellow. The building is a neoclassic mansion of the early nineteenth century which now houses part of the Irkutsk library.

In 2011, Irkutsk celebrated its 350th anniversary. Still, it remains a "young" city. The average age of the city's population is only 31.6 years, and young people and students fill the cafes and restaurants. There are thirty-six institutes and colleges and nine vocational schools. Every day, a total of 166,646 students attend various institutions. In 1949, the East Siberian branch of the Russian Academy of Science set up nine research institutions and a regional Economy Department.

For its anniversary, the town was decked out with attractive poster designs—all very visible on billboards and even park benches. To add meaning to the anniversary, Gazprom, the world's largest producer of natural gas, announced it would construct a water sports center in Irkutsk. The city spent more than $190 million to prepare and celebrate the event, $57 million of which came from the Federal budget.

One anniversary project was to restore a block of houses in historical Irkutsk. All of the wooden houses on this street were refurbished and were scheduled to accommodate businesses related to the travel industry. I stopped at one of the more-famous houses, a perfect example of this type of architecture—two golden-brown gables at the top of the structure in front of two cupolas. The corner boards have a painted overhang and the portico is enhanced by a wooden awning. The shutters are solid wood with a carved face, the fretwork is magnificent, and the inside casements feature awning-covered windows.

Even young, budding artists agree with me; they are out on the sidewalk with their easels and paintbrushes, capturing this fine specimen.

⁓

Time to move on to Lake Baikal, a wonder of the world. If one visits Irkutsk and does not stop at Lake Baikal . . . well, that's like going to Cairo and not heading out to see the pyramids.

The world's oldest, deepest freshwater lake lies in southern Siberia, near Russia's border with Mongolia. Geologists estimate that Lake Baikal was formed about 25 million years ago. Covering 12,000 square miles and with a depth of more than one mile, it contains one-fifth of all the freshwater on the planet, more than any other single lake. No wonder it has such wonderful names: "Blue Eye of Siberia," "the Sacred Sea of Siberia," "the Blue Pearl of Siberia."

Stocked with beautiful and meaty fish, this lake is surrounded by fertile farmland. I realize that memories of wonderful meals play a big role in travel recall. Who among us has not savored a memorable meal on a trip? Aromas and flavors trigger accounts of childhood days. Ah, those beautiful *omul* fish, plucked out of Lake Baikal, placed in a smoker, and handed over to us as "smoked fish," a delightful memory of my childhood. This delicacy was served along with bagels and lox on Sunday mornings in my native Pittsburgh, halfway around the world from where I now stood—a meal to be savored, along with bread, caviar, and country-fresh cucumbers and tomatoes. The same ingredients made it a memorable meal, too, on Lake Baikal.

Omul can be defined as "a trout-sized, white-fleshed fish, belonging to the salmon family, which the Russians eat raw, salted, smoked, dried, boiled baked or fried." For three rubles (about $1.00 U.S.), in 2004 the fish was cooked right in front of us before we boarded our motor-boat. We added some farm-fresh vegetables we had procured on land and heartily devoured this Siberian *repas* as we sailed Lake Baikal.

Our motorboat moved smoothly on the lake. Though warned by the captain to hold onto my hat because of the sudden gusts of wind, I forgot his warning and watched as my Nike baseball cap flew off into the water. Oh well—at least I'd left a gift of thanks for this wonderful masterpiece of nature, this cap (made in Vietnam) that I had bought in Chinatown in Flushing, Queens, New York.

I hope that Lake Baikail will be preserved, especially since environmentalists have been warning us that industrial facilities are ruining this huge body of water.

In building the Trans-Siberian Railway, engineers faced many difficulties, including Lake Baikal, which obstructed and delayed railway traffic. At first, passengers had to use the ferry service across the lake, but it was soon discovered that the ships couldn't cope with the increased traffic.

During the Russo-Japanese War, a track had to be laid across the frozen lake in order to speed the delivery of supplies to the Far East. After Russia's defeat in that war, a large new section had to be put in place because of the shift in borders in Japan's favor. That addition was built by thousands of convicts and poor peasants who laid the rails and then paid with their lives in landslides, bridge and tunnel collapses, disease, and permafrost. As one observer pointed out many perished without seeing the results of their work.

⌒

A Jewish commissar tells a group of Jewish leaders about the founding of Birobidzhan: "This is the most important moment in the history of the Jewish people in two thousand years. . . ."
—*Ken Kalfus,* Pu-239 and Other Russian Fantasies

Next stop, Khabarovsk, in the Russian Far East, where we immediately took a side trip to one of the most exotic and mystical Jewish sites in the world—Birobidzhan.

Heading west from Khabarovsk, on a tree-lined, well-paved road, our car sped along a 120-mile route. Three hours later, we reached our destination: a huge autonomous region, the size of Connecticut and Massachusetts, and located on the main trunk of the Trans-Siberian Railway. Just on the outskirts of the region's main city, we stopped to gaze at a huge sign that read BIROBIDZHAN.

Not unusual, of course, except that alongside this marker in Russian was a similar sign in Yiddish, the former language of the Jewish diaspora. Yes! Yiddish was written and spoken here, even in the days of Stalinist Russia. Today, too, the observer can spot Yiddish on welcome signs, street signs, town posters, the municipal radio station, schools, stamps, and government documents.

One cannot help but be moved when viewing the sign BIROBIDZHAN in large Hebrew letters. Some visitors even go so far as to say they were under the spell of those letters, and felt they were on Jewish soil. That is because, in the words of a Russian Jewish leader, "It was a myth." People, especially with Communist-leaning ideologues wanted to believe that this Jewish utopia was real. Nevertheless, myths die hard.

For instance, at the railway station, the first thing you see in the plaza outside the train station is a huge menorah-shaped fountain. Gigantic lettering on the station roof names the city in both Russian and Yiddish, BIROBIDZHAN. Birobidzhan, the Jewish autonomous region, was established in 1934 when Stalin had the "bright idea" of moving Jews to this bleak, lonely, swampy 13,895-square-mile area near his vulnerable border with China. Supposedly it stood as a new "Soviet Zion," where a proletarian Jewish culture could be developed. Yiddish would be the national language, and new socialist literature and arts would replace religion as the primary expression of culture. It was Stalin's answer to Zionism: Jewish farmers tilling the soil in a socialist republic, except that much of that soil rested on a frozen wasteland.

Tens of thousands of Jewish settlers traveled eastward. After all, they were people who had never before possessed land, and now they were promised their own plot of soil to farm.

In Soviet times, Birobidzhan was always cited by the Soviet government as proof that it was not engaged in systematic repression of Jewish religious practices and Zionist sentiment. Once again, the Russians pulled the ruse known as a "Potemkin village." Grigory A. Potemkin, the favorite minister of Catherine the Great, deceived the czarina about the state of rural Russia by setting up villages that were composed of empty stucco shells that only appeared to be part of a prosperous village.

Likewise, the atheist Soviet Union did not tell their Jews that this Jewish Autonomous Region (JAR) would be a strictly secular Jewish culture; they were not going to be allowed to practice their religion. To the Soviets, the Jews were not a nation. Early on, Stalin ruled that they were a religion, and after the Bolshevik revolution, Jews were denied nationality status.

Stalin invented Birobidzhan to encourage Jews to go there and populate this part of Siberia, which was threatened by Japanese forces in Manchuria. Once the Jews had their own autonomous region, he believed they would forget the lure of Zionism.

So Russian Jews and Jewish pioneers from all over the world, including the U.S., Canada, Argentina, France—good Communists that they were— drained the swamps, cultivated the barren land, established agricultural cooperatives, started a Yiddish newspaper, and opened a theater, schools, and various other institutions. These "true believers" literally transformed a forgotten town into a city—all in the belief that with this "socialist paradise," they would be liberated from the unproductive trades of the so-called Jewish *bourgeoisie*. American Jewish Communists even contributed money to support this Siberian ideal.

But they were all duped.

The Jews in Palestine knew what was happening. According to noted author Amos Oz, many Jews in the days before the State of Israel and on into the early 1950s, strongly voiced their doubts about the Soviet Union. Oz quoted his grandfather in his book, *A Tale of Love and Darkness* as saying in the early 1940s "Russia doesn't exist anymore! Russia is dead. There is Stalin. There is Dzerzhinsky. There is Yezhov. There is Beria. There is one great prison. Gulag! Yevsektsia! *Apparatchiks!* Murderers!"

In the late 1930s and early 1940s, many Jews fled Birobidzhan—anything to escape the misery of this region, as well as to hide from Stalin's mad purges. Estimates vary, but at least 2,000 Jews from the region were murdered during those terrible times. No wonder the great novelist, W. Somerset Maugham, asked, "Can anyone write the word, *Birobidzhan,* without a quickening of the pulse and the pain of unsatisfied desire?"

At its height in the 1930s, the Jewish population of Birobidzhan may have reached 38,000. However, isolation, poor planning, and administrative ineptitude eventually drove many away to nearby Khabarovsk. Moreover, in addition to being untrained for agricultural work, the newcomers were also plagued with brutal winters, swampy land, and few roads. The harsh conditions combined with government mismanagement caused many to leave. Stalin's purges and the failure of the government to support the project doomed it.

At the end of World War II, Jews constituted about one-quarter of the city's total population of 100,000. The Soviet experiment of Jewish nation-building had ended in failure.

During the Communist era, a few Westerners visited this "Jewish homeland," and perpetuated the *myth* of Birobidzhan. To this day, officials proudly call this Jewish Autonomous Region "the first modern Jewish homeland." Such *chutzpah!* Jewish life was condemned and thousands of Jews died there. What good was it?

And still the mystique lingers. For example, every time I mention Birobidzhan to my friend Barbara, her eyes light up as she recalls one of those delightful childhood memories. During World War II when the USSR was our ally, she attended a Communist-leaning kindergarten in Canada. One day she came home and told her parents that she was "going to be a leader to take Jews to Birobidzhan." Her parents weren't exactly ecstatic about it as she told them how her schoolmates sang songs praising the Region.

When I mentioned Birobidzhan to my friend Sam, a teacher, he immediately knew the name. "I haven't heard that name mentioned for years," he told me with an expression of wonderment. "The forgotten city," he said, beaming.

On a walk in 2004 around Birobidzhan, Yelena Belyaeva, a native (but not Jewish) who has studied Yiddish and Hebrew in New York, Tel Aviv, and Moscow, told me, "You can even be late in Birobidzhan; it's a provincial city."

The city is a tidy, well-kept municipality of some 70,000 residents. Its name derives from two small tributaries of the Amur River, the Bira and the Bidzhan. Jewish leaders even joke that the entire JAR region with its 200,000 residents could be considered a "small Kuwait," because minerals and oil exist in the Russian Far East.

Yelena, who teaches Yiddish and Hebrew at the State Pedagogical Institute, the JCC, and Sunday school, greets people with a *Shalom Aleichem!* (peace be with you). They fire back with *Aleichem Shalom*. Later, we viewed a new monument to the great Jewish writer, Sholom Aleichem, fittingly located on Sholom-Aleichem Street. The statue was unveiled in 2004, the city's seventieth anniversary.

During much of Stalin's days, no synagogue existed in Birobidzhan, as religion was perceived to be counterrevolutionary. The first synagogue opened at the end of World War II, but closed in the mid-1960s after it was severely damaged in a fire. Then, in 1968, the "hut synagogue" (so named because it resembled a wooden *shtibel,* or prayer hall) was established on Mayakovskaya Street. This modest structure with a tin roof houses what is often described as a nineteenth-century Jewish village congregation, held together by a small membership.

A second synagogue—today, the main one—opened in 2000 as part of a newly renovated Jewish community center (JCC) at 14a Sholom-Aleichem Street. The congregation soon discovered that it was difficult to hold services in a crowded JCC, so in 2004, they moved into an attractive, newly constructed building, next door to the JCC. The new facility features a prayer hall that seats 122; a beautifully designed ark crafted of wood imported from China; meeting rooms; a kitchen and canteen; a children's center; and a room designated for celebrating the Shabbat and Jewish culture.

Outside of the synagogue and the JCC stands a statue in memory of victims of the Holocaust, as well as a memorial for the Jews who died in the terrorist attack in Mumbai, India, in 2008.

After years of decline, Birobidzhan's Jews face the future with optimism, even though the Jewish population has decreased. In the last decade, it has dropped in the number of Jewish residents. A realistic figure today is about 4,500. Some believe the figure is actually closer to 2,000. None of these statistics can be confirmed.

In 2011, the community eagerly awaited a new rabbi to replace Rabbi Mordechai Scheiner who returned to Israel, according to Rabbi Yaakov Klein of Chabad.

With the fall of Communism in 1991, officials thought that the region's entire Jewish population would emigrate to Israel. And true enough, along with the freedom to practice Judaism openly came a sharp increase in the number of Jews making *aliyah*.

"Now that the Jewish autonomy has real meaning, people are leaving," said Birobidzhan's mayor, Vladimir Bolotnov, back in a 1995 interview with David Landau, published by the Jewish Telegraphic Agency (JTA). His comment recognized the paradox of renewed Jewish life in *Birobidzhan* and *aliyah*. Not everyone has left, however; many have remained behind, and several hundred have even returned from the Jewish state. Today, JDC subsidizes welfare programs such as food packages, home care, medicine, a day care center, and winter relief, as well as several social clubs.

One can still buy *Birobidzhaner Shtern,* a newspaper which is now printed in Russian (with occasional pages in Yiddish); listen to the Yiddish radio program, *In a Mazeldicka Shu (In a Lucky Time);* dine out at the L'Chayim Restaurant on Gorky Street (which serves up non-kosher Jewish and Russian fare); and walk tree-lined streets named after such Jewish personalities as Emmanuil Kazakevich and Boris Miller. And with Zionism no longer taboo here, Hebrew language study is gaining ground. The *Alef Bet* is taught in the state kindergarten.

We stopped to visit the kindergarten, where the tykes in the *Menora* program move us with Birobidzhan's story in Yiddish and Hebrew songs. Afterwards, we join in for some Israeli dancing. Later, we note that State School No. 2 teaches Jewish subjects to 800 students.

Any chance of a Jewish revival of *Birobidzhan?* Fragile at best!

In an article in the *Christian Science Monitor,* Boris Kotlerman—a professor at Bar-Ilan University, who ran a Yiddish summer program for scholars for several years before it died out—is quoted as saying, "The Jewish republic has a good potential for a real revival, but the authorities are keeping the status quo. . . . They're not really interested in pushing it forward. . . . In recent years, Russia has sought to fold its ethnic-minority regions into larger, Russian-dominated ones."

At our farewell, my wife, Riva, was offered a Hebrew school teaching position. "I'm honored," she said. "Let me think about it," she added politely, obviously considering the Siberian winters.

In the Jewish traditional life span of 120 years—in Birobidzhan's case, the year will be 2054—Jewish children will never have to ask parents and grandparents, "Why do they call our province 'the Jewish Autonomous Region'?" They'll know.

⌇

After Birobidzhan, our destination and last stop in Russia was Vladivostok, "Lord of the East."

If you want to observe the vast expanse of Russia—meeting people from the many former Soviet republics in Europe and Asia, as well as citizens from many nations—then I recommend traveling on the Trans-Siberian Railway, the longest railroad in the world, especially because it traverses the world's last great wilderness. Today, largely electrified, it is one of the best ways for the tourist to experience the vastness that is Siberia.

Moreover, to be at the very heart of Russia, to vicariously "live the life of Dr. Zhivago," to ride this, "the big train ride"—all 5,771 miles, from Moscow to Vladivostok on the Pacific Ocean—this is real travel adventure. All of the other train rides in the world "are peanuts" compared to this, remarked fellow travel writer, Eric Newby.

When it was built its main purpose was military, and economic—to open up Siberia for settlers. Even today, the railway is still the backbone of Russia, the only overland route traversing the entire country. It takes more than six days—and the crossing of seven time zones—to do so.

The Trans-Siberian, usually called the "Trans-Sib" in Russia, starts in Moscow, passes through European Russia, crosses the Ural Mountains (which separate Europe and Asia), continues into Siberia's taiga and steppes, and finishes in Vladivostok, located in the Russian Far East coast on the Pacific Ocean.

The first stone for the construction of the Trans-Siberian Railway was laid by the tsarevich Nicholas, (1868–1918), "the last czar" who on May 31, 1891, took a wheelbarrow filled with earth and emptied it onto what was to become the beginning of the great railway line. The line was constructed in stages. Twenty-five years later, in 1916, the long bridge over the Amur River at Khabarovsk was completed and the railway was open for business.

From Khabarovsk, the line runs south following the Ussuri River and the border with China. The region is a mixture of hilly country interspersed with wide flat valleys.

Today, Jewish communities along the Trans-Siberian Railway are being revitalized—a triumph for Jewish persistence and optimism.

⁓

Back in Khabarovsk, we finally boarded our Vladivostok-bound train, ready to roll on the all-electric line that has overhead cables like a streetcar. While sitting in our compartment, waiting to travel the 477 miles to Vladivostok, a female conductor suddenly yanked open our sliding door. Almost unhinging it, she burst into our cabin with the momentum of a 350-pound defensive lineman. *This just might be the crowning moment of our trip on the Trans-Siberian Railway,* I thought.

This conductor, known as the *provadnitza,* sounded more menacing than any drill sergeant. Loudly demanding "Money"—cash for the linen on the two beds in the compartment—she wrote "2-140" on her wrinkled, sweaty palm, barking, "Rubles, *da*—dollars, *nyet."* I calculated that 2,140 rubles was an exorbitant $70 U.S. I decided I was going to stand up to this non-smiling Russian who surely must be a Cold War relic.

After I explained that I had a Russian friend several cars down who spoke her language, she stormed out, pulling the door closed behind her with such force that it bounced back and forth like a steel ball hitting a barrier in a pinball machine. Such tempers these Russians possess in this post-Communist era. I rehearsed the speech I'd give the *provadnitza* when she came back: "No way am I going to shell out $70 for linens for our beds." Riva urged me to pay up or face an international incident.

It's then that I remembered a guidebook warning: "Never get on the wrong side of the cabin crew." They control the roost, so to speak—your tea, meals, snacks, dining-room seat, entrance to the sole bathroom in the carriage (they often keep the other one locked for their personal use).

Saving me from an unpredictable journey was my friend Sasha. I walked down to his compartment, and after he'd heard my tale of woe, he laughed. Turns out she didn't want 2,140 rubles, but 140 rubles, which would cover the cost for two persons. I had confused a dash with a comma.

"I'll talk to her," he said.

I placed 140 rubles ($5 U.S.) in his hand, along with some additional rubles for the conductor. Little gifts ensured a smooth journey.

Later I learned that even if the *provadnitza* had explained the charge more clearly, many travelers still would have believed this to be just another money-making scam; but all passengers have to pay extra for such amenities on Russian trains.

Finally, the train began to chug out of Khabarovsk. The *provadnitza* was in a good mood. I was happy knowing we could enjoy the voyage, which would be bathed in several hours of summer delight.

We followed the Ussuri River and the Chinese border, heading south to Vladivostok, a naval base and Russia's outlet to the Pacific. Our course took us over hills and down into flat valleys similar to those in Montana or rural France. No longer the stark Siberian *tundra,* we saw green scene after green scene. We rambled through a fertile region where wheat, oats, soybeans, and rice grow, and the warm summer rains create a hothouse atmosphere, ideal for agriculture. In addition, this part of the country—the most populous part of the Russian Far East, where 2.3 million people reside—has a worldwide reputation for flora and fauna, including wild grapes, garlic, mushrooms, cranberries, apples, apricots, and strawberries, the latter which we would later devour on our trip through Primorye.

As the landscape unrolled outside our window, the *provadnitza* returned. This time she opened the door with balletic agility, as if caressing an infant. With our misunderstanding annulled, she offered us chocolate with our tea.

Picking up speed, the train hurled itself through the countryside. By now it was 10:15 p.m., and still light outside. Party time! Our fellow passengers were a gregarious lot, with hearty appetites. Russian tradition demands that passengers share vittles with their cabin-mates. Having devoured our box lunches, we handed out chewy fruit and nut bars which we had brought from America, and the Russians enjoyed them.

An American professor and his cabin-mate, a stern-looking Russian army officer, came into our compartment. We called the military man

"General." He offered up some vodka, and after a few hearty *Nazdarovyas*, he began to smile. It was midnight when we turned in.

The engine's humming lulled us to sleep. As we dreamed, we passed sleeping villages, including the town Muravevo-Amurskaya, named after the great Russian explorer, Count Nikolai Muraviev-Amursky (1809–81). He was given the honorific name of "Amurskaya" after the Amur River. The town was formerly known as Lazo, in honor of the Bolshevik revolutionary, S. G. Lazo (1894–1920), who was captured by the Japanese and executed at the station, allegedly by being thrown alive into a steam-engine firebox. Two other revolutionaries, Lutsky and Sibirtsev, met a similar fate. A monument to all three stands at the station.

Nearing Vladivostok, the train entered an area, which, although far from the main battlefields of the Russian Civil War, had witnessed the arrival of more than a dozen nations in 1918, including the U.S., Britain, and Japan, sent to guard the railroad and halt the Bolshevik advance.

To consolidate their position after the October Revolution, the Reds deserted the Allies and signed the Treaty of Brest-Litovsk on March 3, 1918. To the anti-Communists, Brest-Litovsk became the "sellout" of Russia, and the betrayal of trust with the Allied Powers. Those opposed to the Reds would greet the Allied "interventionists" pouring into Vladivostok: the U.S., Britain, France, Italy, Japan, and other nations, a few of whose units had already arrived earlier that summer. The Allies also moved into "peripheral areas" of North and South Russia, as well as in Siberia, eventually to open up an eastern front against the Germans in the long run, and to protect Allied supplies in Siberia from German seizure in the short run. But most really wanted to intercede on behalf of the Whites, a term used loosely to refer to all factions that battled the Bolsheviks. The U.S. tried to follow an independent course; however, its real purpose was to keep an eye on possible Japanese expansionist moves in the Russian Far East.

Germany surrendered in November 1918, and the Allies soon realized they could not overthrow the Soviet regime. Over the next two years, they would withdraw their forces from Russian soil. The effort to punish the Soviets by military force ended.

As the train pulled into Vladivostok, I recalled Osip Mandelstam, the Russian Jewish poet who was arrested for a poetic attack on Stalin. The former was sent to Vtoraya Rechka, a transit camp in suburban Vladivostok where thousands waited for ships to take them to the gulag. He was "arguably the most brilliant poet Russia produced in the twentieth century," and was among the noted Jewish victims of Stalin to be sent to certain doom in the frozen wasteland of Siberia. "With no drugs or proper care, Mandelstam died in Vtoraya Rechka in December 1938, paranoid and raving," writes Anne Applebaum in her prize-winning book, *Gulag*. Later in Vladivostok, I would make it a point to have the guide take us to the city's university, where stands the memorial statue of Mandelstam (born January 15, 1891, died December 27, 1936).

"In the 1930s and '40s, Josef Stalin's regime killed tens of millions of people, a number so large that the mind tends "to shunt it off into the abstract space reserved for statistics," wrote Linda Sue Park in a *New York Times* review of *Between Shades of Gray* by Ruta Sepetys.

With our train journey at an end, we all spruced up. The General donned his medal-bedecked officer's jacket. The *provadnitza* came by and found the beds just as she had made them.

Final act: A photo in front of our train, with our smiling conductor. To me the smile says, "Everything will be fine." But be forewarned: Don't mess with the *provadnitza*. You may not be as lucky as we were.

⁓

"We have not yet found all the Jews in the Russian Far East or even in the small isolated communities near the port," Jewish leader Vladimir Yankelevich told us when we arrived in Vladivostok. There are regions north of Vladivostok, he added, where they suspect Jews live, but they can only get to them by boat at certain times of the year.

"Even if there is one Jew left in a [single] town, all the facilities and opportunities will be held out to him or her," added Nika of the Siberian office of the JDC. She indicated that I would be seeing a few of these distant locations, towns like Nakhodka and Partizansk in the Primorye region, and she points to my itinerary which states "long periphery tour to a number of very distant places in Primorye; living in such places is a real extreme life experience." I'll say!

Thickly forested and mountainous Primorye Province, known as the Maritime Territory, could easily fit into the size of Washington State. Located in the southeast corner of Russia by the Sea of Japan, its residents engage in logging, mining, fishing, and hunting. Experts have also dubbed it the last stronghold of the Siberian tiger. Not just tigers, but some of the world's largest cats.

One day our driver takes us on a trip outside Vladivostok. After a several hour journey we entered Partizansk, located in the southern part of maritime Primorye Province, and about 150 miles from Vladivostok. Founded in 1896 as the town of Suchan, its name became Gamarnik in honor of revolutionary commissar, Yan Gamarnik. However, the name reverted to Suchan after Gamarnik's suicide, which occurred when he faced arrest during the purges of the Great Terror in 1937.

In the Russian and Chinese rift of the 1950s and 1960s, Nikita S. Khrushchev, then head of the Kremlin, did not want Chinese names on his soil to memorialize the Red partisans in the Civil War, so the town received a new name, "Partizansk." In reality, this municipality should be called "Hardship," what with the amount of pollution in the air and in the rivers. Makes me wonder how people and families stayed put in Soviet times; they do so today, I am told, because they can't afford to move, and Jewish seniors feel their age prohibits moving to Israel. Besides, they are either waiting for or receiving their pension. They need help, and the JDC brings home care to them, as well as minimal food packages made up of vegetable oil, crackers, condensed milk, juice, salads, oats, tea, and, of course, medications—all this in a country where life expectancy for males is 63.03 years of age, and for females, 74.87.

Partizansk lies on the branch of the Trans-Siberian Railway that leads to Nakhodka, the port city. I met Sofia at her modest apartment. She was a member of Komsomol, the Communist youth organization in Soviet days. A survivor of the blockade in Leningrad during World War II, like many young people Sofia was sent to this area. She taught math in this city where she found "hills like the jungle." She described the town thusly:

Sand and sky,
Curse and vodka
This is our dear Nakhodka.

But if Vladivostok and Nakhodka seemed to be on the moon, then Partizansk was on the other side of the crescent. In this poor town where the roads are barely passable because of horrific potholes, and the harsh winters wreak havoc on homes, we met the Baraz sisters, Rita and Nila, now retired. People in this country love literature, and Rita and Nila are no exception. They love to read short stories, poems, and the classics, along with painting, writing, and working in their little garden. They often talk about how their father and brothers all "went to the front" in the "Great Patriotic War."

On the way back to the city, I was reminded of the way many non-Jews still stereotype the Jewish people. Our driver had stopped alongside a house where they were selling baskets of strawberries—what turns out to be an expensive delicacy here in this part of the Russian Far East. The driver bargained long and hard.

"You must be Jewish," said the proprietress, finally giving in to his last offer.

I recalled that in Morocco, they at least called me a "Berber" when I bargained.

⌒

Back in Vladivostok, I met Max Zilberman. Although he had grown up in landlocked Belorussia, as a child he was always interested in sailing the seven seas. He eventually did go to sea, actually becoming a captain in the Soviet navy. He was stationed with the fleet on the Caspian Sea, on Sakhalin Island, and finally, in Vladivostok, where he retired—by the sea, of course.

My friend, the Captain told me how he often visits the Jewish center, as do many seniors. Many of them are alone, and look forward to having a hot meal there. "I don't know Hebrew," he confessed—not uncommon for his generation, raised in the USSR—but he was taking a course at the JCC, which at that time housed the synagogue, In his own words, Max "tries his best" to read Hebrew.

⌒

I don't remember where I first heard or read the expression, *Jews on the Moon*. Russian journalists have long said that inhabitants living in the provinces might as well be "living on the moon." After all, Vladivostok, nearly 6,000 miles from Moscow, and the terminus of the Trans-Siberian Railway, remains the first as well as the last place in Russia. Even Lenin is supposed to have said, "Vladivostok may be far, but it is very much our city."

In 1903, a direct rail link was established between Vladivostok and Moscow. The Byzantine-style railway station, now somewhat faded in grandeur, once showed promise with its arched windows, curved portals, and exterior architectural embellishments.

Vladivostok remains the largest and most important city in the Russian Far East. This port on the Sea of Japan occupies a beautiful setting, especially in summer. In winter, icebreakers are needed to open the channels that lead out to the Pacific. The city boasts that its coastline remains unfrozen longer than any other Siberian port, being inaccessible for only seventy-two days per year compared to nearby Nakhodka's ninety-eight. Together, the two ports handle one-quarter of Russia's foreign trade.

Vladivostok lies further south than the French Riviera, but this is hard to reconcile with the fact that the city's bays stay frozen until April. People in Siberia manage to stay alive in winter, even in the face of blackouts with no heat. "Like so many millions of Russians, the hardy souls of Primorye rely on a long tradition of self-preservation," writes Andrew Meier in *Black Earth: A Journey through Russia after the Fall.*

Everywhere you go in Vladivostok, it's either up a hill or down a hill. Hills, hills, and more hills. A big tourist attraction is the childhood home of actor Yul Brynner, born here in 1920. His Swiss grandfather was an important trader. Taxi drivers will happily show you the house as they speed past, although by the time you turn your head and look back, it's gone.

The city was founded in 1860 by Count Muraviev-Amursky. Buried in Vladivostok, he brought Russia to the Pacific, though he also suggested that Alaska be ceded to the U.S.

Standing in upper Vladivostok, the freezing winds off the Sea of Japan chilled me to the bone. I could see that this Russian city possesses an Asian influence in its architecture. After the fall of Communism, city officials had dreams of the port becoming a Russian Hong Kong. Instead of a boomtown, however, Meier notes that the city became corrupt. He is correct; cargo smuggling from China, Japan, and Korea is a common occurrence.

As I walked along the paths of the old fortress atop the sprawling city, I reflected on the city's history. The Russians arrived in the mid-nineteenth century. At the head of the exploration mission was Count Muraviev-Amursky, who, in 1859, chose the site for a harbor from his steamer, the *America*. A year later, a party of forty soldiers landed and secured the region. By 1898, the city had become an important naval base. In World War I, the city was the chief Pacific Ocean entry port for military supplies and railway equipment sent to Russia from the U.S. After the outbreak of the Russian Revolution in 1917, the city was occupied by Allied troops, the last of which were not withdrawn until 1922 when anti-Revolutionary forces collapsed and Soviet power was established in the region. In the years between the two world wars, Vladivostok remained the home of the Soviet Pacific fleet. During World War II, Vladivostok was a major port for shipping lend-lease supplies to the front. After the war, Stalin shut it down to the outside world. In 1991, with the demise of Communism, Washington opened a consulate in this former Cold War flash point.

Today, berthed in the Golden Horn Bay, the Russian flotilla, somewhat diminished and rusty, is still a naval power in these volatile waters where Russia meets China, Korea, and Japan.

It is said that the Japanese once described this city as a "dagger aimed at their heart . . ." While the port resembles San Francisco, Vladivostok has the distinction of being fifteen time zones away from the East Coast of the U.S. I lost complete track of time in this moon-like atmosphere and kept reminding myself that I was in the vast territory of the Russian Far East. I shuddered when I contemplated its boundaries: the Arctic Ocean on the north; the Pacific Ocean on the east; Korea, China, and Mongolia on the south; and Siberia and Lake Baikal on the west.

Atop the city and gazing down into the harbor, I imagined that during her journey, Aunt Clara might have come up here in 1918 to gaze eastward toward America. After trekking across Russia and Siberia during the Bolshevik Revolution and Civil War, Clara found a small Jewish community of several hundred people, and met up with international Jewish organizations that were rescuing Jews fleeing World War I and Bolshevism.

Vladivostok must have seemed like paradise—the most exciting day of her eight-month journey from Odessa. Now all she had to do was board a ship crossing the Tsugaru Strait to the coast of Japan, where she would take a train to Yokohama, on the western side of Tokyo Bay. Hard to imagine an eighteen-year-old-girl alone in Japan in 1918—riding on a *jinricksha* and walking through the mysterious streets of Yokohama until she sailed on an ocean liner to the U.S., and then Canada, where she met my grandfather.

Visuals of past wars were everywhere in this municipality if you looked for them, and I did. Near the railway station, nestled on a platform, was a Russian submarine, open for viewing. Reminded me that in World War II, the navy displayed a Japanese one-man sub in Pittsburgh for all to see. Nearby was an American lend-lease locomotive which was used to transport part of the $11 billion in war matériel sent to the Soviet Union from the United States in that conflict.

As I meandered through the downtown area, I bumped into American sailors. Few around us knew the importance of the Fourth of July, but we did. We shook hands and wished each other a "Happy Fourth." The neat, clean-shaven American marines were quite popular, especially with Russian children. No ugly-American syndrome here. Russian sailors, decked out in their black and navy blue uniforms, reefer jackets, and sailor's vests, were friendly toward their American counterparts.

Vladivostok seeks to become a tourist destination, though economically it is dependent on the used-car trade from Japan. Korean, Chinese, and Japanese businesspeople are frequent visitors to the city. Russia's improving economy is fueled by that liquid gold, oil. Lest we forget, Russia has the largest oil reserves in the world, larger even than Saudi Arabia, and lest we forget again, gas and oil exploration are gradually making Siberia the source of Russia's wealth. This income helped Russia overcome its economic collapse of 1998.

About 700,000 people, including 6,000 Jews, call Vladivostok home. Founded in 1902, the headquarters of the Vladivostok Jewish community were originally located on the wide, attractive Svetlanskaya, the main boulevard where American soldiers once marched in parade near the end of World War I. The building formerly belonged to a famous Russian Jewish family, Skedelsky. The Jewish center occupied only a few floors and officially was called the Jewish Religious and Cultural Community Center.

The synagogue was situated on Komarov Street. Until recently, the building which the Communists wrested away from the Jewish community in the 1930s served as a confectionary shop. Before the Soviets seized the building, they induced Jewish workers to write "letters to the editor" demanding that it should be used as a cultural center and not a house of worship.

Finally, in 2004, the structure was turned over to the Chabad-backed Federation of Jewish Communities in Russia (FJC). The confectionary shop which had occupied the premises had moved, and the cost of repairing the empty building amounted to between $500,000 and $1 million. Renovating the building into a synagogue was possible with the assistance of the Federation of the Jewish Communities (FJC) of the Commonwealth of Independent States (CIS) which is the regional organization whose participating countries were former Soviet Republics at the breakup of the Soviet Union. CIS is a very "loose association."

When the confectionary shop was finally refurbished as a Jewish house of worship, it contained a prayer hall, a *mikveh,* and a soup kitchen large enough to meet the needs of the city's growing Jewish community.

In 2007, the new synagogue was dedicated, seventy years after it had been confiscated by the Soviets. The FJC newsletter reported that the building was "filled with the vibrancy of Jews once again proudly celebrating their identity." Even before it was officially dedicated, the synagogue was used for prayers.

For a while, it has been recognized that the exterior of this historic synagogue bears an etching of the tablets presented to Moses—the sign of the Jewish covenant with God. Soviet authorities did their utmost to erase the actual letters. Recently, during renovations, drilling accidentally bore into the tablets and the original Hebrew letters were discovered underneath a heavy layer of cement. Once the cement and dirt were removed, the first two words of each commandment were once again legible.

The synagogue has been desecrated at times by vandals who scrawl anti-Semitic slogans on the walls, such as "Death to the Jews," along with the Nazi swastika.

The community has begun looking for a site to establish a permanent JCC. Building a community is like watching a baby learn to walk, "step by step," said Rebbetzin Raskin, wife of the former rabbi of the synagogue. Her husband, Chabad rabbi Menachem Raskin, was the first rabbi since the 1920s to officiate in the city, and like most Chabad rabbis, he would have stayed "forever." However, he was expelled in 2005. A short while later, Rabbi Isroel Silberstein succeeded Rabbi Raskin, and in 2009, he too was expelled due to visa difficulties. Chabad officials told this writer that a Russian rabbi would be sent to the community sometime in 2011.

Since the fall of the Soviet Union, it seems that the Jewish community of Russia has yet to train a new generation of Jewish religious leaders from their own population, so Chabad, for instance, relies on foreign-born rabbis, mostly from Israel or its headquarters in Brooklyn.

No one is quite sure if the expulsions represent a dangerous trend toward barring foreign-born rabbis from occupying pulpits in Russia.

And this community with an intermarriage rate of 95 percent certainly needs a rabbi. Because it was isolated from Jewish life for decades, Vladivostok Jewry probably suffers more than other communities. No wonder Jews here are called "Jews on the Moon."

One does not want to spend his whole life on the moon, especially when I see that former president and now prime minister Vladimir Putin, is pressing down on Russian freedom, though not as completely as in Communist days. The Russian government has introduced near complete control of the media, an overwhelming one-party majority in the legislature, and a lack of respect for democratic freedoms and rule of law.

As Keith Gessen, writing in *The New Yorker* (March 23, 2009), put it: "Russia is a safer, more prosperous place than it was ten, or even five, years ago. And in the new Russia, if you mind your own business, drive to and from work, hire a babysitter, and eat out—all as they do in the West—then you really can feel safe entering and exiting your entryway at four in the morning and four in the afternoon."

Reflecting on my frequent trips to Russia, I believe chances are that the country will not return to the terror of the 1930s or to the gulag or to government-sponsored anti-Semitism. But its leaders probably will be greedy and thus grab enough power so that in the future, it just might stay stuck in its Byzantine ways. Power corrupts, and to hold on to power, rulers—or those who are beholden to rulers, as well as their surrogates—often resort to the murder of journalists and human rights activists, such as Anna Politkovskaya, who was gunned down in 2006. There have been other journalists murdered since her death.

While Russia is no longer hampered by Communist ideology, the "political institutions needed for an effective market economy are largely missing, and corruption is rampant," according to Joseph S. Nye Jr., former U.S. Assistant Secretary of Defense and a professor at Harvard. As a Russian told this writer, "The real mafia sleeps in the Kremlin."

In 2009, President Dmitri A. Medvedev issued a sweeping call for Russia to modernize its economy, wean itself from a humiliating dependence on natural resources, and do away with Soviet-style attitudes that he said were hindering its effort to remain a world power. Of course, Medvedev's mentor is Vladimir V. Putin, the former president and current prime minister who is widely considered to be more influential and less interested in reform that might diminish the Kremlin's authority.

No doubt about it, Putin has adopted an assertive foreign policy. In 2008, for example, Russia once again flexed its bearish muscles in Georgia. At the end of that year, relations between Russia and the U.S. reached their lowest point since the Soviet Union's fall, amid great fears of Russian adventurism. However, by the fall of 2009, with the new administration, contacts and relations seemed to warm up, especially after the U.S. scrapped President George W. Bush's planned missile defense system in Poland and the Czech Republic. That move was "seen in Russian official circles as a vindication of the assertive foreign policy," observed BBC News.

Certainly mistrust remains part of the relationship when it comes to Russia. Are the Russian ghosts of czarism and Leninism and Stalinism coming back to haunt the world, as the Kremlin pushes to regain borderlands of former republics, now independent nations, such as Ukraine?

At the end of my most recent trip in 2009 I recalled other thoughts about Russia which, it has been said, is never as weak—or as strong—as it appears. Often it just wants to be heard and respected, and if it is not, it can go into its power mode; or, as Yevgeny Kiselyov wrote in the *Moscow Times* in July 2009, "[Russia can once] again claim it is 'getting up off its knees' and shake its fist at the West."

Change is coming in terms of the trade pattern of the country in 2011. For example, the destination of Russian exports has changed dramatically in the last decade. Trade with Asia has increased at the expense of business with the U.S. and former Soviet Union countries. Today, China remains Russia's largest trade partner, ahead of Germany. Moreover, Russia is part of the *BRIC* nations of Brazil, Russia, India, and China, the four fastest-rising economies. These four recovered quickly from the global financial crisis in 2008, proving they were not as vulnerable to a downturn as the U.S. and Europe.

In economic resources, Russia is the largest global producer of many commodities, and is a large natural resource exporter. And, "because of its residual nuclear strength," its great human capital, its skills in cyber technology, and its location in both Europe and Asia, Russia will have the resources to either cause major problems for nations, or to make major contributions to a globalized world.

So, which way Russia? Will it be, as Professor Nye asks, "an industrial banana republic," or an example of "reform and modernization"?

One may ask, as did the great Russian writer Nikolai Gogol:

And where do you fly to, Russia?
. . . The carriage bells break into an enchanted tinkling, the air is torn to shreds and turns into wind, everything on earth flashes past, and, casting worried, sidelong glances, other nations and countries step out of her way.

Yes, remembering Gogol, I am always looking over my shoulder to see if his chariot or his "dead souls" are chasing me.

For example, after one earlier trip to Russia, we found ourselves landing in the heart of world cuisine, Paris, certainly the city of food, where one never, but never, eats a bad meal. Emerging from the Metro, we entered the first café restaurant we see, Fouquet's on the Champs-Élysées.

And what did the maître d' do? He seated us next to a group of Russian men who were gorging themselves on huge platters of meat, potatoes, fish, and salad. Talk led to more talk. We toasted each other. We discussed our trip—politics, of course. One man berated us for not knowing Russian politics, names of leaders, opposition parties. He accused Americans of being naive, saying abruptly, "You *must* know this," and then, summoning the waiter, added, "Check, please."

The waiter brought the bill. Instead of reaching for his wallet, my new Russian friend lifted his leather briefcase up onto the table, opened the lid.

Eureka!

Stacked neatly inside were new, crisp American dollar bills, shining as if they had just came off the U.S. Mint presses.

James Bond, where are you? I asked silently. Those Russian ghosts of what is amiss in Russia seem to be still following me.

JEWS ON AN EXOTIC ISLAND

Discovering the Magic of Tahiti, Moorea, and Bora Bora

"For as this appalling ocean surrounds the verdant land, so in the soul of man there lies one insular Tahiti, full of peace and joy, but encompassed by the horrors of the half-known life."
—*Herman Melville,* Moby Dick

I will never forget the first time I met fifty-two-year-old Dr. Yonah Poul. Wrapped in a prayer shawl and phylacteries and holding a prayer book, he sat alone in a far corner of the darkened synagogue, just as the tropical morning sunlight began to pour through the stained-glass windows, each reflecting the design of a major Jewish holiday. His head and the upper part of his body rocked back and forth in the traditional mode of prayer for religious Jews.

Fervently at prayer, he was spending the 17th of Tamuz, a fast day, in the small but well-kept, two-story Jewish house of worship. Of medium height, with close-cropped hair and a salt-and-pepper beard, he reminded me of the Rembrandt painting of a Jew reciting his prayers. Not an unusual scene. Other religious Jews throughout the world might be praying that morning and reciting lamentations just as Dr. Poul was doing—except that this prayer hall was located in one of the most exotic, remote islands on the globe: Tahiti, also known as *Tahiti-nui-i-te-vai-uri-rau* (Great Tahiti of the Many-Colored Waters).

Tahiti stands as the largest and most populated island of French Polynesia, a group of 121 volcanic islands and coral atolls, 76 of which are inhabited. These tiny flakes of land are spread out over 1,300 square miles of the glistening South Pacific, in an area about one-third the size of all

Europe. The islands form a vast triangle that extends from Hawaii in the north to Easter Island in the east and New Zealand in the far southwest. Actually, Polynesia—which means "many islands" in Greek—lies at the same longitude as Hawaii, about 2,000 miles south, halfway between California and Australia.

My reading had informed me that if there is any destination where reality comes close to fantasy, the Polynesian islands carry the day. With their guava, mango, orange, and lemon trees, their coconut palms and furrows of fertile land, it's not even a contest. The Pacific's delicate blue sky constantly beckons travelers, who immediately express awe at how the water constantly deepens into a rich turquoise.

I had read Herman Melville's first novel, *Typee: A Peep at Polynesian Life,* in which he describes these islands as "blooming valleys, deep glens, waterfalls, and waving groves, hidden here and there by projecting and rocky headlands, every moment opening to the view some new and startling scene of beauty." The escape from civilization draws travelers long in need of a respite from tedious work and chores. Believe me, these atolls still rank tops when you seek a paradise full of colors such as sapphire blue, dazzling white, and brilliant green.

As a travel writer, I knew there were Jews in Tahiti; it didn't shock me. I had discovered that a synagogue and congregation functioned there, and through e-mail and phone calls, I had arranged a meeting with Dr. Poul, who gave me directions to the synagogue on rue Morenhout, Quartier Fariipiti, located in the bustling port city of Papeete, the Polynesian capital that claims 132,000 residents.

I quickly learned that this synagogue, built in 1993, helps to nourish the Tahitian tradition of love and romance. Its name alone, Ahava v'Ahava ("Love and Friendship"), reflects kindly and accurately on an isle that was made famous by French artist Paul Gauguin's paintings of beautiful Tahitian women and luxuriant island scenery, as well as romanticized by authors Herman Melville, Robert Louis Stevenson, Pierre Loti, W. Somerset Maugham, James Michener, and anthropologist Margaret Mead.

As far back as 1768, navigator Louis-Antoine de Bougainville wrote back to France that the local women possessed "the celestial form of that goddess Venus." French Polynesia seems to have been synonymous with a land of earthly delights, and the mystique of its women quickly filtered through to the outside world.

French novelist Pierre Loti, who arrived in Tahiti in 1872, wrote in his novel, *Le Mariage de Loti* (Loti's Marriage):

> *Oh! the delightful hours, Oh! the soft and warm summer hours that we spent there, each day, near the Fataoua River . . . the air was all charged with tropical scents dominated by the fragrance of oranges heated in the branches by the midday sun . . .*

James Michener's book, *Tales of the South Pacific,* first published in 1947, was adapted into a classic musical romance two years later by Rodgers and Hammerstein, running on Broadway for nearly 2,000 performances. Revived in 2008, *South Pacific* thrilled audiences for another 1,000 performances and received seven Tony Awards.

The show's opening lines will long be remembered:

> *I wish I could tell you about the South Pacific, the way it actually was. The endless ocean. The infinite specks of coral we call islands. Coconut palms nodding gracefully toward the ocean. Reefs upon which waves broke into spray, and inner lagoons, lovely beyond description.*

Welcome to the islands of love. Welcome to Tahiti. Welcome to the capital city, Papeete. Welcome to the Sephardic synagogue, Ahava v'Ahava.

Standing there that first day in Tahiti, as the bright morning sunlight illuminated the synagogue, I could see that its exterior meshed nicely with the island paradise atmosphere. Here was the white-washed house of prayer nestled in the midst of lush, tilting palm trees, date and mango trees. Actually, Dr. Poul insisted that "one of the most beautiful *sukkahs* (booths for the holiday of Sukkot, which celebrates the harvest in Israel) in the world" can be found in Tahiti, since the temporary hut is decorated with tropical flowers and fruits.

Some of the members of this congregation came to Tahiti as adventurers, filled with wanderlust. Certainly Tahiti and the islands of Polynesia meet the qualifications for those who want to live out their days in "paradise," especially if heaven is 4,000 miles from Los Angeles, 7,000 miles from New York City, and 12,000 miles from Paris.

I could see why visitors would tell Dr. Poul and others in the community over and over again, "This is such a wonderful synagogue. It's unbelievable to have so nice a *shul* [Yiddish word for synagogue] so far from everywhere."

As Dr. Poul related to me, the travelers usually rattle off the following questions:

"How long has the Jewish community existed in Tahiti?"

"Are you Orthodox?"

"How many Jews are there in Tahiti?"

"What jobs and what professions do Jews engage in?"

"How and where do you get kosher food?"

"Are there any weddings in Tahiti? Bar mitzvahs?"

"Is there a Jewish cemetery?"

"Is there a rabbi?"

"Are there mixed marriages?"

"Talmud Torah?"

"What about festivals and High Holidays?"

And finally, that very important, ancient Jewish question: "Where do you come from?"

Even in today's beyond-the-jet-age, even in the imagination of today's world travelers, they are shocked to hear that most Tahitian Jews originally hailed from other exotic lands, including Morocco and Algeria.

My ears perked up when I heard the word "Algeria." Ah, *Algerie!* Little did I know nearly fifty years earlier, as I'd walked the streets of the capital city of Algiers, that I would end up meeting Algerian Jews so far from the *casbah*. Over the years since 1962, when Algeria became independent from France, these Jews, still French citizens, had moved to France and then on to French Polynesia.

I wasn't the first writer to meet Algerian Jews in Tahiti. About a hundred years ago, W. Somerset Maugham, playwright, novelist, and short story writer, reported on such a meeting during a visit to the island. When he boarded a cutter in the harbor, the owner of the boat, a man named Levy, spoke French. Nothing unusual about that, until he said he came from

Paris, recalls Maugham. "But he spoke French with a strong accent which suggested to me the Algerian Jew."

While most Jews from Algeria settled in France and Israel in the 1960s, some headed for Tahiti, and specifically, its capital, Papeete. There, they formed ACISPO, a French acronym for "Cultural Association of Israelites and Polynesian Friends."

Today, most Tahitian Jews say they are French, Sephardic, and Orthodox. Many, like Dr. Poul, settled here after French military service. A large number are doctors or businesspeople, most of the latter engaged in the sale of Tahitian pearls.

The congregation, sponsored by ACISPO, claims a membership of about 200 persons—a pretty reliable figure, because that's the number of Jews who show up on Yom Kippur. Even though this congregation functions thousands of miles away from its nearest Jewish neighbors, it desperately tries to keep Judaism alive. And it does so without a full-time rabbi and cantor, except occasionally for High Holidays.

In recent years, the congregation could have hired a rabbi from Israel for Rosh Hashanah and Yom Kippur, but says it lacks the funds to pay for the rabbi's airfare and hotel. When that happens, the congregation has been led in prayer by a *shaliach tzibbur* (volunteer cantor), at no charge. However, in 2009, a rabbi from Paris did conduct High Holiday services.

While 200 congregants may show up for Yom Kippur service, according to Dr. Poul, only about 20 attend Friday-night or Saturday-morning prayers in this house of worship, which contains a *mikveh*. Two of the community's Torah scrolls were provided by the Egyptian Jewish community of Paris, and the other was contributed by a Los Angeles community.

As in all synagogues, the ark faces east, toward Jerusalem. Only later would I learn that Tahiti is "the farthest place on Earth from Jerusalem, the exact antipode."

In an interview in *Hana Hou*, the magazine of Hawaiian Airlines, George Alezrah, an active member of the congregation, told an interviewer that because this house of worship "is just this side of the international dateline, it stands as the last congregation in the world to say the blessings that begin and end the Sabbath and other holy days," which means if that is so Tahiti holds a very special place in the diaspora.

However, Dr. Poul adds an interesting twist. Apparently in geography, the antipodes of any place on earth is the point on the earth's surface which is diametrically opposite it. "Yet," explains Dr. Poul "because of our geographic situation at the antipode, the real direction of Jerusalem is . . . anywhere, because the Holy City is in fact just under our feet! However, because of custom, the ark faces east. But it could be anywhere else."

As in France, the synagogue is governed by Orthodox tradition. A so-called "Committee of Ten" is picked by the President. The latter is elected every two years. The Committee organizes holidays, memorial services, circumcision rites, and bar mitzvahs, as well as manages a Sunday school. It orders kosher wine and *matzot,* manages the building, and often meets to settle disputes among its Jewish members. Several times a year, a "General Assembly of Tahitian Jews" gathers, and members contribute to the upkeep of the synagogue.

This congregation does not waver from Orthodox Judaism, at least when it comes to custom and observance inside the synagogue. Like many congregations in the world that are tourist attractions, Ahava v'Ahava complains about Jewish visitors who arrive on Shabbat from the cruise ships, dressed in shorts and short-sleeved shirts and taking photos, much to the chagrin of worshippers.

Dr. Poul also told this writer about an American Reform female rabbi who was politely refused an *aliyah* and kindly requested to sit in the women's section.

A small Sunday school functions here. Every Sunday morning, two classes are held—one for children under seven years old, and another for bar mitzvah–age students. Miriam Sroussi is the Hebrew teacher.

Half of the community is composed of mixed marriages. In the past, children from interfaith marriages were admitted to the Sunday school, but the Committee recently decided not to accept children born of a non-Jewish mother, as "there were a lot of problems between the Orthodox and more traditionalists," said Dr. Poul, adding that a few of those children are taught at home.

For a dozen years before 2009, a total of six bar mitzvahs were held at the synagogue. But in 2009, two bar mitzvahs were held, including one for Raphael, Dr. Joseph Sebbag's son. And in 2010, three bar mitzvahs were held, including again, another of Dr. Sebbag's sons, Daniel. Dr. Sebbag is a former president and now spokesperson for the community.

One couple held their son's bar mitzvah in the Meridien Hotel here, with a "liberal" rabbi from Los Angeles who brought his own Torah, according to Dr. Poul. Another bar mitzvah was held with a Conservative Movement rabbi in a ceremony at the Western Wall in Jerusalem.

Synagogue members say there's no anti-Semitism here. "Polynesians," explained Mrs. Joseph Sebbag, "believe in God and understand that everyone has his or her own religion." No police or guards at the front door, and a *shamash* lived on the premises. Well I should say kind of a *shamash*. You see Jean Eliyahu Boccobza was a blind octogenarian from Tunisia who welcomed tourists that came to the *shul*. But what I did not know was that Jean Eliyahu was once the hit of Parisian entertainment and jet set. You see, this veteran of the Free French fighting forces in World War II who had helped liberate Paris, founded after the war, a string of glitzy night clubs in the French capital and Brussels. He also established in 1950, the first night club in the French Riviera resort town of St. Tropez. The club was called, *Les Jardins de la Licorne* (The Gardens of the Unicorn) and was frequented by Brigitte Bardot, fashion model and actress, according to Dr. Poul.

In 1975, Jean Eliyahu sold his clubs and later visited Tahiti on his honeymoon. Like hundreds and hundreds before him, he fell in love with the island and settled in Tahiti in 1990. But he soon began to go blind and according to Dr. Poul, ended up a decade later no longer married, penniless, and totally blind. Like Dr. Poul, he became a *baal tshuva*.

The congregation took him into the *shul* where he now lived and he helped out as best he could.

In 2005, Dr. Poul and Jean Eliyahu took a trip to Jerusalem. The latter had been to Israel several times, but it was Dr. Poul's first visit. The two of them enjoyed the trip immensely. Though blind, "Jean Eliyahu was very receptive to perfumes, sounds, music, and voices." Both of them would later describe the visit as "very emotional."

In 2009, Jean Eliyahu passed away. But before he died, he asked Dr. Poul and friends to bury him in Jerusalem. So Dr. Poul and Andre Amouyal, the latter also an active member in the synagogue, accompanied the body to Israel and buried Jean Eliyahu in Givat Shaul in Jerusalem.

Over and over again in my travels in the diaspora, I was to hear the name of Jerusalem uttered with awe, even in Tahiti. The story of this *shamash* and his trip to Jerusalem and his desire to be buried there, hit home when I remembered that once I asked Mrs. Joseph Sebbag, how does she like living in paradise in Tahiti. To which she responded, "paradise is only in Jerusalem."

Services are held at 6:30 p.m. on Friday, and at 8:00 a.m. and 5:00 p.m. on Saturday. They are led by a community member and are conducted according to Sephardic tradition.

I learned that a few times each year, a rabbi comes from the U.S. to teach Talmud and educate the children regarding Jewish customs. Several rabbis from *yeshivas* in Israel arrive to teach and raise funds. At one time, Chabad rabbis from the U.S. and Australia came at least twice a year, but no longer.

On the upper level of the synagogue is the residence of the rabbi, now empty. For twenty years, Rabbi Yosef Ben David of Sydney conducted High Holiday services. When in Tahiti, he lived in the synagogue. He now resides in Israel, I was told.

The synagogue can be difficult to find, as it is not mentioned in many tourist guides. It organizes Shabbat and holiday services, but often has to scout around for a *minyan*. Few *B'nai Mitzvahs* take place, and even fewer *brit milahs;* a Jewish wedding has not been celebrated for some years.

The community has good relations with France, the U.S., and Israel. They are always looking for a rabbi from the U.S. to teach Talmud and instruct the children. No question the community suffers from the absence of a rabbi.

Kosher products arrive from Australia and are sold at the synagogue. The Carrefour supermarket in Faa'a, near the airport, also stocks kosher foods. But one of the disadvantages of living on this beautiful island is that its distance from major population centers always causes anxiety just before the High Holidays, waiting for food deliveries, and hoping the kosher-for-Passover food products will arrive in time from Los Angeles. "Always, it arrives at the last minute," says Dr. Poul.

So, what brought these Jews to Tahiti? Perhaps the weather and good business opportunities. To many Westerners, however, Tahiti means escape. The question is, escape from what? Unless one pries, the reasons remain unknown. What is extremely unusual in such a remote outpost is for an individual suddenly to discover Judaism. Usually it's the other way around, and he or she assimilates.

It does happen, however. Take the case of Dr. Poul, an internist in private practice in Papeete who converted to Judaism years after he had arrived on the island.

As Dr. Poul and I sat outside in the hallway of the synagogue, he told me about his life and that of his father, Eric Abraham ben Yosef Poul. This is a story of two lives that would reach from Siberia to France, from France to Vietnam, from Vietnam back to France, again from France to French Polynesia, and then, on top of that, to military service in the Red Army, French Army, and the French Foreign Legion.

While children in most cases take a different path from those chosen by their parents, there was one aspect of the father-son relationship that intrigued and obsessed me: Both men served in the French Foreign Legion, the *Légion étrangère*—that unique unit in the French military specifically created for foreign nationals who wish to serve in the armed forces of France. Although it's open to French citizens and commanded by French officers today, I knew that over the years, its storied history had spawned a great deal of fiction and had made an impact on popular culture. I was amazed to learn, however, that immediately before and after World War II, many Poles and Jews from Eastern Europe who had fled to France ended up enlisting in the Legion.

Another aspect of the life of Yonah Poul's father obsessed me: As a member of the French Foreign Legion, Eric Abraham ben Yosef Poul had fought in the Battle of Dien Bien Phu, in the First Indochina War. He was not the only Jew to fight alongside the French in that debacle, battling to the bitter end until they surrendered on May 7, 1954.

Born in 1920 in Dubno, in western Ukraine—which was then rife with pogroms—Eric Abraham Poul's parents moved first to Brno in South Moravia (which before World War II was in Czechoslovakia, and today is in the Czech Republic), There, they changed their name from Poulstein to Poul. They then moved to Prague, until that capital was occupied by the

Germans in 1939. The Pouls fled again. Eric Abraham was separated from his parents and believed they and a brother were dead. He was immediately picked up by the Nazi SS, but escaped during a truck transfer in a forest in Bohemia. Somehow he made his way to Russia, where he joined the Red Army, now fighting the Germans.

After the war, Stalin rewarded Eric Abraham and thousands of other Jewish soldiers by deporting them to Siberia; so much for patriotism in the Communist days. In that bleak and frigid land, Eric Abraham, now skilled in the ways of prison breaks, escaped again. This time he began a journey which many take but few survive: He wandered through Siberia, with the Russian secret police hot on his trail. Smuggling himself across the Turkish frontier, he joined the French Foreign Legion in Istanbul. No questions asked! Eventually he was sent to French Indochina, where he fought at Da Lat, Hoa Binh, and Cao Bang. Little did he know that he would soon be defending Dien Bien Phu.

After the French surrender of the jungle fortress in Northwest Vietnam in 1954, Eric Abraham Poul was imprisoned by the Viet Minh for one year. Finally, he was repatriated and sent back to France, where he met his future wife and Yonah's mother, Christiane Porte, born in 1932 in Spain, and now a nurse in a military hospital in the south of France. This Spanish lady—whose father, Rafael Porte, and mother, Antonieta Arinio, were Communists—had escaped from Spain after General Francisco Franco had won the Spanish Civil War. Christiane nursed Eric Abraham back to health. They married, although Eric Abraham Poul apparently never told his wife about his roots.

Eric Abraham Poul, now recovered, reentered the Foreign Legion and served in Algeria as a lieutenant until the French departed that North African land in 1962.

Meanwhile, the newly married couple had a son, Yonah, who was born in the south of France in 1959. Yonah did not discover his father was Jewish until he was twenty years old.

"It's the worst thing to be a Jew," the father told his son, who years later would explain that his father, it seems, "was very angry with Judaism and rabbis." He claimed they prevented the Ashkenazi Jews from resisting against the Nazis.

A few years after Yonah was born, Eric Abraham suddenly discovered that his parents and brother were alive and well in the U.S. In 1963, Eric Abraham and his family flew to America and spent three months with their kin. They traveled to the U.S. many times thereafter, with Yonah spending several summer holidays with his grandmother, uncle, and cousins in Hopkins, Minnesota, a suburban city west of Minneapolis. By this time, according to Dr. Poul, his father's "American family" had become "very assimilated, and didn't want to be Jewish anymore."

Over the next thirty-three years, son Yonah Poul would attend high school in Toulouse; be admitted to the prestigious Saint-Cyr Military Academy, from which he graduated in 1975; study medicine; work in the local hospital; and practice anesthesiology and intensive care in the heart surgery unit of a university hospital in Toulouse. This was followed by a stint in the French Foreign Legion, where he served as a physician with the Fifth Foreign Regiment. He was first stationed in Aubagne, France, near Marseilles, where the French Foreign Legion maintains its headquarters. Later, he was shipped to Tahiti, where he became a "flying doctor" (with the rank of chief doctor/captain) in Moruroa, once used as a nuclear test site by France, and in Hao, a large coral atoll, both located in the Tuamotu Archipelago. He was also employed as chief doctor/captain by the Tahitian Health Ministry, a job he performed for ten years.

Eric Abraham passed away in 1987, and two years later, Yonah married a Chinese woman from Tahiti. The couple had three children, and divorced in 1995. Dr. Poul's mother, now ill, lives with him on the island today.

At about the same time as his estrangement from his wife in 1995, Dr. Poul met Dr. Joseph Sebbag and others in the Jewish community and "fell in love with Judaism." Inspired by Dr. Sebbag, at whose home he has a standing invitation for Shabbat, and moved by Chabad rabbis who often visit the island, he began the Orthodox conversion process. This took him eight years, until one day in 2004 he flew to Paris and went to a *mikveh* in an Orthodox Sephardic synagogue, rue Pani Cao in the 19th arrondissement. He recorded the date, the 10th day of Nissan, 5764/April 1, 2004. During all this time, he continued to meet Chabad messengers from abroad who came to Tahiti. "I feel very close to the Lubavitch way of Judaism. Now, I think I'm a real Lubavitcher just waiting for the *huppah* [wedding canopy]."

Dr. Poul set up an office in Papeete as a general practitioner. He is friends with other Jewish doctors throughout the islands who help treat the people of Polynesia.

When asked if a Jewish community could survive another twenty years, Mrs. Sebbag noted, "We hope so, but maybe it will be a liberal community." As for Dr. Poul, he replied: "I don't know. Jews have been here for at least two centuries."

Indeed they have!

Two centuries, however, is but a mere flash in the history of civilizations. Today we know that the first ma'ohi great warriors and navigators arrived in the Polynesian area almost 4,000 years ago, from Southeast Asia. Guided by sea currents and stars, they began to populate present-day French Polynesia, around 500–300 BCE. Initially drawn to the islands along the north shore of New Guinea, these canoe people ventured farther eastward into the ocean—first, hundreds of miles to Polynesia, and then thousands of miles to the far corners of the Polynesian Triangle.

The original Tahitians were Polynesians who moved from another of the Society Islands, Raiatea, a Polynesian cultural diffusion center. The French policy of assimilation, however, produced a modern people that were basically Polynesian but deeply influenced by French culture.

Though the French eventually would assume control of the islands, the first European to discover Tahiti was the English navigator Samuel Wallis, who on his second voyage to the Pacific in June 1767 claimed the island for England and named it "King George the Third's Island." The natives called their island Otaheite; we call it Tahiti.

Arriving the following year, Louis-Antoine de Bougainville anchored on the east coast of Tahiti in the Hitiaa Lagoon. He immediately claimed possession of the island for France. By the way, Americans owe a debt to de Bougainville. From 1779 to 1782, he served as commodore of the French fleet in support of our American Revolution.

Then on April 13, 1769, Captain James Cook—one of the most outstanding figures in the history of exploration—anchored his ship at Matavi Bay on the northwest side of Tahiti. Cook returned to the island in 1773 and 1777, to much acclaim from the Tahitians. Cook named these and nearby islands the Society Islands after the Royal Society in England. Today the Society Islands are subdivided into the Windwards (Tahiti, Moorea, Maiao, Tetiaroa, and Mehetia) and the Leewards (Huahine, Raiatea, Taha'a, Maupiti, and Bora Bora).

One of the men who sailed with Captain Cook was a seafarer whose name is known for the inhumane way he treated the sailors under him. He is none other than Captain William Bligh, who later would return to Tahiti on his own ship, the *Bounty*.

"Tahiti was in those days a veritable paradise to the seaman—one of the richest islands in the world, with a mild and wholesome climate, abounding in every variety of delicious food," wrote Charles Nordhoff and James Norman Hall in their acclaimed book, *Mutiny on the Bounty*. "In the South Sea," they wrote, "men lose their sense of the passage of time. In a climate where perpetual summer reigns and there is little to distinguish one week from another, the days slip by imperceptibly."

While clouded in myth and mystique, Tahitian Jewish history includes at least one Jew among the early European explorers who reached Polynesia's shores. We don't have the name of this Jew who allegedly arrived with Captain Cook when the latter sailed into Tahiti on April 13, 1769, on his ship, the *Endeavour*. All we know is that he was called *Monsieur Jew*. According to another tale, the doctor to Captain Cook was a John Levy, who also married a Tahitian princess.

Immersing ourselves in the area's facts and folklore, we come up with the story of one of the first Jews to arrive in Tahiti in the nineteenth century, a man who not only made a name for himself, but whose historic story is romantic fiction at its best, including adventure, risk-taking, true romance, and love at first sight.

In 1791, a certain John Salmon fled his native France during the French Revolution on suspicion that he contributed financially to the flight of King Louis XVI to Varennes, in order to escape the clutches of the Revolution. John Salmon landed in England that year and established himself first in London, then in Hastings, in Sussex, where he began life anew as a merchant, as well as a rabbi for the small Jewish community there.

A son, Alexander, grew up in the shadow of his father. Apparently not content with life in the British Isles, Alexander and his two brothers moved to America, eventually settling in California. One account has Alexander running away to sea on a whaler and arriving in Tahiti in the spring of 1841, at age twenty-one. Because of his diplomatic skills, he soon became the secretary of Queen Pomare IV, who introduced him to twenty-year-old Princess Arrioehau, the adopted sister of the queen, supposedly the most beautiful Tahitian woman on the island. She also held the distinction of being from a family of chiefs.

So we have this Jewish adventurer who fell passionately, head over heels in love with the sister of a reigning monarch. But there were problems. It was forbidden for a Tahitian to marry a foreigner. So by royal command, Queen Pomare IV suspended the law, and Alexander and Arrioehau were married and lived happily ever after.

Invested with the Tahitian title of Ariitaimai ("the prince who came from the sea"), Alexander supervised agriculture and introduced coffee to the island. He also played a role in helping France to acquire Tahiti and Polynesia. Meanwhile, Queen Pomare IV had been having difficulties with the French, who claimed title to the island colony on the basis of the landing of Captain Louis-Antoine de Bougainville, who had anchored in Tahiti in 1768. She roused the ire of the French when she deported two French Roman Catholic missionary priests in 1836. This act led the French, in a show of strength, to dispatch a warship in 1842 to demand reparations, and to eventually arrange for a French Protectorate, to which Queen Pomare IV was forced to agree.

Alexander devoted himself "wholeheartedly to the cause of the French Protectorate over his adopted homeland," Tahiti, according to Ida Cowen, author of *Jews in the Remote Corners of the World*. He interceded with the queen and helped to reconcile the two sides. From then on, Alexander, close to the Queen, watched the royal office and looked out for those who might have been hostile toward the French Republic.

Fast-forward to July 1859, when Alexander and Princess Arrioehau's daughter, Titaua, married Scottish merchant John Brander. The union helped Alexander to become a partner in the Brander firm. The two immediately "made a fortune in pearl trading, and had become the most important ship chandler in Tahiti," according to Cowen.

Salmon continued his life of public service to Tahiti. Appointed honorary consul for the U.S., he served as president of the Papeete Lodge of Freemasons, vice president of one of the courts, and a member of the Administrative Council. But according to Cowen, Salmon "formally enter[ed] the Protestant Church."

Alexander Salmon died in August 1866, during a dysentery epidemic. He was only forty-four years old. Queen Pomare followed the burial procession as the entire island mourned his death.

But our story does not end there. One of Salmon's three daughters, Johanna Marau Ta'aroa (1846–1934) married her uncle, who became King Pomare V. He was the son of Queen Pomare IV, who died in 1877. Johanna became Queen Marau (1877–80), and remained on the throne until her husband, the king, abdicated to the French colonial government on the promise of a large sum of money, it is said. So, by the Act of Annexation of 1880, Tahiti officially became a French colony. In effect, the last queen of Tahiti, this daughter of Alexander and Arrioehau, was half Jewish.

Meanwhile, Alexander Salmon's son, Alexander Jr.—known as Pa'ea (Mangarevan for "hobble")—inherited his father's business interests. As co-owner with John Brander of the Maison Brander copra and coconut oil plantations in Tahiti, the Marquesas, and the Cook Islands, set up new businesses on Easter Island, the Polynesian island in the Southeastern Pacific. Because of their vast land holdings, the company and this English Jewish Tahitian in effect became de facto ruler of Easter Island, from 1878 until it was ceded to Chile in 1888.

A hundred years later, Ida Cowen, author, teacher, and lecturer, visited Papeete. During her visit, she met another Alexander Salmon who told her he was so named because of his resemblance to his forebear and his cousins. Although Christian by faith, he acknowledged his family's descent from the scion of the house of an English Jewish banker and rabbi, John Salmon, Alexander's father. This young lad must have been the great-grandson and namesake of yes, our English Jew, Alexander Salmon.

We know that many European Jewish merchants came to Tahiti in the nineteenth century, besides Salmon, with names such as Levy, Cowan, and Cohen. For example, a certain Emile Levy, a French Jewish merchant, sailed to Papeete in 1888 to acquire pearls for the Levy family jewelry store in Paris.

Even today, there are names of Tahitians with hyphenated names, including Ceran-Jerusalemy, a familiar name in Tahiti. These nineteenth-century Jews soon assimilated into Tahitian society and many of them are now Protestants.

Dr. Poul and I discussed the new French Jews coming to Tahiti. What does the future hold for Tahitian Jewry on this island that floats the tricolor of France? Will more Jews come, and if so, will they stay?

Some may find it difficult to believe, but there are people in the world who shun the big cities of New York, London, and Paris for small towns, and yes, even islands. Many Jews who once lived in France have settled on various beautiful and exotic French islands, such as Guadeloupe and Martinique. Tahitian Jews also want a French lifestyle without the noise and pollution, crowded apartment buildings, the Metro, the heavy traffic, and the foul air hanging over the huge metropolitan areas.

Still, despite the beauty of this "jewel of the South Seas," Tahiti, after all, remains an island, romantic though it may be. At one time, the capital city of Papeete, where nearly all the Jews reside, stood as a modest modern town with bars and food stalls. Today, it is crowded with tourists who have dollars and euros to spend.

Among the Europeans, a sense of island loneliness can creep into their mundane lives. I was to see this in Israel, considered by many to be an island, mainly because it is surrounded on one side by the Mediterranean Sea and on three sides by hostile neighbors. So every summer, citizens are compelled to break out, to get away, to travel to *chutz la'aretz* ("outside the Land") to escape the confines of isolation.

As for the Jews of Tahiti, years ago they spent retreats during Shabbat in hotels in nearby Moorea. Now their vacation destinations include mostly Israel, but also the U.S., New Zealand, Australia, and France.

Isolation can bring on an atmosphere of melancholy—the dreamlike sense of lonely and haunting sadness that is familiar even today to all those who know the Pacific islands well.

"It is a delightful land when one is but twenty, but one soon gets tired of it, and perhaps it is as well not to go back after one has turned thirty," wrote Pierre Loti, according to Kaori O'Connor in the introduction to Loti's *The Marriage of Loti—Tahiti*.

Because of the smallness of the community, "We're always together," says Dr. Poul, especially at meetings, meetings, and more meetings. What would a Jewish community be without meetings? It's like a big family, and now with the Internet and Skype, well, "the world is in your home," he adds.

Some things go by the wayside. The community at one time lit the Hanukkah menorah in the largest square in Tahiti, down near the seashore. The program featured Hasidic music, and synagogue members passed out traditional donuts. It stopped when the Lubavitch rabbi, David Partouche—who had flown from London to Tahiti for twenty years, for the Hanukkah celebration—was no longer able to make the journey. Apparently Rabbi Partouche still manages to come at least once a year, it was reported.

Then there remains the lack of cultural, intellectual, and artistic activity on the islands. Mrs. Joseph Sebbag, who is from Belgium, and Ashkenazi, tells me that these islands are "a wonderful place to raise children. We have a good way of life," she declares. But sadly, she adds, for the educated, cosmopolitan French, there's "no theater, no ballet, no culture, no music. Nothing!"

Well, there's always love!

Agreed, says one group of people who don't need any encouragement to come here. You guessed it: honeymooners! To use an old-fashioned cliché, "Love is in the air." This is always true in Tahiti and the islands.

A large number of Jewish young adults arrive in Tahiti each day, mostly from the U.S., but it's not clear how many of these honeymooners actually visit the synagogue. Dr. Poul says that some do stop, but often they are from Brazil, Mexico, Canada, Argentina, Australia, and of course, France.

Honeymooners keep on coming to these Polynesian islands, especially Moorea and Bora Bora, whose beaches lend themselves to passion.

In the days of the eighteenth century explorers, Tahiti and the surrounding islands literally were situated at the ends of the earth.

Not so in the twenty-first century! It's only a flight away.

The reader may ask how I came to realize that newlyweds fly to this enchanted island. Simple. Riva and I followed them and boarded the Honeymoon Express, as I call it, the direct, nonstop Air Tahiti Nui flight.

I was shocked at the large crowd of young people waiting at gate B29 at JFK airport in New York a few summers ago in 2007. There they were, my honeymooners—youthful couples, leaning on each other's shoulders, holding hands, kissing, as they impatiently waited to board the jet which would land them at Tahiti's international airport in Papeete.

I watched them closing their eyes, their minds conjuring up anticipated sexual adventures with lush tropical French Polynesia as their background: The cloudless blue skies above a vista framed in palm trees, lush green vegetation, volcanic peaks, and turquoise lagoons formed by coral reefs. I was sure they also had in mind the mystique of the South Sea Islands and the sensuality and beauty of the Tahitian people. All of this must have been putting them in the mood for love.

"We got married yesterday," said one couple.

"We just got married in May," declared another that steamy humid July day at JFK airport.

Perhaps these recent brides were imagining the smooth, sensuous touch of a Tahitian black pearl—the symbol of fertility, purity, beauty, and longevity. From the moment explorers first landed in Tahiti back in the 1700s, this exotic pearl represented the essence of romance itself for many women.

Since my earliest days of travel, I have always felt it best to arrive at a destination by ship. The eagerness, the anticipation, that finally-getting-there feeling. That's the way I felt on my first journey to Israel, when I sailed into the welcoming harbor of Haifa. Arriving by ship, the vista is true and immediate; it's welcoming, not inhospitable like the cold black tarmac and glass-windowed arrivals building.

Not so Tahiti! But then again, what would you expect from an island paradise?

Like most of the international flights originating in the U.S., our huge jet touched down in the middle of the night at Faa'a, the large airport located a few miles outside of the capital. Deplaning with us were the weary and groggy honeymooners who, as they walked across the tarmac, quickly inhaled the heady scent of fragrant flowers.

It's custom here upon arrival for visitors to receive a typical Tahitian display of hospitality: the flower every Tahitian knows, the *tiare*. Tahiti's national blossom is a tiny white gardenia redolent with the intoxicating perfume of the island. Visitors are handed this flower, which is worn over the ear, after entering the terminal. An important distinction here is not whether a person is young or old, but rather, where they place their flower. If the *tiare* is worn behind the left ear, on the side of the heart, it signals that your love has been won. If it is worn behind the right ear, it indicates that you are unmarried and open to proposals.

The warm scented air made us all drowsy. It was night and sleep beckoned; we were all looking forward to our first day in paradise.

Today's air passengers complain about thirteen-hour trips with the same gusto as those eighteenth-century sailors grumbled about spending months at sea. French artist Paul Gauguin knew a good thing when he saw it; he was willing to spend sixty-three days on a ship that set sail from France to reach the paradise of Tahiti. Gauguin just wanted to end his days in peace and freedom. So he left what he considered to be a culturally bereft Europe to live an unfettered life in the tropical paradise of Tahiti.

Gauguin was forty-three when he arrived on the island. He was to live in Tahiti from 1891 to 1893, and from 1895 to 1901. Then he moved to the south coast of Hiva Oa in the Marquesas from 1901 until his death on May 8, 1903. He rests in the Calvary Cemetery in Atuona, watched over by a replica of his statue, *Oviri* ("Savage").

"The landscape with its pure and ardent colors dazzled and blinded me," Gauguin noted. He left everything in France to find a paradise of tropical beauty: Tahiti's sunlight, freedom, and color. "Already it seems to me that the troubles of life in Europe don't exist anymore," he wrote, "and that each day will follow the other without change until the end."

Before he died, this leading French painter of the Post-impressionist period was one of the few who put Tahiti on the map, for he produced some of his most beautiful and best-known paintings here. He also created another masterpiece—his enchanting journal, *Noa, Noa* (*Fragrant, Fragrant*).

The journal includes Gauguin's sensuous woodblock prints and sketches, his richly colored illustrations, Tahitian myths and legends, affectionate tales of his encounters with the captivating Tahitian people, and fascinating glimpses into the inspiration behind his most famous paintings.

You can stare at the paintings themselves in the Paul Gauguin Art Museum and Botanical Gardens, located outside Papeete in a lovely setting, surrounded by palm trees and green grass, and featuring an inner court. You cannot help but come away with an understanding of his intense love for these islands. You can see for yourself how Gauguin captured the sun-splashed colors, dreamlike atmosphere, and serenity of this paradise.

I imagine standing in an area where Gauguin "sat and stood for hours in the sun, beret on head, cigarette in mouth, bare-chested, barefooted, wearing coarse trousers . . . sketching, painting with the silent Tehura squatting beside him," according to Lawrence and Elisabeth Hanson in their book, *Noble Savage: The Life of Paul Gauguin.*

One of his famous paintings is *Two Tahitian Women,* an oil on canvas housed in the Metropolitan Museum of Art in New York City. Nearly all the paintings in the Tahitian museum are reproductions.

⌒

In Polynesia, Tahiti is known as "the gathering place," or "the starting point." Encompassing a 403-square-mile area, this figure-eight-shaped island contains a larger part known as Tahiti Nui (which means "big") and a smaller part called Tahiti Lti ("little").

As we noted, the synagogue is in Tahiti's main city and the capital, Papeete. This is a municipality that embraces all its citizens, the so-called *demis*—half-Europeans, Europeans, Chinese, and Polynesian peoples, and its tiny Jewish community. While Papeete somewhat resembles a town in France, with its narrow streets where French is heard and touches of French architecture, the municipality only came into its own when the French built the international Faa'a airport in 1960s. The government of France was conducting a series of nuclear tests about 1,000 miles east of Tahiti. Amid local and worldwide protests, the testing stopped. At the same time, the French began work on redeveloping the waterfront. It's still a work in progress. However, the waterfront area does have the feel of a long park, with food and carnival-like attractions.

Today in the twenty-first century, Tahiti, and certainly Papeete, is not the untouched paradise that explorers found over 200 years ago, nor is it the island of Gauguin, Loti, or even Somerset Maugham. Today, this little village moves like a large town, as it is home to 132,000 people, and is the banking and telecommunications center, the government center, and an industrial port. A plethora of hotels welcome visitors, including the Intercontinental Hotel with its over-water bungalows that we shall discuss when we visit our Polynesian paradise, Bora Bora.

While there are fine restaurants on the island, many tourists in town head for the *roulottes* at Vai'ete Square, in the colorful waterfront area. This is like an outdoor food court where tourists mingle with locals who sit at long picnic tables and order hot meals from colorful food vans and trucks (reminding one of tailgating at football games). Cuisine-wise, this is a wonderful place to find a wide variety of menu options, including Chinese, Polynesian, and French dishes; crepes; steaks; chicken; fish; *frites* (French fries); and desserts, including Belgian waffles with Tahitian bananas and Tahitian vanilla whipped cream. Open at dusk, "It's the best deal in town," according to travel agents and tourist boards. They are correct. Also, because this is France, everything comes with bread.

Step up from the waterfront area and you will behold inviting shops, especially jewelry, including, of course, pearls, pearls, and more pearls, pearls by the thousands, and at all prices. Why so many? Well, French Polynesia is home to black pearls.

From the moment explorers first landed in Tahiti in the 1700s, the Tahitian black pearl has represented love. It has been said that nothing can express love as well as this treasure.

Tahitian cultured pearls are a local specialty and Tahiti's largest export. But be careful: Every type of merchant exists, including some—particularly near Le Marché—who have no problem selling you imitation balls of black glass or fiberglass at market prices. Be sure to look for a certificate of authenticity on the wall of the shop, and trust your guidebook to recommend a jeweler or pearl store. Before you go, learn how to judge value, which is based on size, color, luster, and shape. Best advice: Shop around.

The Tahitian black pearl, a symbol of beauty and rarity, was born in the lagoons of French Polynesia, and comes from a species of oyster specific only to the Polynesia, the largest producer of black pearls. These black pearls come in various shades from silver to peacock blue to midnight black; it's all about the way the pearl reflects light.

Later, on a tour to nearby Moorea, our guide took us to a demonstration showing how pearls are born. In our case, a tall, strapping, handsome male resident of the island, with a mane of long black hair and wearing only bathing trunks—it's almost as if he's out of the movie, *Mutiny on the Bounty*—describes how pearl oysters are carefully monitored and nurtured from their birth until pearl harvest time, which is five years on pearl farms. He opened an oyster shell and explained how pearls are formed inside the shells of oysters, and how the pearl begins to form when a particle of foreign matter enters the shell.

The color of the pearl, I later learned, is the same color as the fleshy lip of the oyster just under the outer edge of the shell, according to Stephen G. Bloom in his book, *Tears of Mermaids*. According to Bloom, there are 600 small-family pearl farmers in French Polynesia, along with some giant farms, too, of course. The pearl industry and how it thrives on these isolated pearl farms, such as in the Tuamotu Archipelago, is an exciting phenomenon, the results of which you can see when you visit the several-story Tahiti Pearl Market, at 25 rue Colette, Papeete, which claims to have the largest choice in the world of top gem necklaces. You can customize your own jewelry from a selection of over 200,000 loose pearls and mountings, all within three price ranges of products. I find it fascinating to watch these women salespersons and their clients pore over the pearls, first choosing this one, then that one, holding it up to the light, checking it over and over again.

Indeed, Tahitian pearls reflect sensuality, according to Bloom. "They invert the American concept of the traditional white or ivory pearl. These are pearls, yes, but they are also amulets that are among the most exotic of all jewelry. There's something naughty about them." No wonder a black pearl is called a "woman's secret weapon."

After pearl shopping, saunter through Le Marché, the colorful downtown market in the center of town. This municipal market is not to be missed, and it's where you will meet the people of Tahiti. The first floor of this indoor market has an abundant supply of tropical fruits and vegetables, and fresh fish from the lagoon. The second floor is dedicated to Tahitian arts and crafts, and boasts a large selection of colorful sarongs.

People-watching is a must on any vacation or trip abroad, but it's especially true in Tahiti, where you can appreciate the sensuality and beauty of the Tahitian women in the market.

Gaze at the displays of luscious ripe fruits, Tahitian and Chinese vegetables, scented soaps, vanilla beans, cakes and pies, fruit preserves, shell necklaces, wall hangings, bed covers, and handicrafts.

And I almost forgot—you can get a tattoo here. In case you didn't know it, *tattoo* is one of the few Polynesian words that has worked its way into our language.

Tattoos are not for this writer. I remember my Melville in the Typee Valley on the Island of Nukuheva where he was kept prisoner. His captors at one point try to tattoo him, but he bolts and flees the tattoo artists.

Some people believe that tattooing is dyeing the skin with permanent designs—that it's an art form. For those who are interested, guidebooks tell us that the most elaborate traditions of tattooing are found in Polynesia, where they traditionally use tattoos to protect an individual from attacks by unseen forces, and to protect the person's own sacred power. Another source says tattoos were used in ancient times to indicate social class and to preserve oral histories.

On Tahiti, some tattoo masters still offer tattoos the traditional way, by actually hammering in the ink with an original hand-carved comb designed specifically for each client. Supposedly, they take the time to get to know you and create a unique Polynesian design based on your story. Full of symbolism and often done with traditional instruments, tattoos remain an important part of Tahitian culture.

But for Jews, tattooing is taboo. *Taboo* comes from the Polynesian word *tapu,* or *tabu,* which means something sacred, special, dangerous, or unclean. No wonder it says in Leviticus 19:28, "You shall not make gashes in your flesh for the dead, or incise any marks on yourselves; I am the Lord."

Most honeymooners and vacationers bypass Tahiti, or spend a day or two there at the beginning or end of their trip to Polynesia. They head for the less-populated, less-crowded areas, places that have less city and more accessible beaches, more water sports, more outdoor activities—more of the traditional fun of paradise islands.

I had heard so much about the over-water bungalows that it was time to move on. One thing was for sure: Ida Cowen was right when she wrote about her own departure from Tahiti a half-century ago:

> One sits in the open-air dining room, lulled by the breezes on a terrace overlooking a calm lagoon, and is served by dark-eyed, lustrous black-haired, café-au-lait-skinned Polynesian girls wearing brightly colored print cotton sheaths, with a tiare, a single sweet-scented flower behind one ear.

I began to realize the truth of her statement: "When it comes to pleasure, Tahitians are all business."

I also knew it was time to move on when our guide said to us, "See our sister, Moorea, over there." Across the water my eyes focused on Moorea, an island Tahitians believe was created so they would have something to stare at across the water. Moorea is only forty-five minutes away by ferryboat, or seven minutes by air from Tahiti harbor.

Romantics are sure that this island is shaped like a heart. They love to behold the rocky promontories and sheer, stupendous pinnacle heights of the island. Actually, these pinnacles inspired the mythical "Bali Hai" that was based on James Michener's book, *Tales of the South Pacific*.

Walking and hiking are great sports here. Nearly one hundred years ago, Charlotte Cameron in her travel book, *Two Years in Southern Seas*, wrote: "The Island of Moorea is some 40 miles in circumference. You can get a light cart and horse and drive around it; many people prefer to walk and stop at the different villages."

Today, in the twenty-first century, you can still accomplish that feat. And if you don't like walking, you can rent a scooter and enjoy the passing scenery. If you take the jeep safari, a 4x4 will drive you past plantations, across streams, into deep valleys, and up to waterfalls. If you prefer traveling on foot, it's best to go with a guide along rain-forest trails.

Moorea means "Yellow Lizard." The twin bays of Cook's and Opunohu are launching pads for excursions and days of leisure on fine beaches.

On one such tour in Moorea on a tender, I stood above Cook's Bay,
looking down at one of the sites used in the film *Mutiny on the Bounty,* starring Marlon Brando. The jagged mountains framed the bay where cruise
ships come to moor. Movie fans and history buffs definitely want to go
to Opunohu Bay, which carries significant history. It is where the HMS
Bounty landed to search for breadfruit.

Actually, there are a number of versions of the movie, *Mutiny on the
Bounty.* I prefer the 1935 film starring Charles Laughton and Clark Gable
and directed by Frank Lloyd, based on the Charles Nordhoff and James
Norman Hall novel, *Mutiny on the Bounty.* This film was one of the biggest
hits of its time. The acting is superb, as it is in the Marlon Brando version,
which is in color and gives a "real" picture of the Tahitian landscape, which
is breathtaking. The films, which portray different versions of the book,
reveal the unforgettable story of the infamous voyage of the HMS *Bounty.*

In 1787, having been made a lieutenant and given command of His
Majesty's Armed Transport, *Bounty,* William Bligh was ordered to sail to
Tahiti at the suggestion of Sir Joseph Banks, to obtain breadfruit for transportation to the West Indies, where it was intended to serve as food for
slaves. The 230-ton three-mast ship had been refitted as a floating green-
house. Bligh and crew arrived in Tahiti on October 26, 1788, and they
spent five months there, longer than any Europeans before them. Shortly
after leaving Tahiti, Fletcher Christian's bold mutiny, sparked by the cruelty
of Captain William Bligh, broke out. After his crew set him and nineteen
loyal crew members adrift, Bligh crossed nearly 4,000 miles of open ocean
in a small boat and reached what is now Indonesia.

It's also a good idea to read the book of the same name, *Mutiny on
the Bounty.* I recommend reading *Mutiny on the Bounty,* the first part of
The Bounty Trilogy by Nordhoff and Hall, followed by *Men Against the Sea,*
which relates the epic drama of the nineteen loyal men who were set adrift
at sword-point in the *Bounty's* 23-foot open launch, with Captain Bligh
at the tiller. To this day, the nearly 4,000-mile voyage back to civilization
remains one of the greatest feats of navigation and human endurance in the
annals of the sea. *Pitcairn's Island,* the third and climactic volume, chronicles

the fate of Christian, the mutineers, and a handful of Tahitian men and women, who at last found refuge on the loneliest island in the Pacific.

As nice as it is to contemplate adventures in the lush scenery on the South Seas, Moorea is only temporary. I wanted fantasy, and I found it in Bora Bora, along with . . . who else? Our honeymoon friends.

⌒

Who has not tasted the bread of fantasy once in his or her life? For some, it has been the dream of being adrift on South Pacific waters, moving from island to island. If you have touched down on Bora Bora, you will never forget your stay there, no matter how long. How could you? It's as beautiful as any island in the world—some say the most beautiful; indeed, it provides a textbook definition of bliss.

Recalling it now, Riva and I remember certain aspects of our stay in this vacation paradise: arrival, the lagoon, the accommodations, and, as often happens in travel, that special meal and its location. In our case, a simple breakfast.

The landing on the tarmac was a feat in itself, for the airport is built on a *motu*, a small islet. Off the plane we went, out of the gate and onto a motor launch that conveyed us to paradise. We were about to begin the journey across one of the most luminous lagoons in the world. We felt what thousands have felt before us: a truly exotic travel welcome, not just an artificial greeting by a hotel greeter (as charming as that may be), but a welcome by nature itself. I imagined, even though it was daylight, that I was truly part of the ancient Polynesian art of sailing by the stars, with the feel of the wind behind me and the look of the sea around me.

The beckoning blue lagoon overwhelmed me as the waves broke a path for tourists from abroad. The lagoon is "quite out of proportion to the size of the surviving core of the island," Peter Crawford writes in his book, *Nomads of the Wind*. The lagoon is tinged with myriad hues of blue, including turquoise, lapis, and aquamarine. Since it is open to the ocean by only one pass, the lagoon is enclosed to the east by the *motu,* and to the west, by a reef. Thus, it is so well protected that swimming in its clear, calm waters is like floating in a pear-shaped pool at a resort. No wonder there are no swimming pools on Bora Bora.

Nicknamed the "Pearl of the Pacific," Bora Bora lies 124 miles north-west of Tahiti. Small by most standards, it measures only 18 miles in circumference and is encircled by a protective necklace of coral reefs, making it as close to paradise as any vacation isle in the world.

Two towering volcanic peaks of sheer black rock look down upon you wherever you find yourself. They are located in the center of the island and are called Pahia and Otemanu. Sloping down from these peaks to the beaches are hillsides of lush tropical foliage.

The first European to visit this abode of happiness was Captain James Cook, who came in 1777 after having previously sighted the island in 1769. Bora Bora remained sovereign until 1888, when it was annexed by France. The last queen, Terii-Maevarua II, granddaughter of Queen Pomare IV of Tahiti (whom we met earlier in this chapter), died in Tahiti, in 1932.

Following the December 7, 1941, attack on Pearl Harbor, the U.S. chose Bora Bora as a South Pacific military base. Defensive fortifications were constructed. Although the base was officially closed on June 2, 1946, American soldiers so loved the island and the people that they refused to leave. The story goes that some had to be forcibly removed following complaints from their families. Because of the GIs, the island still has an American flavor. Make sure you ask your guide to show you the graffiti-covered artillery pieces facing the calm, crystal lagoon. Those guns were intended to ward off a Japanese invasion, especially in the dark days of 1942 in World War II. The Japanese never came.

In recent years, Bora Bora, which means "firstborn," has evolved into a mecca for American, European, and, increasingly, Japanese tourists. Most of its 7,000 residents make a living from tourism. The island lives up to its boast that it contains one of the world's highest concentrations of glamorous resorts, most of them located on *motus*, that ring of islets that encloses the lagoon.

It was only when I saw those exotic thatched-roof bungalows over the water on the turquoise lagoon that I found myself agreeing with James A. Michener in *Tales of the South Pacific,* where he describes Bora Bora as "an island of rare beauty, wild, impetuous," and "so beautiful that the gods must have formed it."

I convinced my wife that although we would be living just above the water, we had nothing to fear staying in a over-water bungalow. Even on a stormy night, the protection of the reef breaks the waters to shelter the bungalows on stilts from the winds and currents of the open season sea.

The over-water bungalows pretty much make up the bulk of the vacation housing on the island. Most honeymooners and tourists opt for these over-water huts, today, a standard feature of most resorts in French Polynesia. These accommodations certainly fit in with the island's atmosphere.

From our bungalow's patio, I could see those "forty-three shades of blue" on one side and the lush vegetation and coconut groves on the other. Believe me, even this peripatetic and somewhat-hyper travel writer suddenly felt calm and refreshed. And if you have a decent sense of smell you come away intoxicated with the scent of amazing tropical flowers.

Right from your balcony, you can spot multicolored fish and stingrays. This writer opted to stare at them from up high and not float alongside the creatures in the water, although we met tourists who loved the experience of swimming with the rays and sharks—or so they said.

In the twenty-first century, an over-water bungalow sits like a castle, a hotel room far beyond the ordinary. Built on stilts over a lagoon, these thatched-roof luxury bungalows are perfect havens for lovers. Each one offers a charming sitting room with exquisitely furnished accommodations, including a partial glass-bottom floor to observe the polychromatic fish swimming below; you will also find a spacious bedroom, a private balcony, and a small lower dock for entering the crystal-clear lagoon waters. At night, a romantic touch comes into play as you hear the melodic sound of soft waves rolling onto the shore.

Some resorts deliver breakfast in their outrigger canoe right to your glass coffee table, so you can enjoy a morning *repas* with *croissants* and *café au lait*. Move the coffee table and then remove a square glass floorboard and you can feed the fish swimming in the blue lagoon below, or just plain observe, stingrays, huge sea turtles, and reef sharks.

Instead, we opted for an early-morning walk along the 18-mile road that encircles the island and hugs the shoreline. Our hike amounted to a trek to what is, in effect, a convenience store. It's best to shop early in the day, when the food is fresh and the small market is well stocked to satiate our appetites. We bought a French *baguette,* some yogurt, tuna, hard–boiled eggs, and cheese. Now quite hungry, we are in a hurry to return to our patio for breakfast, where we shall eat what will likely become a favorite memory: "Remember that morning in Bora Bora when we sat on our patio and ate breakfast—all the time gazing out over the blue lagoon under an azure sky as the sun warmed our faces, bodies and souls?" *Le petit déjeuner* in probably the most beautiful island setting in the world. It doesn't get much better than that!

Forgive the sales pitch, but if you are into water sports back home, you must endeavor to reach Bora Bora. You will find plenty of opportunities for water-skiing, jet-skiing, parasailing, paragliding, hang-gliding, windsurf-ing, and sailing, along with hiking, horseback riding, and mountain biking. It's all here. You can head out into the crystal-clear waters in a kayak or an outrigger canoe, or you can go deep-sea fishing, or go and feed the sharks and rays, or take a lagoon tour—all of which provides fun and excitement. The lagoon offers world-class diving in warm, clear waters, full of rainbow-colored fish that dart about playfully.

No matter where you stay or eat, on any bright sunny morning you will be greeted with *Ia ora na,* which in Polynesian means "Good morning," or "Hello," or "How are you?," or "Good-bye and thank you."

When we left our bungalow in Bora Bora and boarded the launch that took us across probably the most beautiful turquoise lagoon on earth, to the airport, it started to drizzle, causing the driver to comment with a smile, "Bora Bora is crying because you're leaving."

We believed him.

Welcome to Vietnam and its Jewish Community

Exploring Ho Chi Minh City and Hanoi

"They made a wasteland and called it peace . . ."

—*Tacitus*

Of all the Jewish holidays, Passover remains the one where you don't want to find yourself in a strange land with strange customs and a strange language. On this celebration of freedom from bondage, Jews sit down with their families and friends at home or nearby. Reading the *haggadah,* the Passover-story prayer book, they tell and retell the story of those days many centuries ago when God brought the Jewish people out of the land of the pharaohs.

Occasionally at Passover, one does find oneself out of town. It happens. In 2009, Riva and I found ourselves spending the holiday in an unusual Jewish community in a faraway, exotic land: Vietnam.

We had landed at Tan Son Nhat International Airport in Ho Chi Minh City, formerly known as Saigon. With 7 million residents, it stands as the largest city in Vietnam, a country bounded on the east by the South China Sea, on the north by China, on the west by Laos and Cambodia, and on the southwest by the Gulf of Thailand.

Greeting me at Immigration was the Vietnamese flag, a five-pointed gold star centered on a field of red. The color red stands for Communism, officially adopted by Vietnamese Communists when they declared independence in 1945 from the French, an independence that would be thwarted by France and the U.S. for thirty years.

Those events, however, occurred more than a half-century ago, a gigantic interval in historical memory. In August 2010, the two former combatants staged joint naval activities in the South China Sea as a sign of increasing military cooperation. The naval drills were part of the fifteenth anniversary of diplomatic ties between Washington and Hanoi. Welcome to the Socialist Republic of Vietnam.

⌒

"What makes this night different than all other nights?" This is the first question in the *haggadah*. Listening to and reciting the Passover tale in Vietnam made my first night in Ho Chi Minh City very different. Indeed, my Passover experience in this Southeast Asian country would turn into a near Chekhov story. Though it was hot and muggy, I felt I was playing the part of the nineteenth-century Russian traveler who walks in from a fierce snowstorm on the cold steppes of czarist land into an utterly new, warm world. I was excited about the prospect of attending a Passover *seder* at Chabad House in this commercial hub.

Of course, the weather was not like Russia's 20 degrees below zero, nor was I about to enter an *izba* (cottage). I was in the Paris of the Orient, in a Communist nation that lies along the southeastern corner of the Indochina peninsula.

Having watched battle after battle, defeat after defeat, during the decades of the 1960s and '70s, the years that America participated in that long conflict, it was difficult to believe that I was walking around Ho Chi Minh City's District 1, the downtown area that includes the Rex Hotel, where Riva and I were staying and Chabad House, a ten-minute walk down Le Loi Street. This district is still called Saigon, even though the official city name of the metropolis, as of July 2, 1976, is Ho Chi Minh City.

I prefer the sound of the name Saigon, which I wanted to use all of the time during my visit—not out of impoliteness, but because it fits my imagination and recall. My guide, Nguyen Trung Thanh ("Just call me Thanh") assures me I can do so. In fact, he later explains, people from the countryside, journeying to this big city, often say, "I'm going to Saigon."

The pace of the city gets to me right away: frenetic, energetic, hectic, and loud, a reminder of my own New York City. It was evening, and the streets and avenues were packed with pedestrians, heading home. The city's downtown is a far cry from the early days of the last century, when novelist and travel writer W. Somerset Maugham visited. He described it as having "the air of a little provincial town in the South of France." In the twenty-first century, Saigon is dedicated to commerce and hedonistic pleasures.

⌒

Ask any recent visitor what they remember most about Vietnam, and chances are it's those darn motorbikes. The noise level in this metropolitan area reaches a crescendo not unlike a major American city. But the sound is different. Here the noise comes from motorbikes and motorcycles that roar past. My eyes and ears picked up these loud-sounding "bees" buzzing down wide, tree-lined boulevards, their horns blaring and warning me to stay out of their way. Making the scene more haunting were the bike riders and their *Star Wars* helmets and hospital-type masks to ward off pollution. Dodging these modern urban cowboys, whose butts are planted firmly in the saddles of their motorized steeds, offered quite a challenge.

The style and shape of the motorbikes vary greatly, but in Vietnam, it's hard to hold more than four on a bike—a fact which ironically helps advance population control by the government, as they only offer stipends for families with two children. The point is that with three children, Mom and Pop can't place themselves and the three tykes on the same bike. Not only would they have to buy a second bike, but they also would not receive a welfare grant for the third child. Practicality usually convinces couples to limit their families to just two children.

Because of its late start in family planning, Vietnam has nearly 90 million people, a huge pressure on a small land area of 128,000 square miles. And gender ratios are becoming increasingly imbalanced, with far more boys being born than girls, according to the United Nations Population Fund. Add on to that a thousand-year-old tradition that favors men over women in a country where men carry on the family line and care for elderly parents, and one can see how difficult it must be to change.

I never realized how much the roar of those bike engines would affect me. But they do. Months later in America, whenever I heard the sound of a moped or motorcycle, I was reminded of Ho Chi Minh City.

I am not long in Saigon when it becomes clear that the former capital-ists of the 1960s are back in favor. This vital city has taken off into the stratosphere of a free market economy. One commentator even went so far as to affirm that Vietnam's economic reforms, especially in Ho Chi Minh City, are definitely in vogue. The fact is, the country's largest population of ethnic Chinese, once persecuted for their economic suc-cess, once again have a great deal of economic influence and acumen in a system sometimes described as crony capitalism. The new system propels a reborn Saigon, energetically driven by work and money. As the com-mercial heart of Vietnam, the city accounts for more than a quarter of the country's retail trade.

My guide, Thanh, is part of the new entrepreneurial spirit that per-vades Saigon. After graduating from foreign language school at Hanoi Uni-versity with a BA in English, he boarded the Reunification Train in 1992, with no money, two pairs of pants, and a few shirts. Arriving in Ho Chi Minh City, he obtained a position with the Far East Tourist Company and worked in the then-burgeoning tourist industry. In 2010, he joined up with a partner from Belgium and they bought the company that he had signed on with during the previous decade.

Guides reflect the mood of the country—the desires, dreams, and aspirations of a nation, especially those nations ruled by dictatorial sys-tems. In the early 1990s, just after the fall of Communism in the former Soviet Union, the first words out of the mouth of our Russian guide as we climbed into the car for a tour of St. Petersburg were: "Let's make a deal."

Saigon's Thanh, who was highly recommended and reliable, came across as discreet and tactful. A good and honest businessperson, he desires to build a network with travel contacts in the U.S. After all, Vietnam is an "in" destination for Americans, fourth on the list of visitors to this country that now trades with the world.

I stopped at the Rex Hotel, situated on the corner of Le Loi and Nguyen Hue boulevards. Surrounding the intersection were department stores, shops, and boutiques. Vietnam increasingly has become a shopping haven, with designer clothes, silk goods, high-quality handcrafts, ceramics, and lacquer products, all inviting purchase and at excellent value.

Francophiles feel at home in former French colonial cities such as Saigon or Algiers. The wrought-iron balconies, the redecorated villas, the outdoor cafes, the not-uncommon sound of the French language, are all reminiscent of the warm atmosphere of *dolce* Paris.

Just across the way from the Rex stand the opera house and the city hall. The latter's obvious French colonial style reminds one of the town halls that grace many a French city center.

People-watching remains a great pastime for the traveler, especially here, in a city which has managed to maintain a French presence and Asian motif. Saigon certainly ranks up there with the best when it comes to gazing at the passing scene. Sitting in the coffee shop of the Rex recalls pedestrian-watching at Café de la Paix on rue de la Paix in Paris, where legend has it that if one sits at the cafe, one is bound to run into a friend or acquaintance as the establishment is so well-known and popular. Same here, *mon ami*.

⟜

Stunning Vietnamese women window-shopped before entering mall-like boutiques and stores. Merchants were busy negotiating, pleading, and convincing. Like their brothers and sisters on motor scooters, pedestrians set a fast pace as they moved quickly on their way to work, then much slower on their return from work. Meeting a friend, rendezvousing with a lover, making a sale, expressing joy, anger—everything imaginable in the daily struggle of life. The visitor can see it all.

But it's not only the pretty ladies and handsome men jostling for position on crowded sidewalks. Inevitably the stone statues of political figures pop up, and in Ho Chi Minh City, it is, you guessed it, Ho Chi Minh himself. The statue near the Rex Hotel shows "Uncle Ho" comforting a young girl who is looking down on a book he is holding. In France and America during the 1950s and '60s, Ho was seen as "the devil incarnate," that old, wiry, revolutionary founder of the Communist Party and leader of North Vietnam, recognizable by his characteristic goatee. Ho, who died on September 3, 1969, never lived to see the 1975 reunification of North and South Vietnam. Later, I would pay him a visit as he lies in repose in his mausoleum in the capital city of Hanoi.

⟜

Like Lenin and Mao Tse-tung, "Uncle Ho" would be shocked to learn that his Marxist ideals were relaxed only two decades after his passing—in a 1986 program called "Renovation." Suddenly, with a green light to open up, to trade, the Socialist Republic of Vietnam, with labor costs even lower than China, snared multinational corporations that opportunistically pounced and established beachheads. Following closely on their heels, the professionals, businesspeople, and venture capitalists trotted in, and among them were the Jews, those Jewish entrepreneurs who spotted potential in an overseas market. With them came teams of doctors, especially from Israel, who without fanfare work in developing countries.

Some 10,000 to 15,000 Jewish businesspeople and tourists travel to this Southeast Asian country each year, according to estimates provided by Rabbi Menachem Hartman of Chabad House. Only 150 to 200 Jews reside in Vietnam year-round, all of them temporary residents, except for a few converted, native Vietnamese who have married Jewish foreigners. About 100 Jews make their home in the capital, Hanoi.

Since Chabad House is only a ten-minute walk from the Rex Hotel, I still had some time to scout the area before the Seder began. I strolled down Dong Khoi Street, once known as rue Catinat in the former world of bars and brothels. Just as in yesteryear, cafes, restaurants, and boutiques, made famous by author Graham Greene and others, all thrive in the twenty-first century.

Some say the Rex Hotel served as the headquarters of the United States Information Agency (USIA) during the Vietnam War. Others claim it housed the CIA from 1962–70. We do know that in the 1960s and 1970s, the Rex's popular rooftop bar served as a watering hole for journalists, who received daily press bulletins known as "The Five O'Clock Follies." Today, the bar still offers superb views of the streets below. Of course, U.S. military officers have long since gone, their place taken by tourists.

As I walked down the broad and shady Le Loi Boulevard toward Chabad House, with its handsome trees, I passed boutiques, malls, and stores, all the time observing young Vietnamese, who, having parked their motorbikes on the corner, were standing around and conversing. Other young adults walked along the avenue, males and females dressed in trendy Western clothes of the day, and even more obvious, shopping in new malls and department stores. Meanwhile, the Passover *seder* beckoned. I quickly made my way through the torpid streets, the high humidity slowing my pace. I imagined that the air I would inhale when I stepped through the door into Chabad Lubavitch House would be the warm air of an imaginary Eastern European *shtibel* (small house of prayer).

Located in an upscale neighborhood, surrounded by stores and shops selling clothes and books, as well as a few office buildings and even a nearby hospital, Chabad House, which doubles as a synagogue and home for Rabbi Hartman and his family, is well situated. The first-floor hall is a long room which contains an *Aron Kodesh* (Holy Ark). Several long narrow tables have been put together and covered with white tablecloths. Dishes and utensils have been placed on the tables for the guests at the holiday meal. About forty Jews would be attending this second-night *seder*.

So here I was, in the home of the *Do-Thai* (Vietnamese for "Jew"). I and my coreligionists—plural—are called *Nguoi Do-Thai*. To my historically battered, sensitive diaspora ears, *Do-Thai* sounds much better than *Jude, Juif, Zhid!*

This night, I would help make a *minyan;* in this case, only ten Jewish male worshippers were needed to fulfill the required quorum. Women are not counted for a *minyan* in Orthodox Judaism. The people gathered here represented a small part of the Jewish diaspora. A few Chabadniks, in dark trousers and white shirts, with white *tzitzits* dangling over their belts, were part of the group. Atop their heads were black skullcaps or black hats. They hailed from Brooklyn, the headquarters of Chabad Lubavitch. Other fellow Jews originated from the U.S., the UK, France, and Israel. A few local American businessmen made up the rest of the group, dressed in washed-out, short-sleeved sport shirts—certainly not the dressy white shirts and possibly ties and jackets one would see at an American Jewish family *seder*. I'm wearing a white dress shirt and blazer.

Before the *seder* began, we recited the evening prayers. The beseeching sounds of the deep male voices reverberated against the walls. Soon we were about to celebrate the second Passover *seder*. The first *seder* was held in a hotel the night before, with about 150 in attendance. Tonight's *seder,* we were told, would be less formal. I counted about forty present. I scanned the group and assumed the men were the regulars. Every synagogue boasts a core of devoted ones who come to pray each day or on weekends.

But something was missing from this holiday gathering. It did not take a rocket scientist to discover what it was: Not one person in attendance was a citizen of Vietnam. Everyone in this room was an expat, or, as Rabbi Hartman prefers to call them, "temporary residents." And most of them were American citizens, he informed me.

In Vietnam, foreigners can only get a visa as a temporary resident. No homegrown residents were here at this gathering; they were all expats or travelers just passing through. An expat is defined as a person temporarily or permanently *residing* in a country and culture other than that of his/her upbringing or legal residence. The word comes from the Latin *ex* ("out of") and *patria* ("country, fatherland").

The word *temporarily* begs the question: Are expats the loneliest people in the world? In six decades of foreign travel, this was my first experience at a synagogue or Jewish gathering where everyone in attendance, including the rabbi, was from somewhere else. This wasn't Odessa, for instance, where the people are Ukrainian Jews, nor was it Santiago, where they are Chilean Jews. This was the most unusual Jewish community that I had ever seen.

And yet, is it a community? Does it meet the standards of community, defined as a group of people living in the same locality and under the same government and having common interests?

Meet the Jewish community of Vietnam, of which about half are inter-married. Not everyone is here to make money, at least outwardly. Some, I am told, have fled what one might call the American drive for the almighty dollar; they desired to escape American life and its proverbial rat race. They have been drawn to the so-called exotic Vietnamese way of life. Another definite group clearly settled here for business reasons, according to one of the Hasids, Rabbi Zalman, who was helping Rabbi Hartman.

After prayers, I noticed two Americans talking. One fellow country-man was born and raised in The Bronx, New York. We immediately felt an affinity, since I live in Westchester County, which borders on The Bronx. We exchanged notes, for example, on how far my former hometown of Chappaqua is from his former borough. He brought another American into the discussion. When the evening prayers were over, my Bronx friend, who was big and broad-shouldered, with a good deep voice, suddenly got up and left. I was told he had to be at his factory early in the morning. Still, to leave before the *seder* began seemed strange. Yet Rabbi Hartman, obviously a man of patience, asked the Bronx fellow to come the next morning to services, which began at 10:00 a.m.

"Yes, that's possible," answered the Bronxite.

I got the impression that the rabbi needed people to make a *minyan*. Actually, I would miss the big guy during the *seder*, for many of the people didn't seem to know each other, and those that did seemed to focus on the people they recognized. Seemed like a very in-group.

Even though I was with total strangers, I felt good that I was reading the story of Passover. The *seder* went fast as we sang and drank the ceremonial wine. Going around the room, each one of us recited a paragraph in Hebrew; those who felt uncomfortable in the holy tongue gave their rendition in English. Quite progressive for Chabad, to read in English, I thought.

I sat across from Andrew, an architect, who worked with the young Swiss Jew who sat next to him. The Swiss man studied in Israel and read Hebrew very well. The Israelis at the *seder*, with their homegrown accents and their easy reading of the *haggadah,* made me even more homesick. Their Hebrew pronunciation reminded me of Israel, where many moons ago I spent my first *seder* overseas—on a kibbutz, no less. I was moved again, as we would soon say, "Next year in Jerusalem," and this time, it would be recited even more fervently.

According to Andrew, the expats included several Jewish families who lived here full-time. "As you know, as an expat, we have chosen to live abroad and are probably less risk-averse than other nationals of our home countries," he told me.

Andrew had lived in Ho Chi Minh City for seven years. When he first came to Vietnam he designed and built robotic equipment. He acquired a small engineering company designing software and electronics for the machines. He recently opened a small factory, as well as a non-kosher restaurant for expats, and started a design company that he still manages. He and his wife have invested in a number of local ventures—"some successful, others not."

Originally from Kingston, New York, he moved to Lexington, Kentucky, in 1977, when he was ten years old. He is very active in Chabad and goes every day to pray. He believes Chabad is one of the "greatest resources that a traveling or expat Jew has to keep in touch with their faith, where they can talk and meet other Jews, eat kosher food, and learn Judaism."

For those who keep kosher, not to worry regarding a trip to Vietnam. You can purchase fresh food at Chabad House. Rabbi Hartman explained that Chabad can also dispatch kosher frozen food to other cities, such as Hanoi and Hoi An.

Andrew told me that Chabad boasts about ten active members and forty "occasional" visitors. Chabad has a kosher restaurant that offers traditional Jewish and Israeli cuisine, as well as a few kosher versions of Vietnamese cuisine.

I learned that a *minyan* is held on Friday nights and Saturday mornings. Weekly services can be organized when someone has *yahrzeit* (memorial anniversary). Between fifty to sixty people show up for the Friday-night Shabbat meal. Activities are offered, including a woman's group, a Torah study group, a youth group, a singles group, a weekly Hebrew School, and ten weekly classes. The nursery school functions off and on.

A few years ago—2008, to be exact—Chabad moved out into the wider community and took the holiday festivities to the people, as it does throughout the world, especially during Hanukkah, when it lights huge menorahs in downtown public squares or plazas. One media outlet described the Ho Chi Minh Hanukkah attendees as a group of "more than 100 locals, foreign businesspeople and backpackers, who came to the event in Saigon Park. The party, replete with dancing and the public menorah lighting, represented the first holiday celebration held outside Chabad House, directed by Rabbi Menachem and Rachel Hartman."

According to Andrew, "Living and working in Vietnam is a challenge if you stop and think about it. But the same could be said about living and working in Atlanta, or New York, or Philadelphia. People, of course, adapt to their environments—Jews probably more than others, considering our history," said Andrew.

⌒

Rabbi Hartman's son Levi recited the four questions with such fervor, such strength. Standing on a chair, he reminded me of my granddaughters, Sarah and Julia, the youngest at our family *seder*. They are cousins, and a day apart in age, so they both offer up the questions.

Tonight, Levi moved us all.

Before we started the second half of the seder, the rabbi asked each of us to talk about one of the remarkable *seders* in our lives, and where and when they occurred.

A young British man talked about a family *seder*. After the hunt for the *afikoman* (ceremonial *matzah*), he recalled, it was discovered that his young brother had retrieved the special *matzah* without notice, which is customary, but then put it in his back pocket and later couldn't remember where he had put it. Finally, moving around the table and sitting down, he heard the crunch of the unleavened bread in his pocket, which had broken into little pieces of what looked like crushed cracker. The English lad laughed as he finished; the story to him is funny, exciting, a family event; it seemed to give him pleasure. Maybe that's what the rabbi wanted—to recall happiness, joy.

I raised my hand to tell about a Passover *seder* I attended in Odessa. The rabbi said he was sure that spending Passover in Vietnam would be added to my list of most memorable Passovers. I agreed.

The *seder* was going well. The two Chabad assistants, sent by the organization to help Rabbi Hartman, expressed happiness in their singing and spontaneously banged the table with joy. Lubavitch Hasidim believe Jews should be joyful, and they were joyfully ecstatic on this night. Everyone was drinking wine during the sumptuous meal. *L'chaim*—"To life!"—is proclaimed over and over again. The rabbi said you could always "make a *l'chaim*." One of the assistants, Rabbi Chaim, was very pleasant; he was from Brooklyn, too. "We come to help," he said.

Sitting across from me was *chabadnik* Rabbi Zalman, also aiding Rabbi Hartman. To me, he possessed a spiritual face, pale, yet wise, with a long, unruly beard. During the evening, everyone congratulated him. He was getting married in a few months. *Mazel tov! L'chaim!* We all wished him well as we sipped a little wine.

I found out that Rabbi Zalman is what might be called a "Chabad advance man." His goal is to bring *Yiddishkeit* (Jewishness), as he puts it, to an entire city, an entire country. A few months before Rabbi Hartman arrived, Rabbi Zalman went from city to city, making contacts, finding out Jewish names. He had heard there were about sixty Jews in Vietnam in 2006.

"If you build it, they will come" seems to be Chabad strategy. It worked in China, where in one location Chabad opened with a list of ten Jews. Now, according to Rivka Chaya Berman, "[T]heir programs have taken off, with more than 100 families in touch with Chabad of Shenzhen."

Rabbi Zalman's scouting was considered successful. In 2006, Chabad opened in Vietnam, which was then coming into prominence as the "next Asian tiger economy."

"We are looking to set down the infrastructure of Jewish life in Vietnam according to Torah and Jewish law instead of waiting to see a Jewish life form there," said a Chabad representative in Hong Kong, Rabbi Mordechai Avtzon, who directed the opening of the new venture. "A lot of people moved their businesses here and now we have many more Jews," he is quoted as saying. "Chabad reminds Jews they are not far away from Judaism, a Jewish presence." And of course, they are always on the lookout for Israeli backpackers, even though they do not flock to Vietnam as often as they do to neighboring Thailand.

⁓

At times during the *seder* I felt like Big Brother was watching me, as a security monitor at the front of the room drew my attention from time to time. Chabad House is at the end of a narrow alleyway. I wondered if anyone else was nervous. I didn't see any security guards around, but maybe they were hidden. Here we sat in a Chabad House, much as the Chabad rabbi and his wife had sat in Chabad headquarters in Mumbai, India, in late November of 2008, during the days of the brutal terrorist attack in that Indian city. The two were murdered by gunmen from Pakistan.

What, me worry? I thought. *You betcha.* I watched the monitor.

Two French Jewish young ladies, both Sephardim, talked of their Passover customs. One related to the group that the oldest unmarried daughter in her family washes her feet in wine at the *seder*, apparently a Sephardic tradition at Passover. Never heard that before! Her family is from Tunisia. The oldest is obliged to do this, she explained. The other French girl told how during the Passover *seder*, the whole family gets up from the *seder* table and walks outside, looking for Eliyahu Ha-Navi, Elijah the Prophet.

My own family is Ashkenazi. However, I personally like the custom of walking out, though I think that there have been Passovers when we in North America have had light snow and chilly temperatures.

My neighbor at the table was from Los Angeles. He hardly talked, although he did tell me that he had a house once worth $2.5 million; now, because of the housing market crash in 2008, it's worth $1.5 million. Ironic; the U.S. recession is following us all the way to Vietnam, a Communist country. He warned me to keep a special eye on my wife's purse when we toured the city. Some motorbike riders scoot by and grab women's purses. I told him I had heard similar stories fifty years ago in Rome and Naples: Italian young men, besides pinching girls' *derrieres* would drive their Vespa motorbikes down the streets and snatch a woman's pocketbook, and off they scooted, with the poor damsel left behind, shouting on the sidewalk.

I took him seriously, remembering a quote from a guidebook: "Do not take any valuables onto the streets of HCMC, as bag and jewelry snatching is a common and serious problem."

As the centuries go on, unfortunately, crimes against tourists don't change. As a traveler, I recognize that every nation has its thieves. I have heard stories about gypsy kids surrounding you in Paris or Moscow and grabbing your wallet or your wife's purse. Warnings are offered to urge you to be alert; thieves sometimes work in teams, with beggar women carrying babies as a decoy. Pushing a bicycle across the pavement is another common ruse; while you stop and wait, your pockets are being emptied from behind.

Robbery can happen anywhere, even in my hometown of New York. My French photographer friend visited New York City and had the old ketchup (or mustard) trick pulled on him near the famous New York Library lions at 42nd Street and Fifth Avenue. When he went to wash off the stain in the nearby men's room, putting down his camera equipment for a moment, voila—the bad guys rushed in and grabbed it. Ah yes, travel. Traveler beware!

Still, as a destination, Vietnam remains pretty safe, tourist people tell me. I can't dispute that.

One family unit—I think the only one at the forty-person *seder*—became very spirited, and delivered a prepared skit. Actually, this was one of the cutest parts: The father dressed up as Moses, and the daughter as

Pharaoh. He kept saying "Let my people go," and she repeated "No!" each time, just as Pharaoh did. The act resonated, as we have just recited the ten plagues. He and his family live outside Saigon in a small city. He seemed happy, though he hinted that his wife was not too pleased about living so far away from the U.S., and in a city outside Saigon.

We left, and I thanked Rabbi Hartman for inviting us.

After this trip, I think I shall be sure to stay home for Passover. I want to hear granddaughters Sarah and Julia recite the four questions.

⌒

Weeks later, I e-mailed the rabbi, and even though I knew he came on a one-way ticket, I asked him how long he planned to stay in Vietnam.

"Our plan," he replied, "is to stay here till the coming of *Moshiach;* hopefully our work here will speed his coming."

⌒

Walking back to the hotel later that night, we traversed the now-quiet streets. I wanted to get back to reading Graham Greene's *The Quiet American,* which Thanh, my guide, had given me.

Is this really Vietnam? My mental flashbacks revert all the way back to the Vietnam of my youth, that terrible decade of the 1950s during the First Indochina War when the French fought Ho Chi Minh. Then came the disruptive 1960s and 1970s, when the U.S. took over and engaged in a wrenching war that ripped America in two. You were either violently opposed to the war and supported or marched in massive demonstrations, or, if not, you kept quiet or served in Vietnam in what came to be called the Second Indochina War, with U.S. troops leaving in 1973 and South Vietnam falling to the Communists in 1975. Depending on when you begin, Vietnam stands with Afghanistan as the longest war in American history, and an undeclared one on top of it. The war still haunts us.

"In human terms at least, the war in Vietnam was a war that nobody won—a struggle between victims. Its origins were complex, its lessons disputed, its legacy still to be assessed by future generations. But whether a valid venture or a misguided endeavor, it was a tragedy of epic dimensions," wrote Stanley Karnow in his book, *Vietnam: A History*, a quarter of a century ago.

Someplace along the line, American tourists to Vietnam will recall the war—that is, if you are old enough. But whether senior or young person, comfort yourself, dear traveler: There is no animosity toward Americans here. On the contrary, the war is not even an issue. The Vietnamese will treat you kindly; they'll even be friendly. Nowhere will you meet up with people or guides who spout wartime propaganda. They will show you their country, sell you their souvenirs or goods, and eagerly take your dollars. Americans are welcome in Vietnam; tourism is a big income producer, and the Vietnamese are hospitable by nature. And you will have a good time.

That is not to say that the Vietnamese government in its own subtle and sometimes not-so-subtle way won't remind tourists and their own people, "This war happened, and we won, and don't you forget it."

Every country flaunts its monuments of victorious wars even as it honors its dead, whether it is a war of liberation, as the Communists called their struggle, or a fight to "stop Communist aggression," as presidents Truman, Eisenhower, Kennedy, Johnson, and Nixon titled it.

Or put another way, as Seth Mydans wrote in the *New York Times* back in 1999, "[S]ometimes these [war] spots seem to be memorials to wartime propaganda as much as to the war itself." That's why perhaps Vietnam opened the War Remnants Museum, which once carried the name Museum of American War Crimes. In Ho Chi Minh City's War Remnants Museum, as well as the Cu Chi Tunnels, located just outside the city, I have the feeling that most American tourists are certainly affected by what has been called the "catalog of horrors. For those interested in history, or for those who grew up in the 1960s, I learned that visiting Vietnam is like walking across an old battlefield from wars fought oh, so long ago; like visiting the hills and pastures of Gettysburg, the countryside of Chateau-Thierry and Belleau Wood, the beaches of Normandy, the Belgian forests of Bastogne, and Mount Suribachi on Iwo Jima.

Even upon landing in Saigon, the name of the international airport itself, Tan Son Nhat, is the very same airbase the U.S. Air Force used during the war. Seeing flight destinations up on the board, such as Danang, Camran Bay, and Hue, bring back those anguished photos that are seared in your mind. The monk's self-immolation; the little naked girl, Phan Thi Kim Phuc, running down a highway after napalm had been dropped. There's the bare-chested GI with a cigarette dangling from his dry, sweaty lips, young, oh so young, with an M5 in his hands; was he wounded at Khe Sanh or Saigon in the Tet Offensive? There's a medic and a buddy carrying out a stretcher of a wounded soldier from the jungle, and oh yes, the police chief shooting right into the temple of the captured Vietcong, the latter's face brutally distorted.

Back home during the war, I, like most U.S. civilians, wanted only to forget, and with time, the memories dimmed. But now the reminders are back with me, full force. After all, this is Saigon, the capital of former South Vietnam, now part of united Vietnam. Nearly every guide will take you to the War Remnants Museum; all the local travel agents assign it. "It's history," they say, and history is written by the victors.

First stop, the Presidential Palace where on April 30, 1975, Saigon fell to the North Vietnamese.

I ambled along with hundreds of school kids out on an outing to this symbol of the old regime, a palace kept as a museum. I walked over to the young ones to get a closer look. They were well-fed, with fresh, rosy-red cheeks. I took their picture. They flashed a "V" for victory sign.

Alas, there was the T-54 North Vietnamese tank, number 843—the same tank that I saw on the television news years ago, when the news clips showed this armored vehicle rolling up to the palace and crashing through the palace gates that spring morning in 1975. As the tank rolled through the gates into the spacious courtyard, one of the crew jumped down and rushed up the stairs to unfurl the red-and-yellow Vietcong flag from a balcony.

Once the armored vehicle was inside, North Vietnamese soldiers arrived. General Duong Van Minh, South Vietnam's temporary president, impatiently awaited the conqueror. He surrendered to Colonel Bui Tin, the ranking North Vietnamese officer who was actually a correspondent for a Hanoi military newspaper. According to Stanley Karnow, the officer, Bui Tin, gave a short speech:

> You have nothing to fear. Between Vietnamese there are no victors and no vanquished. Only the Americans have been beaten. If you are patriots, consider this a moment of joy. The war for our country is over.

Leaving the chamber, Bui Tan roamed through the building until he found General Nguyen Van Thieu's private office. He sat down at the desk and composed his dispatch, datelining it: THE PUPPET PRESIDENTIAL PALACE.

Now in his fifties, he had enlisted in the Viet Minh just thirty years before. He had fought as a regular in the Red River Valley and at Dien Bien Phu, and he had trekked the length of the Ho Chi Minh Trail, shuddering under the American bombing. Twelve hours earlier on a bridge at the entrance to Saigon, he had survived a tank skirmish.

He finished his article and strolled into the park behind the palace, stretching out on the grass. He gazed up at the sky, exalted.

That was thirty-five years ago, and here I was, snapping photos of the tank, which must mean to the Vietnamese what raising the flag at Iwo Jima means to Americans: Victory!

Ironically, in 1990, Bui Tin left Vietnam to live in exile and reportedly expressed his dissatisfaction with Communist rulers.

⁓

Not surprisingly as we visited the War Remnants Museum, we learned about the horrors and atrocities the Vietnamese have listed as committed by the U.S.

One caption highlights that infamous quote by General LeMay: "My solution to the people would be to tell them, the NV, 'Frankly that they've got to draw in their horns or we're going to bomb them back to the Stone Age.'"

Another sign in the museum declared: U.S. COMMITTED CRIMES OF WAR. It is signed by Bertrand Russell.

As if the Vietnamese were totally innocent! No record here, whatsoever, of North Vietnamese atrocities carried out on U.S. and South Vietnamese troops, or the new nation's horrible relocation centers which held thousands of intellectuals after their victory.

Inside the museum, there are displays of gruesome photos of alleged American atrocities and the after-effects of Agent Orange defoliation. In 2010, the U.S. promised to do more to help Vietnamese deal with the lingering effects of Agent Orange, a chemical the American military used as a defoliant during the Vietnam War.

Lined up on the museum grounds stand the captured American booty: planes, helicopters, bombs.

The Cu Chi Tunnels are a big hit with tourists. Located in the woods at Ben Dinh, 45 miles northwest of Ho Chi Minh City, the tunnels are a 75-mile-long underground maze where thousands of fighters and villagers could hide. One immediately sees that the short-in-stature Vietcong were able to hide from the enemy and often defeat him because they could burrow deep into the jaws of the earth and literally build underground battle stations. Consisting of a three-level network, not only did they possess sleeping quarters, kitchens, mess halls, meeting rooms, and an operating theater, but even a tiny cinema.

The Cu Chi Tunnels are recorded as one of the most famous battlegrounds of the Vietnam War. These tunnels were used as a base from whence the VC mounted, for example, the Tet Offensive in 1968.

Some tourists are amused by all this; it's like a walk through the park. It's fun climbing down camouflaged holes in the ground leading to the tunnels below, observing booby traps that the GIs encountered. Some of the tunnels have been widened, and I watched one thin lad—hands above his head—lower himself downward into the deep maze of tunnels below, including passageways which enabled resident fighters to move from one village to another. After the war, steps were added and lighting installed so tourists could wriggle in for a look.

One of the highlights of the trip was the firing range where one can try their hand with ancient AK-47s. Thanh, my guide, believes the firing range brings back history and shows "how terrible war is." Maybe, but I think younger tourists enjoy firing the weapons. The park and jungle and amusement-park atmosphere of firing a "heavy-duty" weapon mitigates the harsh propaganda film visitors are shown before entering the area of the tunnels.

According to Stanley Karnow in his Vietnam: A History, in the Second Vietnam War (U.S.), 58,000 Americans died and about 300,000 were wounded. The South Vietnamese lost 224,000 souls, with 1 million wounded. Together North Vietnamese and Vietcong losses came to about a million dead and 600,000 wounded.

More than 4 million Vietnamese soldiers and civilians on both sides were killed or wounded from the late 1950s to the mid-1970s—roughly 10 percent of the entire population.

The thirty years of warfare were over in 1975.

But have both sides excised the ghosts of the past?

I believe in the second decade of the twenty-first century the animosity is gone on both sides. Remember that 60 percent of Vietnam's population today was born after the Americans pulled out in 1973. More and more people in the U.S. realize that Vietnam is a country, not a war. Today's "scooter-propelled youth" make busy Saigon a comfortable place for Americans, who are treated as friends. As noted, the Vietnamese I met in Vietnam showed no animosity toward me, and I've never heard of any other Americans being mistreated. The war is long over. People in both the countryside and the cities want their country to become a prosperous nation, not a battlefield.

"Both sides were at fault," said Kurt, a Swiss who married a Vietnamese woman. I met him in the local cafe after my visit to the tunnels. The couple have a small child and are here to visit his mother-in law. He loves the country, and recommends the beaches.

"The war, it's all over," echoes Willie, an ex-GI who is living with a beautiful Vietnamese lady. He indicates that he is following the Buddhist way of life, which, according to him, means "being a good person."

"Hey," he said, kind of looking around to see if there were any Vietnam soldiers nearby, "he had a job to do, and I had a job to do. No animosity. It's like we are long-lost brothers," he said as he boarded the back of the motorbike driven by his charming girlfriend. He waved good-bye and clasped her supple body as the bike sped away in an evening mist, with shadows falling upon Saigon.

As one guidebook put it, "Forget yesterday, look to tomorrow."

But the past does not go away completely, and Vietnam has a long history. In 939, the Chinese ended their rule over the Vietnamese. The latter then set up an independent state. Centuries later, Roman Catholic missionaries from France began to arrive in what was called Dai Viet. In the 1600s, these religious orders converted thousands of Vietnamese to Catholicism, and between 1858 and 1883, France took control of Vietnam.

No, the Jews did not arrive in Vietnam with the Jewish GIs. Nor did they just come aboard with Chabad in 2006.

Jews entered Indochina with the French in the latter half of the nineteenth century and settled in Saigon. *The Jewish Encyclopedia* mentions a French merchant and ship owner named Jules Rueff in the 1870s as being "one of the pioneers of French influence in the country." Between 1883 and 1886 Jewish soldiers and officers fought in the French Army in the Tonkin Campaign.

An interesting Jewish personality in Vietnam was diplomat Harry Samuel Waterman, the U.S. Consul in Saigon. As early as 1929–32 he warned the U.S. about the growth of Communism in Vietnam. Nobody listened!

In 1939, the total Jewish population in Haiphong, Hanoi, Saigon, and Tourane numbered about a thousand individuals, as well as eighty Jews in Tonkin. Jews were targeted after the takeover of Southern France and some of the French territories by the Nazi collaborators known as Vichy France. The anti-Semitic Petain regime even went so far as to issue a "Statute on Jews" whereby French Jewish citizens were limited to certain occupations and professions. During the war, Jews were fired from their jobs, and Jewish children were not allowed to comprise more than 2 percent of public school students.

With the end of World War II and the Japanese defeat, the French returned only once again in 1945–46, to be entangled with Ho Chi Minh and his Communist forces for nearly a decade.

⁓

As the year 1954 dawned, nine years after the end of World War II, the *American Jewish Yearbook* listed the Jewish population of French Indochina as 1,500. That community—let alone the people of Southeast Asia, or the world, for that matter—had no idea that one of the greatest battles in the post–World War II era was about to begin. They would call it a clash of civilizations, a turning point in colonial history. It would rank up there with the sieges of Port Arthur (1904), Corregidor (1941), and Singapore (1942). Those defeats would mark the beginning of the end of Russian, American, and British hegemony in Asia, and this 1954 battle would mark the final French involvement in Indochina.

The ghost of Dien Bien Phu would not only hound the French, but would haunt the U.S. military and its advisors for decades to come. Perhaps if the U.S. who at that time disregarded French appeals for help in 1954, had studied Dien Bien Phu closer, it would have not gotten involved a decade later and yet, at the time, U.S. officials truly believed that they had to stop Communism in Southeast Asia.

Dien Bien Phu, which means "seat of the Border County Prefecture," is a small and very green North Vietnamese valley, located 200 miles from Hanoi. I present it here because the memories and people I meet in other countries sometimes follow me in my travels, and although I have mentioned the good doctor, Dr. Yonah Poul, and his father in my chapter on Tahiti, where Dr. Poul resides, the story of his father at that doomed fortress in Dien Bien Phu now bears telling.

Dr. Poul had told me that his father, Chief Sergeant Eric Abraham Ben Yosef Poul, spent six years in Vietnam fighting with his French Foreign Legion unit, the 13th section of the 3rd company, in battles in Nan Bin, Dalat, Hoa Binh, Cao Bang, and finally, Dien Bien Phu. He was wounded in that French jungle base in 1954, and kept as a prisoner of the Communist Viet Minh for one year.

Still, according to Dr. Poul, his father "spoke about this country with big emotion. He loved it very much—the same for its inhabitants; very kind people, despite the war!"

It all began on November 20, 1953. In a bold airborne operation, the French garrison was dropped 200 miles west of Hanoi. They set up two airfields, bunkers, and a tent city in this jungle valley. From the beginning the French got it all wrong. The fortress at Dien Bien Phu was to have been a stepping-stone, serving as an air-supplied mooring point—a vital barrier designed to block the Viet Minh from moving into Laos. The French also wanted to lure the Viet Minh into a pitched battle in which the former's supposedly superior firepower would annihilate General Vo Nguyen Giap's guerrillas.

"My father told me that the Legion's officers knew the battle would be a failure and a waste," said Dr. Poul, "that it was the wrong place to fight a very mobile and numerous enemy, despite the fact that the French were really brave and good soldiers and fought like lions! A lot of Legion officers died in the battle; it's not the same with the Regular French Army, whose officers are far away from the battlefield," noted Dr. Poul, adding that the Legion is like *Zahal* (Israeli Defense Forces), where the officers are always first.

"My father," he continued, "told me that Dien Bien Phu was hell, with the bombs night and day, and the mud, and not enough bullets for your gun, and not enough clean water, and not enough food, and not enough cognac and cigarettes, and all your friends dying all around you and there's nothing you can do."

So even with some of the best units of the French Army in Indochina, the French High Command underestimated the Viet Minh's capabilities. Outnumbered five to one, the garrison at Dien Bien Phu never exceeded 13,000, while the Viet Minh had a siege force of 49,500. The French had been trapped in an inaccessible valley with little artillery, and they lacked aircraft.

Yonah Poul's father served in the fortified battle station located on Hill 506, otherwise known as "Beatrice," which was an outlying satellite strong point. It has been rumored, but never verified, that these strong points had been given the names of the mistresses of the commander, Colonel Christian Marie Ferdinand de la Croix de Castries.

On March 13, 1954, the Viet Minh threw thousands of their troops into the battle and unleashed a savage artillery bombardment and frontal attack on Beatrice, with its inadequate 500-man garrison. Beatrice was surrounded by impenetrable jungle hills which concealed the Viet Minh's heavy guns. Vietnamese troops had "shown phenomenal muscle in dragging artillery up to the heights above the valley," according to Karnow. A day later, March 14, the fortress fell. Knocking out and overrunning this defensive post, killing the commanders and taking prisoners, was a harbinger of what was to come.

Sergeant Poul was wounded, taken prisoner, and sent to a jail near the South China Sea. Later, he was repatriated to France to a hospital where he was treated by his future wife, Christiane Porte. She nursed him back to health.

Meanwhile, the siege would continue. The Vietnamese, who had decided to wipe out the enemy at all costs, strangled the French force by encircling them with tunnels and trenches, thus tightening the noose around them.

"You can kill ten of my men for every one I kill of yours. But even at those odds, you will lose and I will win," said General Giap.

At the last moment the French pleaded with the U.S. and Britain to bomb the Viet Minh positions from carriers in the South China Sea. The U.S. would not come to the aid of the French and use heavy bombers, with missiles or nukes.

Although the bravery of the defenders at Dien Bien Phu was legendary, especially the paratroopers of the Foreign Legion, of which Sergeant Poul was a member, it was not enough to save the situation. A breakout was impossible, and there was no chance of a relief column getting through to help them.

"Giap's timing was perfect," wrote Karnow. On the afternoon of May 7, 1954, at 5:50 p.m., the Viet Minh's red flag went up over the French Command bunker at Dien Bien Phu. The last French words were: "We're blowing up everything around here. Au revoir."

The 167-day siege was over.

"The news of the disaster covered France like a thick blanket," wrote Bernard B. Fall in his classic, *Hell in a Very Small Place: The Siege of Dien Bien Phu*. The end of France's colonial empire had arrived.

The next morning, May 8, 1954, the French sued for peace. Eight years later, they would pull out of Algeria. After centuries of subjugation, "the Asians had beaten the white man at his own game." And the road from Dien Bien Phu would lead to the American disaster.

⁓

As for Sergeant Poul, he was lucky he was captured before the end of the siege, and not when the French surrendered on May 7. Reminiscent of the Bataan Death March, 10,000, captured French troops began a 500-mile-long trek to the prison camps north of the Red River. "For the exhausted and mostly wounded survivors of the battle of Dien Bien Phu, this became a death march," according to Fall, who estimated that about 3,000 men out of a total of 16,544 eventually returned from Dien Bien Phu. "Over 3,000 died in the battlefield area and a few hundred . . . disappeared in Eastern Europe. But the rest, close to 10,000 men, died on a trek or in the prison camps in less than three months' time. This is a hard statistical fact which cannot and should not be overlooked," Fall wrote.

About 2,000 lay dead all over the battlefield in unmarked graves.

Even though he apparently was not on that infamous prison march, God only knows how Dr. Poul's father survived. We do know he was "in a small bamboo cage in a bayou, with dirty water coming in to just under the chin, with snakes, and just some old rotten rice to eat every day," according to Dr. Poul. The prisoners spent hours standing under the sun, "while the Communist commissars spent hours and hours teaching them [brain-washing], and a lot of the prisoners died of diarrhea and other infectious diseases," said Dr. Poul.

By the way, Sergeant Poul had been hit by a piece of shrapnel. His captors treated his wounds before throwing him into his cell, according to Dr. Poul.

By the late 1950s the *American Jewish Yearbook* included no mention of a Jewish population in the region. The Jews had gone with the French colonial administration in 1954, after the Geneva Conference which divided the country at the seventeenth parallel, with Ho Chi Minh ruling the north and a separate Vietnamese government in the south. Within five years after Dien Bien Phu, however, Hanoi authorized a South Vietnamese Communist insurgency against the Saigon government. By 1965, both the U.S. and North Vietnam had committed themselves to an all-out war. The conflict would prove to be incredibly costly in terms of both money and lives lost. The U.S. quit in 1973. Two years later, on April 30, South Vietnam surrendered to North Vietnam. Except for a dozen Jews in Saigon during the American war, the only Jewish community was that of the U.S. military personnel. About 30,000 American Jews served in the armed forces in Vietnam, among them Colonel Jack H. Jacobs, who won the Medal of Honor for heroic service.

Vietnam today is a very "in" place. Historic pagodas and faded French colonial buildings have been restored. Hotels and restaurants have been returned to the private sector. The tourist industry is growing at almost 20 percent annually, and millions of visitors are drawn to the country each year.

The world economic crisis caused some Jewish investors to close down their factories, but by 2010, the economy began to lift, and with it came new Jewish businesspeople and tourists.

Saigon is indeed a place where you can find everything. Sometimes it is difficult to decide which market to visit—the ones set up between streets lined with stalls and vendors spreading their wares on the sidewalk, or the indoor markets. This distinction becomes clear when you visit the wholesale markets, where an impressive amount of goods are lined up. In particular, a number of them can be found in District 5, Cholon, which is in the Chinese district.

Visit Binh Tay indoor wholesale market in districts 5 and 6. *Binh Tay* means "big market," an indication of the role played by the entrepreneurial

Chinese in Vietnam's economy. But *big* is not the word to describe this indoor supply of goods; in some cases it seems like the stacks almost touch the ceiling. *Humongous* is more like it. Well-known for its great bargains, Binh Tay is located in Cholon on Hua Giang Boulevard, and is ideal if you want to spend a day haggling over souvenirs.

Despite many wars and upheavals, Binh Tay Market has remained an important center of commerce for the locals. Farmers come here to trade their daily wares. All of you shoppers out there will find better bargains here than in the *souk* in Marrakech, or the Great Bazaar in Istanbul. Blouses, bags, shoes, rugs, suitcases, wallets, pillboxes, jewelry, crafts, spices, and food—including delicacies, baked goods, and coconut candy. You will find perfume, beads, ribbons, snake wine, an alcoholic beverage for medicinal purposes and found in Southeast Asia, as well as an ice cream shop to refresh you after you are all shopped out, shall we say—although that is not a condition that Westerners reach quickly, if at all.

You may think that shopping is merely a matter of getting the price, bargaining a bit if possible, buying an item, wrapping the goods, saying thank-you, and walking away. Not so simple in Asia. Shopping sometimes reveals cultural differences. Asian markets, especially in Vietnam, have different sales techniques. At booths, they sometimes grab your hand to bring you over to their booth to buy their wares. It's a cultural thing; they like the feel of your skin.

"When you go to the market, they try to snare you by holding your hand and pulling you into their shop," our guide Thanh told us. "By doing this, the owner of the shop wants to express the close relationship that he and you theoretically have had for a long time. You and he have broken the air to come closer. Then you may buy something in the shop."

"If they see you have smooth, white skin, they will touch you and say, 'Oh, how white and smooth you are,' and this is also another way to get closer to you. Sometimes they do this to compare their Vietnamese skin and yours. Or they will rush up to you and hold your shoulder to walk with you and steer you to their shop. On the street, when you are going to cross the road and traffic is so heavy that you feel you can't make it, they will come and hold your hand and lead you across the heavily trafficked street. Seniors will touch children's heads and say, "A good boy," or "A good girl," said Thanh, who now encouraged us to move on, as the lunch hour was approaching.

As noted, after crossing the huge roundabouts with motorbikes racing at you for a direct hit, one is content to find a place to sit and enjoy a cup of tea or a drink. We found one. And we discovered something else, too—signs that a very important neighbor of ours had already been here.

Having learned that travelers to distant lands often bump into a neighbor, or at least meet someone who knows so-and-so back home, we were not too shocked to see a photo of familiar faces when we entered the PHO 2000 at 01-03 Phan Chu Trinh Street in District One of Ho Chi Minh City. I immediately spotted the framed photo, as it was hanging auspiciously on the establishment's main entrance wall: It was a picture of my neighbors in Chappaqua, N.Y., President Bill Clinton and daughter, Chelsea, now Mrs. Chelsea Clinton Mezvinsky.

No, we did not meet the Clintons in Saigon that day. But just as folks say "George Washington slept here," we are proud to say that we ate at an establishment that boasts, "The Clintons ate here." Well, at least Bill and Chelsea did. Indeed, we learned that when they were there, the police roped off the whole square so the Clintons could cross the street without the burden of facing any motorized horsemen.

Not only was their photo there, but encased under glass at a nearby table in the center of the dining room was the Clintons' November 19, 2000, lunch menu.

President Clinton, who visited Vietnam in 2000, and did much during his administration to improve relations between these former enemies, lived about a mile and a half away from our house on Meadow Lane in Chappaqua. As villagers we saw the ex-president, Secretary of State Hillary Clinton, and daughter Chelsea from time to time, in Lange's Little Store deli, or at Starbucks, or in the Rite Aid drugstore, or one late evening, strolling down King Street.

At PHO 2000, Chelsea ordered vegetarian noodle soup, mineral water, and iced coffee with milk. President Clinton chose chicken noodle soup, spring rolls, and fresh mango.

They chose well, as noodle soup, known as *pho,* and spring rolls are Vietnamese specialties. I learned that *pho* is an important element and a delicious choice in Vietnam. It's a classic dish that combines white noodles, slices of beef, and spring onions in a rich broth. There are eight to ten variations of the soup, with the greatest number based on beef. Seafood and vegetarian options are available as well.

By the time we were about to leave Vietnam, we realized we had forgotten we were visiting a country still run by a Communist Party and still led by a Politburo, the most powerful governmental unit in Vietnam. The days of rigid Communist doctrine seem to be gone, however; the country has adopted a new constitution and set up a new National Assembly. Still, the U.S. worries about the country's human rights record as dozens of lawyers and activists have been arrested over the past five years for challenging the government, according to Seth Mydans in the *New York Times,* April 4, 2011.

Many nations have problems with neighbors and Vietnam is no exception. Tensions rose in 2011 between China and Vietnam in the South China Sea as both nations seek advantage over a potentially resource-rich sea.

We flew up to Hanoi, the capital, the city which was about to celebrate its thousandth anniversary in 2010. Ho Chi Minh's mausoleum, designed by Soviet architects, was modeled on Lenin's tomb in Moscow.

The main attraction in Hanoi, of course, is this mausoleum, although the restaurants, the beautiful lake, and the shops in various neighborhoods also attract visitors. There is less gaiety in the capital, for it's a serious city compared to Ho Chi Minh City. But it has its attractions, and there is a lot to see in Hanoi, including the water puppets; Hoa Lo Prison, Americans know it as the Hanoi Hilton, where former presidential candidate Senator John McCain was held prisoner; the old quarter; and the very worthwhile boat trip to Halong Bay.

Before visiting Ho's mausoleum, we sought out some fun and relaxation: a visit to the water puppets. We purchased tickets in advance, for the water puppet show at Thang Long Theatre is usually quite booked. This is a unique traditional Vietnamese art, which originates from rural festivals. The puppeteers—both men and women—stand waist-deep in the water to manipulate the puppets, making them move about, talk, laugh, and even dance on the surface of the water. Their technical skills are outstanding.

Like all puppet shows, the mood was light and gay, and just as intriguing as watching the manipulation of the puppets in the water was enjoying the instruments and the exotic music that came forth. The audience loved it, and we walked out with smiles on our tired faces after a long day touring.

⁓

Next day, we waited in the hot sun to see Ho, the father of the nation. Even in the heat we must stand still in relatively long lines, and move along with almost military precision. Schoolchildren went first, of course. Uniformed veterans with their green uniforms and red epaulettes joined the line. I took pictures, and they knew I was an American.

Finally, we entered the darkened room where Ho lies in state. Total silence. The guard moved us along. It was all over in less than a minute, and we filed out into the bright sunshine with a picnic atmosphere, where schoolchildren belted out lovely childish shrieks. They love to be photographed.

I recalled that in previous years, I had visited the embalmed Lenin in Red Square, and Mao Tse-tung in Tiananmen Square in Beijing. Now I had seen Ho.

From the mausoleum, visitors are directed across Ba Dinh Square to Ho Chi Minh's house, built in the compound of the former Presidential Palace. The palace, now a party guesthouse, was the residence of the Governors-General of French Indochina and was built between 1900 and 1908. Ho Chi Minh declined to live in the palace, saying it belonged to the people. He stayed in what is said to have been an electrician's hut in the same compound, from 1954–58, before moving to a new stilt house built on the other side of the small lake. The modest house was designed by Ho and was furnished with rare hardwood furniture. It is airy and immaculately kept. He conducted meetings under the house, which is raised up on wooden pillars, and slept and worked in the rooms above from May 1958 to August 1969. Behind the house is Ho's bomb shelter. He died in his house in the former governor's residence in 1969, where he lived alone.

The guide met us and offered up a joke, the type of joke that is often heard in authoritarian countries where, in private, people can mock their leaders verbally, although they will never criticize the government in public—at least, in print. Loosening the safety valve, it might be called. I heard the same type of jokes in Cuba. Here's a Vietnamese version of this kind of joke, which the guide told us after we had left the mausoleum where Uncle Ho lies in state.

"That was very interesting," we told the guide.

"Tell me," he answered, "did he wave back at you?"

We all laughed.

I turned back to snap another photo of that imposing mausoleum, reflecting that Ho, Mao, and Stalin would all be shocked to see that their lands are not only deeply involved in "dreaded" free market activities, but also, that they are now being taunted in front of tourists from capitalist America.

Well, the joke is on them, *n'est-ce pas?*

THE LAND OF GOLDEN PAGODAS

The Religious Wonders of Burma

"The Irrawaddy flowed huge and ochreous, glittering like diamonds on the patches that caught the sun; and beyond the river stretched great wastes of paddy fields, ending at the horizon in a range of blackish hills."
—*George Orwell*, Burmese Days

"You will be on the soil of many countries," disclosed my fortune cookie.

I take predictions like that seriously. Before I knew it, Southeast Asia, with its mysterious and fascinating lands, beckoned me. I knew that this treasure trove had to include Jews, no matter how few. I would not be mistaken during my search for the scattered tribe; I would indeed find them. I wanted to meet my people and learn how they lived and survived.

So I headed for exotic Burma, now known as the Union of Myanmar, where little has changed since British colonial times over a half-century ago. Having read Rudyard Kipling and George Orwell, I was intrigued by this nation that straddles the Asian highway connecting China and India with Southeast Asia.

I even began to hum Kipling's imperial British poem:

On the road to Mandalay,
Where the flyin'-fishes play,
An' the dawn comes up like thunder outer China 'crost the Bay!

And then we arrived!

Welcome, dear reader, to Yangon, once called Rangoon, until recently the nation's capital. Here I gazed at the stately buildings of the Strand and the golden finial of the Shwedagon Pagoda. Here at night, my spirits rose as I observed the alluring golden beams from the shimmering bell of the Sule Pagoda, which, along with the Shwedagon, constantly reminded me that I was in a mystifying land, a land where people have lived since prehistoric times, a land filled with Buddhist shrines.

But an important task awaited me. Where to find my people?

Next day, standing atop the Theingyi Zay Bridge overpass in the city, my spirits rose. We listened to the exhilarating roar of hundreds of buyers and sellers at the Maha Bandula street market below. The sounds emanating from their throaty voices reached a crescendo as they announced their wares. Arguing, bargaining, pleading, these skilled and persuasive Burmese merchants hovered over their goods, carelessly spread out in carts and on blankets. A buyer's dream: watches, jeans, T-shirts, toys, CDs, DVDs, fried beans, vegetable tempura.

Previous journeys had landed us in *souqs* in Mumbai and Kochi in India, as well as in Marrakech and Fez in Morocco. But nothing compares to this outdoor bazaar on Maha Bandula Street between 26th and 31st Streets in Yangon. Yes, we now knew we were in the Orient, in a metropolis that once traded with the world and possessed gems, teak, timber, and oil.

Another sight caught my eye as I looked out at the scene below: a two-story, white stone building, fittingly with blue painted around the windows and a few horizontal blue stripes on its whitewashed walls—as in, blue and white, the colors of the Jewish people as manifested on the Israeli flag. All that was needed was the six-pointed Jewish star on the middle wall of the building. The star wasn't there, but once you are at the main street entrance you can see above the white walls an archway with a seven-branched candelabra, and the name spelled out in large blue letters. It's a Jewish house of worship. Everyone in the neighborhood knows that the structure standing in this exotic but now tired city of Yangon is the *Musmeah Yeshua Synagogue,* which means *"Brings Forth Salvation,"* located at No. 85 26th Street.

All the Jews are gone now—all, that is, except a remnant.

In Europe, formerly large Jewish communities that survived the Holocaust and have shrunk to meager populations are called "remnants." Personally, I don't like that word, although perhaps it fits' here. Officially, only eight Jewish families are known to exist in this entire country of more than 50 million, a country which lies between Thailand and Laos on its eastern side, Bangladesh to the west, and India and China on the north; Andaman Sea to the South.

The 150-year-old *Musmeah Yeshua Synagogue* remains open thanks to one "just" man, Than Lwin. Jews know him as Moses Samuels, the man who carries the load of Jewish history on his shoulders. Every day he walks a few blocks from his home to open the doors of the synagogue and keep Judaism alive in Burma/Myanmar. He tends to its needs, raises money, and supervises repairs.

Usually, no one shows up for a *minyan*. Happily, from time to time a *minyan* does take place—the result of someone having to recite a memorial prayer, or, on occasion, when a group of Israeli, American, or Australian Jews arrive during the tourist season. When that happens, Moses frantically calls the few Jews in the city to come quickly to the synagogue and meet the guests in this building, one of 188 sites on the list of Yangon Heritage Buildings.

If his son, Sammy is at home, he conducts the Sephardic service, as Moses cannot read Hebrew.

⁓

"Our family is still here," says sixty-one-year-old Moses Samuels, who opened the synagogue for me, as he does for any visitor. Born in Burma, his parents were from Iraq. Moses and son Sammy run Myanmar Shalom Travel and Tours together, and the firm's profits go to the synagogue. Moses is the managing director of the Yangon office, and Sammy is the marketing and travel consultant in New York (www.myanmarshalom.com). They offer tours for individuals, groups, businesses, and special interests, and tours that focus on culture, beaches, trekking, and of course, the "Special Jewish Experience," which goes hand in hand with their motto, *Join us to keep the Jewish spirit alive in Burma.*

Sammy, whose name in Burmese is Aung Soe Lwin, graduated with high honors from Yeshiva University in New York City, where he now lives.

Moses and his wife Nellie also have two daughters, Kuzna and Dinah, who returned to Myanmar after their studies in the U.S.

Over the years, I have met many such men and women and their children who have felt the burden of keeping a synagogue alive. A father and son in Seville, Spain, come to mind. Every Friday night the two opened that city's only house of worship, which was located in an apartment building. Even now in the U.S., in those gentrified Bronx and Miami neighborhoods, elderly men and women keep synagogues functioning in neighborhoods that have been abandoned by fellow Jews. It's their life, they say; someone has to do it.

"It's the connection," declared thirty-year-old Sammy, who is in the U.S. working on an MBA, and who for a number of years served as a computer programmer for the American Jewish Congress. "Being in the synagogue gives us our tie to Judaism. We love Burma so much, and we want to keep the Jewish spirit alive."

For at least a decade, Sammy and Moses have kept a Jewish presence in the country which once included between 1,500 to 2,000 Jews, and is now, as noted, down to eight Jewish families, of which eight Jews live in Yangon.

Over and over again throughout my travels, I would hear this phrase: "Keep Judaism alive." But to do that, these people need dedication, especially if all they have in the way of Jewish life is an often-vacant synagogue. In the case of the *Musmeah Yeshua Synagogue,* in Burma, it was built in 1854 and rebuilt in stone in 1896; it also features a cemetery whose oldest tomb dates back to 1876.

A rabbi has not served here for over forty years. Several times a year, Chabad, which is organized in nearby Cambodia, Thailand, and Vietnam, sends an emissary. Apparently, Chabad would set up a headquarters here if they thought enough Jews lived in or visited Myanmar.

Despite the fact that only a few Burmese Jews remain in Yangon; that only a few Israelis work in their embassy; that groups of Jewish travelers only occasionally show up here from November through April—this small number of Jews still tries to convey the message to the world: *We are still here.*

But for how long? I asked myself.

Like Benjamin of Tudela, my namesake, I wanted to record and learn what I could about the Jews of Burma in the early twenty-first century. But first I have to know what happened in the twentieth century to this once-flourishing community of several thousand Jews who lived in peace, thrived here in comfort and stability, without anti-Semitism, and, in the words of a former Jewish Burmese, "fostered the conviction that God was in his heaven, and all was right with the world," especially since the Jews lived most of the time under the benign mantle of the British Empire.

The "happy and beautiful days" for Burmese Jewry ended when the Japanese brutally bombed Rangoon on Christmas Day, 1941, and invaded the country at the outset of World War II, causing the Jews to flee to India. Only a small group remained in Burma to protect *Musmeah Yeshua*. When peace finally came, several hundred returned. They found bombed-out buildings, their homes occupied and looted. "The once-stately colonial city of Rangoon was gone, demolished by bombs, fire and theft, and deep in filth and garbage. Dalhousie Street, long the center of Jewish commercial life, was in ruins," wrote Ruth Fredman Cernea in her book, *Almost Englishmen: Baghdadi Jews in British Burma. The* synagogue still stood, unharmed, its *sifrei Torah* (Torah scrolls) undamaged and ready to serve the shattered community, according to Cernea.

Burma's Jewish community was "devastated and never recovered," she added. "Judaism enjoyed a "brief flowering" after the country's independence in 1948 and the establishment of cordial Israeli-Burmese relations. Those ties were based on the warm friendship between prime ministers David Ben-Gurion and U Nu. The latter was the first head of state to visit Israel just after its birth.

The final blow to the now-weakened Burmese Jewry came in 1962, when General Ne Win, once described as "a military man to his fingertips," overthrew civilian government, set up a military dictatorship, nationalized industry, declared a policy of strict self-reliance and strict neutrality, and disassociated Burma from outside influences, including those of the Jewish state. His new "Burmese Way to Socialism" had ushered in xenophobia, and the position of minorities in Burma quickly deteriorated, as did the nation's economy. With their businesses forcibly nationalized, Jews emigrated. Burma had fallen on bad days.

Now, a half-century later, even though the raucous noise of the Burmese street vendors was doing its best to smother my homesick thoughts in this far-off land, I somehow imagined this synagogue full of worshippers sitting on these wooden benches praying for their families, their health, their businesses, their lives. Hailing from Baghdad, they were known as the *Baghdadis*. A smaller group arriving from Calcutta and Cochin, in India, were called *Bene Israel*.

As in days of yore, the synagogue's beautiful stained-glass windows were wide open; it was hot. Birds flew near the top of the ceiling, they cooed and whistled. It wasn't hard to imagine that these winged creatures symbolized the souls of Jews who once lived and worked in this neighborhood.

At *Musmeah Yeshua,* I learned an amazing fact, a Jewish "Believe-It-or-Not" story: Moses and Sammy told me that at one time, the synagogue possessed 126 Torah scrolls on shelves mounted onto the wall of a small, circular room which served as the Holy Ark. I was shown the last two remaining Torahs embedded in wooden boxes, covered with beaten silver, designed in the style of the Torah scrolls familiar to Babylonian Jews.

How could that be? How could one synagogue have 126 Torahs? Most congregations possess about a half-dozen. Why so many?

In Burma, it was a great honor for a family to donate a Torah to the congregation and inscribe the family name on the scroll. On *Yom Kippur* and *Simchat Torah,* all 126 were removed from the Ark and carried in a procession around the crowded hall of worshippers. Moreover, when the family had to recite *yahrzeit* (a memorial prayer), they would come to services and remove their contributed Torah, in honor of the soul being mourned. Sometimes, the Torahs were taken out by schoolchildren and paraded through the streets of Rangoon to their day school.

Young Sammy Samuels reminded me that much of the surrounding district is a Muslim neighborhood, a fact that I noticed while driving through the crowded streets near the Jewish cemetery, which is a half-hour by foot from the synagogue.

Often in Southeast Asian countries, various streets and even entire districts market a single commodity, such as shoes. Here on 26th Street, paint is product number one. And because the heat is unbearable in tin-roofed huts, much business is done out on the street and not in the shop. Cars can hardly pass down the narrow roadways.

Around 1880, *Musmeah Yeshua* received permission to build stores along Dalhousie Street, the market street now called Maha Bandula, where

I stood on the overpass and heard the crushing din from the marketers. Later I was to discover that Dalhousie was Lord Dalhousie, Viceroy of India, who in 1852 led British forces in annexing Lower Burma.

⌒

To this day, Moses Samuels collects rent from these street shops—about forty-eight dollars a month, which helps to cover the maintenance costs and municipal bills for the synagogue, as well as the nearby cemetery where 700 bodies lie in repose in a burial ground of moss-covered tombstones.

And it is the cemetery that is providing another opportunity for Moses and Sammy to involve the Burmese Jewish diaspora, such as it is, to rise to the occasion and help the two keep a Jewish presence in a country in which their parents, relatives, and friends thrived, lived well, and got along with their neighbors, who in turn treated them kindly, and still do, with no trace of anti-Semitism.

The old Jewish cemetery on 91st Street is in itself a repository of Jewish life and history in Burma. Small pebbles rest on the tombs, a traditional practice in Jewish cemeteries, whether Ashkenazi or Sephardic.

I took a few pictures, standing quietly outside the gate marked with a Star of David, which also adorns many of the tombs. My camera lens captured a symbolic scene: the Jewish cemetery gate with its Jewish star, a mosque in the near background, and in the far background, a Christian church. A Burmese monk habitat also is located on the left side of the cemetery. I realize that in Southeast Asia, tolerance of other religions is not something mouthed in slogans, nor is it staged for photo ops. Different religions are respected.

A lifesaver, however, has come onto the scene in the last few years to help keep up the synagogue and the cemetery, in the form of a dedicated woman and a business group.

Despite U.S. financial sanctions against the repressive Myanmar regime, and the latter's reluctance to accept outside aid, the US–ASEAN Business Council obtained approval from both governments to aid the synagogue. So far, it has raised funds from businesses and individuals to help pay for painting the walls and repairing the roof, severely damaged by Cyclone Nargis in 2008. The council covers the costs of maintenance, about U.S. $2,000 a year.

Frances Zwenig of the US–ASEAN Business Council is the driving force behind the Myanmar Synagogue Project. She also helps with other problems facing Yangon Jewry. For instance, it is a given that where old synagogues and cemeteries occupy pricey downtown real estate, problems arise. A number of years ago, the Jewish community received word from the municipal government that the cemetery would have to be moved. However, according to Sammy and Ms. Zwenig, the actual command to relocate Yangon's Jewish cemetery to Mingalar Taung Nyunt Township, just outside the city, has not been issued.

Still, the community wants to be prepared. Does not the Talmud say: "The Jewish tombstones are fairer than royal palaces" (Sanh. 96b; cf Matt. 23:29)? A new resting ground has been cleaned up and prepared to receive the graves. "The reburial will be carried out according to religious law," Sammy confirmed. He has already consulted rabbis in New York.

Stuart Spencer, a successful insurance executive with Chubb, and based in Hong Kong, certainly belongs among those Jews who say they want to give back to the community, and actually do. He represents those Jews who take an interest not only in locating the roots of their parents and grandparents, but who constantly visit and help, donating funds to assist with the upkeep of that community. Spencer's mother was born in Burma and left at the start of World War II when she fled to India. He donated the funds to prepare the site of the new cemetery. "Hope for the best, prepare for the worst," he said. He gave sufficient funds to level the grounds, wall in the burial area, clean up the premises, pave an access road, and to install a gate and a sign, so that when the municipal government order comes, the community will be ready.

Protestant graves have been moved; not so the Muslim or Jewish. But if the time comes, there will be an "orderly, systematic, *halakhic* exhumation of 700 tombs," Spencer told me. Sammy already has photographed 700 gravestones.

Spencer is enthusiastic about helping the community. He wants his own Hong Kong synagogue, the *United Jewish Congregation,* to reach out to *Musmeah Yeshua,* and send some of their congregants to Yangon to help repair and engage in projects to maintain this most beautiful synagogue.

Moses and Sammy have been engaged in projects such as turning a vacant room off the entrance into a display of historic photos of the community, as well as handmade Judaica and postcards. Also recently cleaned and made kosher is a *mikveh,* though it's not used.

⁓

Back out on the street, the city was hot; the humidity was like steam pouring from the air. As I moved about the city and spotted the different pagodas, I saw saffron-robed monks and heard the tinkling temple bells of Burma.

I took a break and again walked around the neighborhood. Dalhousie Street leads to the Sule Pagoda, not far from *Musmeah Yeshua,* and visited by Jewish visitors who then saunter over to the synagogue. Another passageway is Mogul Street, four blocks from the synagogue, once occupied by Jews, then Muslims and Indians who lived here. Located on these two streets were the Jewish shops, occupied by tailors, wine and liquor traders, coffee and fruit vendors, as well as antique dealers. Today, gold and diamond shops have replaced those former residents. Gone are the residential quarters. Gone are the Jewish traders.

⁓

Yet, amazingly, although few in number, Jews are still here. As I exited the synagogue I noticed that above the gate on the inside wall was the Jewish star I had been looking for, and the Hebrew word, *Shalom* (peace). Visiting landmarks or sites in foreign countries often ignites childhood memories for tourists; the same is true for travel writers. Standing in this Sephardic house of worship, I was captivated by the awe-inspiring surroundings, which recalled my younger days attending Hebrew School in Pittsburgh, Pennsylvania. I used to dread when my teacher would send me on an errand from one part of the synagogue to another. I would have to tread through the congregation's empty downstairs *Beth Hamidrash* (prayer hall). Except for a dim memorial light above the Holy Ark to show the way, the hall was completely dark. If there was one time in my life when I possessed the fear of God, it was then, especially in the evenings when I had to grope through that dim prayer hall.

Memories of my old synagogue and Hebrew School and Jewish holidays with family still kindle my mental images of America, thousands of miles away. I was in Myanmar a few days before Passover, and at that moment in this synagogue, I spotted a *haggadah.* This particular Passover prayer book is special. Marked *Haggadah Shel Pesach,* this tome also recalled my childhood years. Emblazoned on its cover are the words PRODUCED BY MAXWELL HOUSE COFFEE—GOOD TO THE LAST DROP. KOSHER FOR PASSOVER.

Back in the decades of the mid-twentieth century, thousands of Jewish homes in the U.S. used these very same *haggadahs,* which were mass-produced by Maxwell House Coffee. Somehow, either through the Jewish Welfare Board (JWB) in the U.S. or the Joint Distribution Committee (JDC), or former GIs who passed through after World War II, these *haggadahs* found their way to *Musmeah Yeshua.*

Now it was dusk. Perhaps it was the lack of electrical power, because it always seemed to be dark in Yangon. It reminded me of evenings in the former Soviet Union's satellite countries. Even in the pale light, one noticed that apartments needed repairs. Buses were crowded. Except for a few main roads, traffic flowed easily. Travelers flock here because the country has changed little since British colonial times. The pagodas and the majestic rivers captivate voyagers. But it's the Burmese that make a visit to this land exciting. The people! "Ultimately a trip to Myanmar is mostly about the people," exclaims the *Lonely Planet Guide.* They are the wonderful people who welcome strangers, the men and women of this exotic land surrounded by Buddhist *stupas,* Hindu temples, Christian churches, and Muslim mosques, and yes again, the last remaining synagogue, *Musmeah Yeshua.*

I asked myself again: What is it that sometimes makes people in a poor country so nice, so pleasant—a phenomenon that I also witnessed in Cuba. Does poverty and repression bring warmth and hospitality? Couldn't be. I quickly came to the conclusion that these good people one day will live in prosperity and freedom, and I am sure that they will remain as kind as they are today.

As for my people, most of the original Jews who came to Burma were from Iraq, via India. This is certainly evident in the interior of *Musmeah Yeshua,* which is similar in style to the grand Magen David Synagogue in Kolkata (Calcutta): a soaring ceiling, memorial lamps suspended in midair, pale beams over a central carved *bimah* located in the center of the prayer hall, and surrounded by benches for the worshippers. Above them is a women's gallery.

Before World War II, Jews lived in and around these streets in Rangoon, the city which only became the nation's capital city in 1885, after the British completed the conquest of northern Burma. During their sixty-year stay, the British transformed the city, locating it strategically, facing the ocean and serviced by the Irrawaddy River—navigable for 900 fertile miles. Rangoon helped Burma become the world's largest exporter of rice.

Within decades of the British arrival, life for Jews would be wonderful. Jews mixed with Christians, Burmese, Hindus, Muslims, and Chinese. Anti-Semitism did not exist, according to personal testimonials from Cernea's book.

In the 1920s, Jewish travel writer, Israel Cohen, author of *The Journal of a Jewish Traveler,* estimated that there were 500 Jews in Rangoon, most originating from Baghdad. Describing this affluent community as "generous" to Jewish causes, he tells us about a visit to a congregant's residence. "The house was a palatial residence in the suburbs, surrounded by extensive gardens, and comprising a small farmyard with cows and poultry for the household's consumption. Thirty-six Burmese servants served the establishment. They are trilingual," wrote Cohen. "They spoke Arabic among themselves, Burmese with the natives and English with the Europeans," he added, noting that a Jewish day school contained 140 students.

Nearly a hundred years after Cohen's visit, when I met Moses Samuels, he was wearing the traditional Burmese *longyi,* a tightly wrapped skirt made from a cylinder of cotton cloth. Men's *longyi* often have a checkered pattern and are bound in front. The majority of men we saw wear the *longyi,* which is very practical in this tropical heat. Myanmar's isolation and low wages have kept this frugal dress mode in use.

Burmese women favor calf-length *longyi* in solid colors, stripes, or flower prints, topped off by a form-fitting waist-length blouse. Observing the women of Burma, including our guide, I noticed they look as if they all have skin problems, until I learned that it is *thanaka,* a paste made from the bark of the thanaka tree and smeared on the face, usually in circles. Burmese women, including Jews, wear it as a kind of powder, as it absorbs sweat and protects their skin from the sun. Ground into a paste, *thanaka* has a faintly sweet fragrance and a texture like fine wet clay. Men don't wear this cosmetic, although some small children do for sun protection.

Some Burmese women also chew a wad of betel leaves (from the betel vine, known to be a mild stimulant) in their mouth. Originating in India, this addictive habit stands out as the Asian parallel to tobacco chewing. This accounts for their teeth being purple, and yellow, too—that is, whatever teeth they have remaining.

After World War I, many Burmese Jews—far from the centers of European Jewish life, and living in a totally different civilization—felt that if they wanted to adjust, the best and natural way was through intermarriage. Cohen, for instance, found a merchant born in London who had married a Burmese woman, as well as an elderly gentleman born in London married to a Japanese lady.

He also discovered a little coterie of Anglo-Jewish bookmakers in the city who traveled regularly between London and Rangoon. Ah, yes, Jewish occupations are varied.

The first Jew in Burma was not *Baghdadi* but probably a *Bene Israel.* Solomon Gabirol served as a commissar in the army of King Alaungpaya (1752–60). More Jews followed. A Jewish merchant named Goldenberg, from Romania, engaged in the teakwood trade and accumulated great wealth. Solómon Reineman of Galicia, who visited Rangoon, wrote *Solomon's Travels,* in 1884, including a chapter on Burma. In those long-ago centuries, Jewish gem merchants visited lush and exotic Burma for diamonds, rubies, bejeweled gold ornaments, pearls, and golden bangles. With them came Bengalis, Chinese, Malays, Turks, Arabs, Siamese, and Gujaratis. To this day Myanmar is considered the land of star sapphires, emeralds, rubies, and jade. We were taken to a jewelry store, probably an official one; no bargains there. Maybe in other markets, such as Scott Market. We didn't buy.

Jewish community growth and the impetus to settle in Burma came in the decades around 1830 when David Sassoon arrived from Baghdad with his coreligionists, known as *Baghdadis.* Others arrived from Calcutta and Cochin in India and were known as *Bene Israel.*

Sassoon brought with him the investments and connections of an extensive trading network—often based on opium—which Jews would extend to other Asian lands.

The *Baghdadis* built businesses, communal institutions, cemeteries, and synagogues in this hospitable land of gentle hosts. Other *Baghdadis,* some originating in Baghdad, moved on to Singapore, Jakarta, Bangkok, Saigon, Manila, Tokyo, Hong Kong, and Shanghai. As traders, they serviced the ships that docked in the busy harbor of Rangoon, whose population in 1872 was 98,138, including 83 Jews. By 1901, the population had reached 248,060, including 508 Jews, who were "well poised to take advantage of the economic opportunities offered by the British Raj," according to Cernea. A Hebrew school, Zionist groups, and many charitable and communal organizations were functioning at this time. A second synagogue, *Beth El,* was opened in 1932, but closed down after the Japanese invasion.

The Burmese Jewish community was not oblivious to dispute. Antagonisms between class and countries of origin, along with issues related to religious practices and skin color often induced splits and disunity in Jewish communities in Southeast Asia.

In her book, *Jews in Remote Corners of the World,* Ida Cowen—who visited Burma in the early 1960s—put it this way: "Brown-skinned and speaking the Indian Marathi tongue, they [the *Bene Israel]* were fine-featured, dark-eyed and dark-haired. The lighter-skinned *Baghdadis* were condescending toward these darker-skinned coreligionists."

And Cernea points out that in the early twentieth century, tensions between the *Baghdadis* and *Bene Israel* increased, especially in Bombay and Rangoon. By this time, "the *Baghdadis* had become firmly associated with the British lifestyle and the *Bene Israel* were even more identified with India."

In the 1930s, mind you, only 60 Jews were *Bene Israel* out of a Rangoon Jewish population of about 2,000. Try as they might, the two groups could not resolve conflict. "Feelings ran deep," wrote Cernea. Tension was so high that a group of *Baghdadis* bolted from *Musmeah Yeshua* and founded the *Beth El* congregation, which existed until the Japanese invasion, according to Cernea.

Rangoon Jewry was marked by "disagreements, bickering, dissensions," wrote Cowen, and yes, even lawsuits, one of which was Civil Regular Suit No. 85 of 1934, in the High Court at Rangoon. The *Bene Israel* went to court, asserting that they were being "discriminated against in *Musmeah Yeshua*, and that their participation in the synagogue was limited." They "were not permitted to vote," they claimed; they "couldn't purchase synagogue honors and go up to the *bimah;*"and they weren't allowed to carry the Torah during the Simchat Torah holiday procession, according to Cernea.

The *Bene Israel* won their case.

⁓

Even with those tensions, Jews were so integrated into Burmese life that two served as mayor, one in Rangoon and one in Bassein. The Sofaer family donated the iron gates to the Rangoon Zoo, and Mordechai Isaac Cohen gave the cast-iron bandstand in Bandoola Square. Both are still standing. A street was named after Judah Ezekiel, an employee of the British East India Company and a noted philanthropist.

The good life began to end with the coming of World War II and stopped altogether in the 1960s, as a result of the military coup. As Cowen wrote, gone were "the days of dissension and factions with the Rangoon Jewish Community. Now Jews cling together . . . to whatever remains of Jewish life among the pagodas. . . ."

⁓

Ah, the awe-inspiring pagodas! Kipling was right: The Shwedagon Pagoda is a "a golden mystery . . . a beautiful winking wonder that blazed in the sun." The dean of travel writers, Norman Lewis, considered this pagoda "the most brilliant spectacle" he had ever seen.

Yangon's enormous, gold-plated Shwedagon Pagoda is the holiest Buddhist shrine in Myanmar; indeed, the chief place of pilgrimage in the Buddhist world and a tourist's delight.

Yes, even this peripatetic traveler relaxed and walked calmly during my visit to the pagoda. Actually, I had to walk slowly; no shoes, no socks, no orthotics. No hustle and bustle here. Besides, in such an atmosphere, anxiety was diffused. I was visiting a wonder of the world: a religious shrine on the one hand, but also a quiet retreat for the Burmese people. Tension all but disappeared in the Shwedagon Pagoda, with its glittering bright-gold bell-shaped structure and golden dome, resplendent in the sun and dazzling the visitor. The pagoda—a landmark dominating the city skyline—remains the heart and soul of Yangon.

I followed the advice of our guide and visited late in the afternoon when shadows cast a mystic blanket over the shrine with its glittering gold *stupa* gilded with eight tons of gold. I walked around the pagoda's circular promenade bordered on both sides by small shrines of carved wood, with Buddhas of various sizes and small fountains. The informality allows one to stroll undisturbed and observe the pavilions. For tourists, the pagoda can be anything the individual desires it to be, including a place of spirituality, prayer, meditation, contemplation, reflection, discussion, observation, or none of the above.

I had to stop and remind myself that this is a religious shrine. Not hard at all. Women sitting and praying. Monks in deep thought. Families pouring sacred water over a Buddha's head. Teenagers and seniors lighting and relighting incense candles.

Like Israel Cohen, ninety years later, I noticed the small picturesque shrines, "some of carved wood, others containing white-painted Buddhas, and some a Buddha twenty-five feet high, while within them were many worshippers, especially women, whether kneeling or prostrate, with flowers and lighted tapers in their hands."

God's children were here, seeking consolation and guidance, perhaps a refuge in Buddhism, which preaches patience and compassion. The people of Myanmar need comforting. Their nation remains among the poorest in the world. Myanmar ranks 132 out of 177 countries in the 2007 United Nations Development Program's Human Development Index. Most experts, who doubt the government's statistics, think the reality is worse.

The breathtaking golden monument puts me in a trance as I walk clockwise around the *stupa*, which is the solid, cone-like type. While legend has it that the *stupa* may be 2,500 years old, archaeologists believe the original *stupa* was built by the Mon tribe between the sixth and tenth centuries. Earthquakes caused it to be rebuilt many times, and its current form dates back to 1769.

According to legend, the *stupa* was built to house eight hairs from the head of the Buddha, and is adorned with 5,448 diamonds and 2,317 rubies. At the very tip of the structure is a 76-carat diamond. The platform covers 12 acres.

The original height of the pagoda was 66 feet. From the fourteenth century, Burmese monarchs rebuilt it and re-gilded it until Shwedagon reached its present height of 326 feet. It has ten different sections, including the base.

Here at Shwedagon you can see the Burmese people enjoying cool breezes. Family groups pick their station. Parents come here with their young children, some of whom are novices of Buddhism and dressed in monk's garb. We had mixed feelings when we watched parents adjusting the burgundy monks' robes for their children, who were perhaps four or five years old.

I was told by our guide that most men in Burma have spent some time, months or years, as novices and monks before entering what one might call everyday life. Burmese women in monasteries are known as nuns. Earlier in my tour I had visited a monastery, in this case a Monastic Education Center in assembly in Yangon. There I had observed young girls in their pink monastic gowns, reading texts. We stared at each other. The chairman of their monastery had delivered a message during a celebration a few years back: "May there be peace and prosperity in the world." A good message for all of us.

In the early 1920s, fellow Jewish traveler Israel Cohen also went to the Shwedagon Pagoda. He, too, had to take off his shoes and walk barefoot. "I sensed that for the people, the shrines and images were not only a center of spirituality, but also served as the site where quietly, silently, men and women could demand freedom from oppression that dwells in the hearts of all men and women," Cohen wrote.

I traveled to Myanmar with no illusions. I knew it was a repressive regime. The military dictatorship is probably the longest-lasting military dictatorship in the world. Unlike other countries under military rule, the army here doesn't just watch over a civilian government. In Myanmar, the military *is* the government and the law. Army officers and their troops do everything; they are the state. Civilian government has withered away.

This country has been so isolated that Americans do not pay too much attention to events here. Most of my fellow citizens to this day do not know that Burma is now called Myanmar, let alone know about embattled leader Aung San Suu Kyi, Nobel Peace Prize winner and symbol of democracy, Burmese patriot and "prisoner of conscience," who twenty years ago was placed under house arrest in Rangoon and finally freed on November 13, 2010.

I never make it a practice to tell anyone what country to visit. Individual choice is important, especially since the mere mention of a certain nation can lead a friend, relative, or acquaintance to say, "I'd never go there and give them my money!"

Still, visiting Burma raises moral questions, as the bulk of tourist revenue might just fall into the government's treasury. On the other hand, interaction with the people of Burma and its culture helps to encourage change. Independent travel, staying at boutique hotels, shopping in family-owned workshops, and eating at small restaurants is the best way to put money directly into the hands of locals, it has been reported.

Both sides have their defenders.

Sammy encourages Jewish tourism. He says he "strongly believes tourism benefits the Burmese people."

I agree with an article Sammy wrote for the *Baltimore Jewish Times,* in December 2009: "Whatever the politics of visiting Burma, the tourist will find a nation of gentle folk and smiling people, rich archaeological sites, glittering pagodas, colorful bazaars, and joyous festivals." Some travel observers say that for tourists, Myanmar today is similar to Thailand forty years ago.

Kipling is correct: "This is Burma, and it will be quite unlike any land you know about."

Old Burma still exists. Today, Myanmar may be seething inside, but outwardly, it is a quiet land. *Calm* is the best description. The markets may be noisy, but in the pagodas, especially in another pagoda, the pagoda of the reclining Buddha, you can hear a pin drop. People reflect. People pray. Their faith will sustain them, I am sure of that. And I believe our mere presence as tourists will communicate to them that this is truly "one world."

Tourism halted after the 1988 uprising, but quickly recovered after 1992 because of liberalized visa regulations and an expanding tourist infrastructure. Indeed, the regime opened up to tourism for badly needed dollars.

Actually, none of my family or friends voiced anger at our traveling to Myanmar. There was one person, however, who called me up the night

The interior of the Grand Choral Synagogue

The Grand Choral Synagogue in St. Petersburg

Above: The new state-of-the-art, four-story, 75,000-square-foot YESOD building in St. Petersburg Below: A group of women dancing the hora inside the YESOD

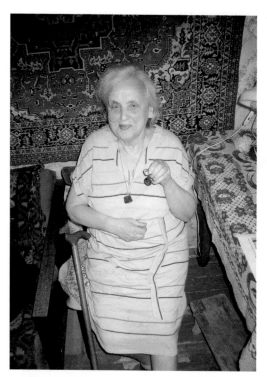

Dora, a survivor of the Leningrad blockade during World War II, shows her medals.

Entrance sign to Birobidzhan, in Yiddish and Russian. Yiddish was written and spoken here, even in the days of Stalinist Russia. Today, too, the observer can spot Yiddish on welcome signs, street signs, town posters, the municipal radio station, schools, stamps, and government documents.

Clockwise from top left: Author with Admiral Max Zilberman, Ret., in Vladivostock; a synagogue in Vladivostok that once again occupies the premises of the confectionary shop shown here. The building was wrested away from the Jewish community during the Communist era but returned a few years ago; the JCC in Birobidzhan; the Feinberg Building in Irkustsk that houses a Jewish kindergarten.

Dr. Yonah Poul standing before the Holy Ark in Tahiti

The Ahava v'Ahava ("Love and Friendship") synagogue in Tahiti

Above: Riverboat outside of Hue
Below: Motorbikes on the streets of Hanoi

Author and wife, Riva, in Cambodia on their way to Vietnam

Ho Chi Minh's mausoleum, Hanoi

Musmeah Yeshua Synagogue, which means "Brings Forth Salvation," is Burma's only synagogue.

Inside the 150-year-old Musmeah Yeshua Synagogue

Author and wife, Riva, in front of the Taj Mahal, Agra

Fathpur Sikri, the Panch Mahal section of this Mughal Palace Complex, in Uttar Pradesh

The wedding party around the wedding cake at the reception of Isaac Divekar and Siyona Garsulkar at the Magen Hassidim synagogue in Mumbai

Above, left: inside the historic Paradesi Synagogue, Kochi; above, right: Magen Hassidim synagogue was built in 1931 and is considered one of Mumbai's most noted Jewish houses of worship; Right: In the Sunday School of the JCC, Mumbai

Author outside a home in Essaouira, Morocco. Notice the amulet used by Jews and Arabs, known as a *hamsa* in Arabic.

A group of Moroccan Jews from Israel praying at Rabbi Pinto's tomb in the large Jewish cemetery in Essaouira

Lubavitch school in Casablanca

Inside the Temple Beth El, Casablanca

Museum of Moroccan Judaism, Le Musée du Judaïsme Marocain, located at 81, rue Chasseur Jules Gros, Casablanca

El Patronato Synagogue and Community Center, Calle 1, between 13th and 15th streets, Havana, is the largest, with 500 members, and is the headquarters of the Jewish community here.
Photo Courtesy of Julian Voloj/JDC

An Israeli Dance Festival at Patronato Synagogue
Photo Courtesy of Julian Voloj/JDC

The sanctuary of Bet Shalom/ El Patronato features a large aisle down the middle, wood paneling on the wall behind the *bimah* (raised platform), and rows of benches where men and women sit together.
Photo Courtesy of Julian Voloj/JDC

Service at Patronato Synagogue
Photo Courtesy of Julian Voloj/JDC

The Western Wall in Jerusalem

Riva, author's wife, in the Old City of Jerusalem

Above: Author and grandson at the tomb of the Rambam (Maimonides) Tiberias

Left: The ancient city of Tiberias overlooks the beautiful, blue Lake Kinneret, also known as the biblical Sea of Galilee.

before departure and literally pierced my heart with fear, so much so that I almost panicked.

"When we landed at the airport for our visit," she related that night, "soldiers pointed their machine guns at us; they demanded our prepaid vouchers. People spied on us. They were mean-looking. Watch out," she warned. "Even the guides are spies."

Sometimes, fear and politics have a way of creeping into a travel experience. With me, it's *de rigueur.* I must tell the reader that when I travel, I am paranoid. "That's no way to travel," you may retort. But it seems to me that this paranoia has saved me on many occasions from being mugged or robbed, from break-ins or being pickpocketed, et cetera. I even go so far as to put a chair up against the doorknob of my hotel-room door at night, hoping that if an intruder enters, the chair will fall and the noise will frighten off the thief.

After the woman's warning, I immediately shredded any evidence among my papers that even alluded to the fact that I was an author or journalist, as the latter usually don't obtain visas to Myanmar. If reporters—who don't declare they are journalists—are caught, or under suspicion, I was told, their computers and notebooks are confiscated and they are shipped out on the next plane.

Landing at the Yangon International Airport, I saw no army, military, or soldiers at the airport, pointing guns; there were no tanks. Nothing! Actually, passport officials were businesslike, but in a pleasant way. Riva and I traveled freely; nobody ever stopped us on the street.

We didn't discuss politics. Nor did anyone ever criticize America or Americans per se, except to mention the sanctions "your country and other Western nations placed on Burma"—a shame, they said, because that's what has caused the lack of tourists from the U.S., UK, and Japan. The almost-nonexistent use of cell phones was attributed to foreign sanctions. But I later learned that to obtain a cell phone one needs a license and to travel abroad, one needs official permission.

Certain taboos reign. Nobody mentioned the name Aung San Suu Kyi, the daughter of Burma's independence hero, General Aung San. The general fought against the British and the Japanese in World War II. Karen

Connelly is probably correct when she writes in her book, *A True Love Story: Burmese Lessons,* "[General Aung San] was a brilliant young statesman whose early assassination left Burma vulnerable to the military he'd helped create." His name is now the prefix for his daughter's name.

Today, they simply call Suu Kyi "The Lady." She remains the symbol of Burmese freedom, the conscience of Burmese society. When she received the Nobel Peace Prize in 1991, it propelled this opposition leader to international acclaim and advanced the cause of Burmese democracy.

Perhaps the Burmese people, who often gave us smiles of welcome, come here to the Shwedagon Pagoda to escape the streets of Yangon where they cannot even mention the name of Suu Kyi. I could not help but think of her famous August 26, 1988, address here, calling for democracy. Suu Kyi spoke on the grounds of the gold-encrusted Shwedagon Pagoda to an estimated crowd of several hundred thousand people, calling for a "multiparty democratic system of government." Emerging as the leader of the pro-democracy opposition, she was forty-three then; now, she is sixty-six.

"Burma has managed to remain an obscure, eccentric tyranny until 1988, the year that Daw Aung San Suu Kyi came home," wrote Christopher R. Cox in his book, *Chasing the Dragon: Into the Heart of the Golden Triangle.* Suddenly, "The Lady" appeared everywhere.

In March and April of 1988, the military government cracked down hard on students. In the second week of August, soldiers opened fire, salvo after salvo onto demonstrators, a killing that continued until the next morning. Thousands of people died as the army drove the pro-democracy crowds from the streets. The military assault that followed was even more brutal than the more publicly viewed repression that occurred in Tiananmen Square, Beijing, China, a year later. Burma rule was a "bulletocracy," as Justin Wintle declares in his book, *Perfect Hostage: A Life of Aung San Suu Kyi, Burma's Prisoner of Conscience.*

After the suppression, the junta installed the State Peace and Development Council (SPDC), who continued to rule the country with an iron hand. Senior General Than Shwe served as the country's top military leader and headed the SPDC. In 1989, the military regime officially changed the old British colonial name, Burma, to Myanmar. The army cancelled the results of a democratic parliamentary election in 1990 that was overwhelmingly won by the National League for Democracy (NLD), the party led by San Suu Kyi. Her party has never been allowed to govern. She has spent nearly all of the last two decades in some form of detention.

In 2007, demonstrations again erupted, this time with a large turnout of the country's Buddhist monks. Once again, the government cracked down.

In 2009, the military regime in Myanmar tried Suu Kyi who had been under house arrest for allegedly violating the terms of her six-year house arrest. The new charges drew widespread scorn and the British ambassador called the case "a show trial."

The charges were brought against Suu Kyi after an American adventurer, John Yettaw, swam across a lake in central Yangon and spent a night at the waterfront home in 2009. The trial was widely condemned as a ploy to keep Suu Kyi, whom some call the "Gandhi of Burma," locked up until after the elections in 2010. Perhaps international outrage influenced the military regime, which could have thrown her into jail with three years of hard labor. Instead, her sentence was commuted to a new term of house arrest of up to eighteen months. The term ensured that she was confined during the 2010 elections.

And then the unexpected. If anyone wanted proof of the esteem she is held that day came on Saturday, November 13, 2010, when this popular and beloved pro-democracy advocate was freed from her last stint of house arrest a week after the elections. Eyewitnesses say that when Suu Kyi appeared at the gates, her voice was drowned out by the exuberant crowd which had pushed past the barricades.

"Children danced, monks meditated," and after sustained applause, Suu Kyi spoke to supporters for the first time. "There is a time to be quiet and a time to talk People must work in unison. Only then can we achieve our goal," she said, according to the British newspaper, *The Guardian*.

A few days later, more than 10,000 persons showed up to hear her say: "I believe in human rights and I believe in the rule of law. I am for national reconciliation and for dialogue," she said, according to various press reports. With her popularity undiminished and once again a free person, she was expected to travel outside Yangon.

By the way, Mr. Yettaw, who had been sentenced to seven years of hard labor, was released in August, 2009 to Senator Jim Webb of Virginia, who, while agreeing it would be wrong to lift sanctions against Myanmar, says there is room for engagement. Like thousands around the world, Senator Webb has called on Myanmar "to end the isolation of its people so that they can live in economic prosperity, under an open political system."

Chances are that the sanctions will not be lifted, even though they may not be working. They certainly have not brought about "regime change," because neighboring countries, especially China, continue to trade and make deals with Myanmar.

"Change is unlikely," wrote Professor David I. Steinberg in *Contemporary Southeast Asia,* in 2007, "without a significant shift in internal Myanmar policies."

We should note, however, that the government again had introduced elections in November, 2010, the first in twenty years. Even though now in civilian garb, a number of the generals were returned to power in a new parliament. Put simply, the army will not go away, even if the top generals did take off their uniforms and don double-breasted suits and appear as if they are elected civilian office holders.

In March, 2011, Thein Sein was sworn into office, officially launching a nominally civilian government after 50 years of military rule. He succeeded Senior General Than Shwe, who had been paramount leader since 1992, as the new head of state. But it was obvious that the new cabinet lineup included several ex-military men, many of whom were ministers in the military junta. The 2010 elections, were widely criticized as a sham to perpetuate the military which has ruled Burma since 1962. Suu Kyi's party boycotted the elections, calling them unfair.

But the elections and new parliament is a step, even if it's not exactly forward. The hope is that those commanders, especially the younger ones, just might allow the country to slide into a more-open economy, as well as end the nation's isolation. The new government intends to privatize 90 percent of state-owned enterprises by the end of 2011 and this for the most rigidly state-dominated economy in Asia after North Korea. Burma, by the way, has oil and natural gas to sell and foreign investment is arriving.

Meanwhile, Suu Kyi has returned to the front lines of the battle for democracy. In a visit to Myanmar in late spring of 2011, Senator John McCain noted that Suu Kyi is planning to travel through the country on her first foray outside Yangon since being freed from house arrest in November, 2010. Suu Kyi's last attempt in 2003 "to travel freely was marred by violence. So the new government's ability and willingness to prevent a similar outcome this time will be an important test of their desire for change," noted Senator McCain.

So, it was worrisome when in early summer of 2011, both the NLD, which the government had dissolved for refusing to register for the election, as well as Suu Kyi, were warned by the new military-backed government to halt all political activities.

After so much bloodshed in the past, it is unlikely the people will take to the streets, though that potential action can never be discounted completely. "However, it would take an economic catastrophe or some egregious act of ignorance or villainy by the authorities at some level to trigger a popular response," wrote Steinberg.

I left the Pagoda, in full agreement with what I'd read in a guidebook: "[O]nce seen it can never be forgotten, and once experienced it will hold you spellbound forever." I walked over to have dinner and watch a show of folk songs and dances on a riverboat designed to resemble an old-century war boat, the kind that used to ply the Irrawaddy River, now a tourist spot. I knew that several kingdoms arose and fell in the region from 1000 CE to 1800 CE. I knew that Jews had been here as traders coming across the Indian Ocean. I had been reading Jeffrey Hantover's *The Jewel Trader of Pegu,* about a melancholy young Jewish gem merchant, Abraham, born in Venice, who in 1598 comes to the lush and exotic Burmese kingdom of Pegu and falls in love with a Burmese woman.

Now, more than 400 years later, who knows if Jewish life will survive in Myanmar. I have noted that the gates of the Golden Age of Jewish life in Burma began to close with World War II and the Japanese invasion, which caused one of the most historical and terrifying flights of civilians fleeing a war zone. "At the time it was the largest migration in history," wrote Cernea. More than a half-million people walked hundreds of miles through jungle, over raging rivers. Eighty thousand died along the way. Chaos reigned.

Flight is a terrible thing, and in many countries where they have resided, Jews have often had to flee at a moment's notice. That is one of the reasons they entered the diamond business—because it enabled them to run away pretty quickly by putting their entire inventory into their pockets.

Along these lines, the story is told that after the Japanese bombardment in December 1941, a Jewish man grabbed his violin—the sole possession he took with him—and set out. Because he took his musical instrument, he was able to survive his trek through the Burmese-Indian jungle, across the high mountains and the swollen rivers. You see, at each village, he would play songs on his violin and be paid in food and shelter.

This traveler might have made it to safety, but if he returned to Burma he would never have recognized his homeland as a result of the War.

At the end of World War II, the "scorched earth" policy practiced by the invader and the Allies had rendered a third of all cultivated land unusable.

Burma enticed me for historic reasons, too. As an elementary school student during World War II, and as a World War II buff during my adult life, the story of the Burma Road—the artery that the U.S. used during that war to supply China and thus hold back the Japanese—fascinated me. Hacked out of the jungles and mountains in 1938 to connect Siakwan in China's Yunnan Province with the railhead at Lashio in the north of Shan State, the Burma Road carried supplies to the Chinese army after Japanese forces had captured the coastal ports.

I didn't make it to the Burma Road on this trip. Next time. As a traveler, one must always leave a destination not seen for a return voyage!

Fighting in Burma during World War II was a man whom I have admired ever since I read about how he helped the Jewish people before the State of Israel was established. This historical favorite of mine was Orde Wingate, indeed "a righteous gentile," who had died in an air crash in Burma in 1944 while commanding the Chindit guerrillas against the Japanese. I guess my fondness of the man who was called the *Hayedid* ("the friend") comes from the Zionist in me, because Wingate was a passionate, deeply religious person and a strong supporter of Zionism.

I visited the Wingate Institute for Physical Education and Sport, named in his honor in Netanya, Israel, which I will discuss further in chapter 9.

As a young British Army captain, Wingate trained members of *Haganah,* the Jewish paramilitary organization which became the Israel Defense

Forces upon the establishment of the State of Israel in 1948. He made his name in the pre–Jewish State era after he led *Haganah* troops, including Special Night Squads, in counterinsurgency operations during the Arab Revolt in Palestine in the late 1930s.

I digress . . . even though by now, readers must know that it seems to me a positive in travel to tie together new sights in one country with memories of another. One journey recalls a first trip, another journey recalls a second, and a third, and before the traveler knows it, he/she will be calling up memories of past vacations and travels in other exotic lands.

Burma/Myanmar is made up of many minority groups in a country dominated by the Burmese people. Those that come to mind are Karen, Shan, Rakhine, Mon, Chin, and Kachin, all of whom have been the source of ethnic tension and have fueled intermittent separatist rebellions. Military offensives against insurgents have uprooted many thousands of civilians.

All along the Indo-Burma frontier, in the lands of Northeast India and Burma, a "remarkable . . . movement" is under way, according to Tudor Parfitt in his book, *The Lost Tribes of Israel: The History of a Myth*. He notes that several hundred have formally converted to Orthodox Judaism.

Christian missionaries, such as Francis Mason of the American Baptist Foreign Mission Society, who arrived in Burma in 1814, became convinced that the populous *Karen* tribe of Burma is descended from Jewish stock. Some individuals, mostly Christian, even went so far as to believe that the Karens are one of the Lost Tribes of Israel. The cause of the *Karens* has been taken up by *Amishav*, which means "My People Are Returning," a religious nonprofit organization operating mainly in India and in Spanish-speaking countries.

My visit marked the fifty-fifth anniversary of diplomatic relations between Israel and Myanmar. Since both nations achieved independence, twenty Israeli ambassadors have served in Myanmar and nineteen Myanmar ambassadors have served in Israel.

I was fortunate to meet Israeli ambassador Yaron Mayer at the Embassy at 15 Khabaung Street in Yangon, which no longer is the capital. The isolation the military leaders want to maintain was reinforced when in 2005 they chose an unknown, never-heard-of city, Naypyidaw, 200 miles north of Yangon. Much of that city is still under construction. Completion is set for 2012, though it is doubtful embassies will move there.

History takes sharp turns. Israel-Myanmar relations, so strong and promising in the first decade and a half of their history, had been forged to last a long time. Both were born in 1948, though Burma is slightly older. Burma's Independence Day is January 4, 1948, 4:20 a.m., the very hour of the day chosen as most favorable by the country's astrologers. "Events [in Burma] often are scheduled on astrological or numerical calculations that are incomprehensible to the outside world," explains Steinberg. For instance, among General Ne Win's disastrous policies was the decision to change the currency into multiples of nine, his lucky number. He even went so far as to change traffic from the left to the right side of the road on the advice of an astrologer, to ensure his success.

The early fondness between Burma and Israel came about because of two great statesmen: U Nu, who guided the nation for a dozen years, and David Ben-Gurion, who led the *Yishuv* (pre–State of Israel) to independence and served as prime minister for about half a dozen years. The two were what one might call "democratic socialists."

Burma voted "no" to Israel's United Nations admission early in 1949, though she did an about-face and granted full recognition to the Jewish state in December 1949. In 1953, David Hacohen became Israel's first minister to Burma.

In the early days, Burma needed technical and agricultural assistance and it turned to Israel. The latter needed friends, especially in developing countries. Israel provided assistance in housing, medicine, industry, military aviation, and agriculture.

U Nu became the first foreign prime minister to visit the newly independent State of Israel in 1955, and David Ben-Gurion, Israel's first prime minister, spent one of the longest official trips abroad for an Israeli prime minister, with a two-week sojourn in 1961, which included studies in Buddhism. Other prominent Israeli visitors were President Yitzhak Ben-Zvi, Moshe Sharett, Golda Meir, Abba Eban, Moshe Dayan, and Shimon Peres, president of Israel.

Thousands of students from Myanmar received training in Israel and scholarships for studies there as well. Many Israelis visit Myanmar every year—certainly not as much as India or Thailand, but still, the natural beauty and wonders of this Southeast Asian land, as well as Myanmar's unique classical Theravada Buddhism, attract them, according to Ambassador Mayer.

Israel aided Myanmar after Cyclone Nargis, in 2008, and is still taking part in reconstruction projects, according to the ambassador, who added that the Jewish state and Myanmar have maintained good relations over the years. Readers will recall that the cyclone killed hundreds of thousands, and the military regime in Myanmar incurred worldwide ire because for weeks it was hesitant to allow relatively large foreign-relief efforts.

Actually, the promising period of Burma-Israel cooperation died at the same time as did the lingering hopes of the Jews remaining in Burma in the 1960s. Burma crawled into its military shell and kept most nations at arm's length, including Israel.

Still, according to the ambassador, "Israel has a good name in Burma."

Before leaving, I conjure up sights of the Reclining Buddha, and Burmese skirted men and women walking around the Shwedagon Pagoda in bare feet. Then that great repast in a native restaurant where four people ate a full fish meal for nine dollars. I enjoyed shopping for rubies, sapphires, and emeralds even though I didn't buy any. I loved the dance performance on the riverboat, and visits with the few people who may turn out to be the last Jews of Burma. I hope not. I always say that a Jewish community or its presence does not disappear until the last Jew is gone.

Back in Yangon, Moses Samuels still feels that the day will come when Jews will return to Burma and the synagogue's beautiful original wooden benches will once again be filled with worshippers.

I ask Ms. Zwenig if Burmese Jewry can survive.

"If Sammy comes back," to Myanmar, she replies.

I ask Stuart Spencer if Judaism can survive. He agrees with Ms. Zwenig and repeats, "If Sammy comes back."

It's not unrealistic. Over the years, Sammy—who has been dubbed "the last hope for the Jews of Myanmar"—has told friends and journalists that he intends to return to Myanmar and live there permanently, once he finds a Jewish wife. Like his father, Moses, who promised his father, Isaac, Sammy in turn has given his word that he will keep the synagogue open.

"We need tourists to energize us," says Sammy, noting that travelers offer donations. "Tourism," he adds, "means the legacy of Jewish history in this Golden Land will be kept alive."

To many, an open market economy would also be beneficial for Myanmar. Perhaps, here, too, Moses and Sammy can set an example in their own small way. Sammy wants to lead the way. He has opened a chocolate store called Chocolate Heaven, located in the Pearl Plaza in Yangon. One of his featured items is the Israeli chocolate, "Elite." He is inquiring about the possibility of importing Israeli wine into Myanmar. According to Sammy, most Burmese wine drinkers are familiar with Israeli wines. Sammy notes that even some government officials have asked his father if he stocks Israeli wines. Since Moses and Sammy are in the travel business, they have good connections with restaurants and hotels. As the young entrepreneur recently put it: "Introducing them to Israeli wines would be unique."

In the many interviews I held with Sammy and others, I discovered that it is not beyond the realm of possibility that Myanmar could open up and allow businesses to invest, following the example of Communist Vietnam and its "crony capitalism." Then former Burmese Jews, along with American and British Jews and Israelis might return and invest. Seeing that Jews were at least living in Myanmar, Chabad might set up a facility. With that scenario, "Our community could actually grow," Sammy says hopefully.

Wishful thinking, you say? Who believed Communism would ever fall? Or the U.S. and Vietnam would become "allies?"

Sammy who in 2011 turned 30, realizes that the future rejuvenation may be a long way off. Until then, he'll need all the help he can get, for as Rabbi Marvin Tokayer, author of *The Fugu Plan: The Untold Story of the Japanese and the Jews During World War Two,* and a leading authority on the Jewish experience in Asia, put it: "This just may be the last page of the history of the Jews of Burma."

Only time will tell.

"Incredible India"

Living among the Jews in Mumbai, Delhi, and Kochi

"A flag unfurls: it is saffron, white and green."
—*Salman Rushdie,* Midnight's Children

To reach the India of my people, I flew nonstop, 8,000 miles in sixteen hours.

A few days later I stood in the village of Chendamangalam, not far from the historic city of Cochin, now called Kochi, in the southern State of Kerala, on the Malabar Coast of India.

The extreme heat warmed my face, and the lush landscapes, sun-drenched beaches, idyllic backwaters, and palm gardens delighted me. Earlier that morning, I had seen rowboats, sailboats, cargo skiffs, steamers, and naval vessels pass frequently in front of the hotel. They were cruising along a nearby vast system of waterways.

Kochi, I learned, is an important spice port whose surroundings contained an ancient and still-functioning fishing industry. Once, traders from Yemen and Babylon exported dates and olive oil in exchange for peacocks and spices. An idyllic scene, especially since I had just arrived from the frigid northeastern United States. It was December.

Now, before me stood the intricate patterns of the facade of the two-story, whitewashed, restored synagogue, with its arched windows and a pair of tall, solid-wood doors that opened into the house of worship. I found myself staring at the single tombstone just in front of the building. The Hebrew letters on the tombstone spelled out *Sara bat-Israel* (Sara, the daughter of Israel). This certainly resonated with me, as it was my mother's and a granddaughter's name. The Hebrew date on the gravestone of this Cochin Jewess recorded the year, 1269, making it probably the oldest Hebrew text in India and another piece of physical evidence of Jewish life in India dating back hundreds of years.

Her grave was probably relocated to Chendamangalam from Cranganore, or, as it is known in medieval Jewish geography, Shingly, which is the ancestral home of Cochin Jews. As we shall see, legend has it that the Jews arrived in the Cochin area at the time of the destruction of the Second Temple in 70 CE. Historically, I have learned, Jews probably landed in Cranganore (Shingly) in the eleventh century, and established communities in Parur, Mala, Mattancherry, and Chendamangalam. Various sources maintain that Sara's grave was relocated to Chendamangalam from Shingly when a group of Jews fled that town. *Sara bat-Israel* might have been among them on their march from Cranganore to Chendamangalam. Now this former house of worship is a museum, the congregation long gone.

At a kiosk, just in front and to the side of the synagogue, stood two tall, middle-aged, dark-skinned Indian men with deep mystical eyes. Dressed in *lungi,* a sarong-like rectangle of cotton worn from waist to ankle, they stared at us almost without blinking. Both of them looked exactly like the men in the photo I had brought with me of the Jewish community of Chendamangalam, which had departed for Israel a half-century ago, leaving the synagogue desolate until its restoration fifty-five years later.

I wondered whether these two gentlemen were just observing another group of tourists who were visiting the synagogue of one of the oldest Jewish communities in the diaspora. Or, were they silently telling us what most people in the world do not know—that the Jews who lived in India for about two thousand years were on good terms with their neighbors, and that these two men would like them to return. These gentlemen probably did not know that Indian Jews now living in Israel are one of the few diaspora communities that look back kindly on their former land, and even today, while they call Israel their fatherland, India, they say, is their motherland.

Then and there, I realized there were two Jewrys in India: One is the Jewish India of the past, which existed in these small towns around Cochin, where only about fifty Jews remain today, and where those remaining are doing everything in their power to restore those empty synagogues, so that long after they pass on, Jews will be remembered. The second is today's vibrant Jewish India, which holds the future of Judaism in India, and is located up north in the huge metropolis known as Mumbai, once called Bombay. That Judaism, I discovered, will survive. I never once asked the question in India that I usually ask in all small, exotic Jewish communities: *Will there be Jews here in twenty-five years?*

"We didn't know there were Jews in India."

Those are often the first words visitors utter when they meet Elijah Jacob, country manager of the Joint Distribution Committee (JDC), in his office at the Jewish Community Center in Mumbai.

And when this writer returned to the U.S., I heard the question: "Indian Jews, are they brown-skinned?"

"Yes," I answered.

"Jews never looked east," explains Rabbi Marvin Tokayer, scholar and author of *The Fugu Plan: The Untold Story of the Japanese and the Jews During World War Two.* "We're blinded by the West and Europe," continues the rabbi, who has led tours to exotic Jewish communities throughout the world, especially Asia, since 1982, and has even set up a Foundation for Remote Jewish Communities (FRJC).

Asian Jewry "is an unknown Jewish experience, not taught in Jewish schools. Most people think the stories I tell about India are *bubbe meises* (grandmothers' tales)," Rabbi Tokayer declares. The rabbi is backed up by Jewish historian, scholar, and author of *Who Are the Jews of India?*, Nathan Katz, who stresses that Jews "are not Western, but global. Jewish history does not begin and end in Europe. It is also richly Asian, both in origin and destiny."

I remembered something else about India and my people, a theme that followed me wherever I went in this subcontinent: India is a country without anti-Semitism. "Indian Jews lived as all Jews should have been allowed to live in the diaspora: free, proud, observant, creative and prosperous, self-realized, full contributors to the host community," wrote Professor Katz. "Moreover, the Indian chapter [in Jewish history] is one of the happiest of the Jewish diaspora," he added. India was and is "the most hospitable country in the world toward Jews." Not one Jew whom I met in my sojourn in India, north and south, contradicted that theme.

I also discovered what most travelers do not realize until they reach India: This nation of 1.3 billion people, already a global power, is one of Israel's best friends. According to an international opinion survey conducted in 2009 on behalf of the Israel Foreign Ministry, India is the most pro-Israel country in the world.

In the nine-nation tour that makes up this volume, India was one of the few countries where, as an American Jew, not only did I feel very comfortable about the Jewish past, but also about the Jewish future. The fact that India is a supporter of Israel and growing closer to the U.S. only enhanced my feelings. One likes to be among friends. No animosity here, such as in Europe or Africa or other countries in Asia.

I certainly was not alone. Among the thousands of foreign Jews passing through India, on business or vacation, are some 40,000 to 50,000 Israelis, many of whom are backpackers who journey to India after their military service, on a spiritual quest.

But first I had to find out about "Jewish India" today.

The Indian Jewish population peaked in 1950 to around 30,000 to 40,000, after which emigration to Israel reduced the number to 5,000. Of the nearly 5,000 Jews in India today, about 4,000 reside in Mumbai and the nearby suburbs of Thane and Dombivli. The balance lives in the Konkan Coast villages: Pune, Ahmedabad, Kochi (Cochin), Delhi, and Kolkata (Calcutta).

One of the reasons Jews survive here, explains Antony Korenstein, JDC country director, is that "it's not hard to be Jewish in India and maintain Jewish identity in this mystic land. You can be what you want to be. No one can stop you from being Jewish." Indian culture is so very different from Judaism that those who remain Jewish "still live in a bubble," he adds.

Professor Katz, too, emphasizes that very point: "The Jews made their places in India in part by fidelity to their own traditions—by being good Jews."

For the first time since Indian independence sixty-four years ago, Indian Jewry has begun to stabilize itself. Now they are staying put, despite the Mumbai terrorist attack of 2008, according to Elijah Jacob, whose organization, JDC, helps seniors and less-fortunate Indian Jews with monthly cash assistance, medical programs, and medicine, as well as conducting and sponsoring a wide range of educational and social programs. In fact, a few Indian Jews are returning to their native land from Israel to take advantage of a fast-growing market economy, with its Western-style malls and skyscrapers. This is not the first country in our *search for the scattered tribe* in which we see the phenomenon of Jews returning to their native land for commerce; Russia and Morocco are two other examples.

"Jews are sharing in and riding the economic wave," observes Korenstein, referring to the prosperity tsunami that is occurring in India today. "Never has there been a better time to have been born in India," proclaimed an Indian businessman on TV. He is correct indeed.

"India is history," wrote the late Jawaharlal Nehru, leader of Indian freedom from Britain and first prime minister. And it possesses "a very long memory."

So, too, do the Jews maintain a very long recall. Jews have been an integral part of the Indian mosaic for centuries. This "land of the Ganges" was known to the Jews of antiquity as well as to those of the Middle Ages. References to India are inscribed in the Book of Esther and Maccabees, as well as the Talmud.

Legend, folklore, and tradition trace the earliest Jewish contact with India to the time of King Solomon, whose navy, it is said, visited India, and to the period at the time of the destruction of the Second Temple in 70 CE. The Romans record Jewish settlements on both coasts of India in the first century. And it is believed that St. Thomas the Apostle sailed to India in 52 CE to convert the Cochin Jews. Yet, throughout history and until this very day, the largest number of Jews of any country east of Iran resides in India, and, except for the Portuguese period, Jews lived in the subcontinent without persecution.

As I searched for the scattered tribe, I tried to remember the uniqueness of India, which boasts a tradition that has lasted through five thousand years of history as the seat of an ancient civilization, the creator of two world religions, Buddhism and Hinduism, and the country that preaches tolerance.

This history went with me as I walked through bazaars and marveled at the palaces, forts, temples, mosques, and synagogues; as I watched thousand-year-old rituals in Mumbai; and as I inhaled history at the National Gandhi Memorial Museum, close to the Samadhi, the memorial where Mahatma Gandhi was cremated on January 31, 1948, in Delhi, and the Gandhi Museum in Mumbai.

Until I arrived, it was hard to believe that India stretches from the tropics right up to the temperate regions, from near the equator to the base of the Himalayas. Located in southern Asia, with about 1.3 billion people—a billion more than the U.S.—India ranks in population as the second-largest nation in the world, comprising 17 percent of the world's population. Again, only China exceeds it, and India will pass China by 2025.

So, dear reader, something else is walking alongside the twenty-first-century traveler, and that is the feeling that you, the tourist, are not just visiting monuments and ruins, castles and forts of the past, but that you are also an eyewitness to an ancient nation rising as a phoenix to become one of the world's great powers.

I witnessed an economic boom that shows that India is on the move with a 9 percent economic growth rate, four times that of the U.S. In short, "India is claiming the twenty-first century as its own," according to Sam Miller, BBC correspondent and author of *Delhi: Adventures in a Megacity.*

Under the current Indian umbrella of change, I found economic dynamism, cultural diversity, and democratic institutions. I also found ecological strain, heated politics, poor infrastructure, and yes, at times, even ethnic rage. Long centuries of invasion, oppression, and colonial rule have left their marks, especially in the trauma of independence after India was born in 1947, leaving a bloody aftermath due to the partition of India into two independent countries—India and Pakistan—that left deep scars in India for the next six decades.

The poverty and inequality that exists in wide segments of India's population stared out at me. Lives continue to be influenced by the ancient Hindu caste system, which assigns each person a place in the social hierarchy, although discrimination on the basis of caste is now illegal. I learned that various measures, similar to Affirmative Action programs in the U.S., have been introduced to empower disadvantaged groups, and to give them easier access to opportunities for education and employment.

For me, falling in love with "incredible India" was not difficult at all. I found it totally different from my usual visitations to Europe. I tried to leave my Western mind-set at home. It wasn't easy, and it often didn't work. But it surely helped in traveling, eating, walking through markets, attending ceremonies, and above all, recalling the days of the Mughals, the Raj, and Mahatma Gandhi.

Over sixty years ago, just before midnight on August 14, 1947, Jawaharlal Nehru, the first prime minister and leader of Indian independence, intoned:

Long years ago we made a tryst with destiny, and now the time comes when we shall redeem our pledge, not wholly or in full measure but very substantially. At the stroke of the midnight hour, when the world sleeps, India will awake to life and freedom. A moment comes, which comes but rarely in history, when we step out from the old to the new, when an age ends, and when the soul of a nation, long suppressed, finds utterance. It is fitting that at this solemn moment we take the pledge of dedication to the service of India and her people, and to the still larger cause of humanity.

"The twentieth century began with India firmly under British imperial fiat. India was the jewel in the crown of an empire that stretched from South America to the South Pacific. The same century ended with the economy of independent India on a Y2K-fueled [computer] roll," wrote Daniel Lak in his book, *India Express: The Future of a New Superpower.*

Jawaharlal Nehru would agree: India is indeed "incredible."

⁓

"As long as Bombay exists, there will be Jews in town," goes an old adage.

So, let us begin our journey to India and the Jews of that nation by visiting Mumbai, the first city in India, where 22 official languages and 200 dialects are spoken every day, the nation's transportation hub, the business and financial capital, and the economic powerhouse of India, which includes the Bollywood film industry.

Soon, more people will live in the city of Mumbai (formerly Bombay)—the fifth-largest city in the world—than on the continent of Australia, wrote Suketu Mehta in his book, *Maximum City: Bombay Lost and Found*. About 20.5 million people live in Greater Mumbai, about 21 million in Australia.

A reliable way to test the vitality of a particular city is to observe how many arrive each day looking for jobs. About 2,000 persons a day pour into sprawling Mumbai to find work. To further make the point, nearly 40 percent of the nation's taxes are raised in populous Mumbai, which changed its well-known Portuguese name of Bombay, meaning "beautiful bay," back to its old name of Mumbai.

Mumbai remains India's most cosmopolitan city. Migrants come into the city drawn by its reputation as India's "city of dreams," where one can become rich. But it is also a city infamous for its poor: A recent study found that roughly 62 percent of the population lived in slums, including one of Asia's biggest, Dharavi, which houses more than 1 million people. This is a city of temples, bazaars, and restaurants alongside acres upon acres of slums, their dirty, miserable shelters patched together from rags, scraps of plastic and paper, reed mats, and bamboo sticks.

Real estate prices are among the highest in the world, pushing many working-class residents into slums, even as developers have brazenly cleared land for a new generation of high-rise apartment towers for the affluent. High-rise structures are considered necessary, given the city's limited land, yet the rising towers have further insulated the rich from the teeming metropolis below. No wonder this vast urban area includes huge high-tech parks which boast huge global corporate headquarters.

Discussing the Jewish community, Elijah Jacob told me that if I really wanted to see the Jewish community, I should come to an event that would certainly give me a snapshot of the community and its state of mind: an Indian Jewish wedding and reception.

I was happy to join the community in celebrating the marriage of Isaac Divekar and Siyona Garsulkar at the Magen Hassidim synagogue, built in 1931 and considered one of the city's most noted Jewish houses of worship. A large courtyard faces the front of the structure, whose facade is brown and white, with a Star of David near the top of the building and a replica of the Ten Commandments just below the star.

Groom Isaac Divekar, an accountant for a large investment firm, and bride Siyona Garsulkar, a human resources professional, were escorted by their family into the synagogue. Garbed in colorful saris, orange, magenta, pink, to name a few, the women escorted the wedding party into the long synagogue, filled with wooden benches. The bride wore a beautiful, long, flowing white gown. A cantor conducted the service in this Sephardic synagogue, with its wooden *bimah* in the middle of the main floor and a decorative ark. A large balcony for women overlooks the synagogue.

Afterwards, the gathering headed out to the reception at the huge, well-kept soccer field at the Sir Elly Kadoori High School. Once it was called the Israelite School for *Bene Israel* children, later renamed in honor of its Iraqi Jewish benefactor, Sir Elly Kadoori. Nearby is the Sir Jacob Sassoon High School. Today, the majority of students in both schools are Muslim.

I snapped a photo of the happy, smiling family standing around a huge wedding cake. Behind them the stage was bedecked with flowers, decorations, and ornaments, with plush red sofas for the wedding party and family. Gracing the banquet tables were rice, lentils, two vegetables with curry, cottage cheese and mixed vegetables, dry vegetables made with potatoes and peas, *chapati* (Indian flatbread), and puris. There were also plenty of sweets and desserts like *gulab jamun* and ice cream.

When I interviewed Divekar days later, he underscored the first big change in the Indian Jewish community: Young Jews are remaining. Unlike their brothers and sisters who in previous years often left the country in search of greater opportunity and Jewish life elsewhere, these young couples are happy residents of this huge metropolis.

"There are more job opportunities in India now," Divekar declared, citing call centers and outsourcing from the United States. Young Indian Jews see their native land as a place of opportunity, and *aliyah* has practically ceased.

In 2007, only 49 Jews left the country for Israel, down from 291 in 2006—though the latter figure includes the 229 Bnei Menashe from northeast India, according to Ze'ev Schwartzberg, head of the Ethiopia and India desk of the Jewish Agency for Israel's *aliyah* department. The Bnei Menashe are tribal people who live on both sides of the Indo-Burmese border and who claim to be descendants of the ancient Israelite tribe of Menashe, displaced by the Assyrian conquerors in 722 BCE. The Indian government prohibited conversions in India, and the Beth Din said groups could not be brought in and converted in Israel; they had to be converted before arrival in India. Due to pronouncements both in India and Israel, the whole procedure has stopped, and 7,000 members of Bnei Menashe remain in India.

Schwartzberg said that 90 Indian Jews left for Israel in 2004, and 143 the previous year. India's booming economy and the Arab-Israeli conflict are keeping *aliyah* down.

Like their fellow Indian compatriots, young Jews are part of the economic boom because many work in call centers, familiar to Americans who have long since become accustomed to picking up the phone, dialing an 800-number for computer guidance or bank account balances, and talking with a young person in an Indian call center.

Today, we are all familiar with the idea of call centers and outsourcing. According to the *Wall Street Journal:* "India's success in the global market for business process outsourcing, or BPO, as it is known, is undeniable. What began as a business opportunity is now an economic sector that earns the country more than U.S. $13 billion a year in foreign exchange. Both revenue and employment in call centers and other BPO firms doubled each year between 2000 and 2005. By 2007, for instance, IBM's employment in India was about 73,000."

However, for young adult Jews who are fiercely wedded to Judaism and to their native land, night-shift work in the call centers can slow down Jewish activity in synagogues. "It's hard to get the young people to activities if they sleep during the day and work at night," a synagogue leader told me. Divekar did point out that Jews are allowed time off from work for Jewish holidays and festivals.

As part of what is dubbed "the fastest-growing middle class on the planet," life is sweet. And Jews are part of this group that in 2011 will reach a high GDP of 9 percent.

Isaac Divekar, I discover, could be a descendant of Samuel Ezekiel Divekar, an officer in the British East India Company who was taken prisoner while fighting the Muslim Tipu Sultan, King of Mysore. The Divekars came from the village of Dive on the Konkan coast.

Tipu Sultan had a military skirmish with the British and took prisoners in 1783, among them Samuel Divekar and his brother, who were *Bene Israel*. Tipu Sultan planned to execute all of the prisoners the next day.

The prisoners were stripped and lined up the next morning, awaiting execution, when Tipu's mother, who had good eyesight, noticed that Samuel and his brother were circumcised. When the two told her they were *Bene Israel,* she begged her son to spare the pair, because they are referred to in the Koran as the Chosen People of the Almighty. Many claimed that if the *Bene Israel* brothers had called themselves *Yahud* (Jew) and not *Bene Israel,* they would have been executed, because the Koran looks negatively upon Jews.

According to legend, the sultan freed Divekar and his brother. They had less than a half hour to get away, and they successfully made it to freedom. They vowed that because they had survived, they must do something for their people, so in 1796, they built the first *Bene Israel* synagogue, Sha'ar ha-Rachamim, on Samuel Street in Bombay. The synagogue and street name are still there.

I can see why Jews settled in Mumbai. You only have to stand at the formidable stone archway of the Gateway of India in this hyper city, and you, too, will feel the breath of history.

URBS PRIMA IN INDIS (First City of India) says the plaque outside this huge archway at the water's edge. Sir David Sassoon (1792–1864), the Baghdad Jewish merchant, industrialist, and philanthropist, who did so much for Indian Jewry and Jews throughout the Far East apparently put up a great deal of the funds. Before aviation became the norm, travelers entered India by sea through this arch. A turning point in the history of the Jewish settlement in Bombay was reached in 1832 with the arrival of David Sassoon. Sassoon and his followers, mostly from Iraq, had a profound spiritual and financial impact on Bombay and its Jewish community, including the construction of the Sassoon Hospital and Magen David Synagogue. This *Baghdadi* synagogue built in 1861 and located on J. J. Road in the Byculla neighborhood still stands today and is known as David Sassoon Synagogue. Sassoon was accompanied by *Baghdadi* jewelers and entrepreneurs who soon moved into cotton, jute, tobacco, shipping, real estate, manufacturing, and the opium trade in India.

The Gateway was built in 1911 to commemorate the visit of King George V and Queen Mary to India and was officially opened in 1924. It became redundant just twenty-four years later, however, when the last British regiment left India through its archway and ended England's rule over the Empire's "crown jewel."

Every day, thousands of Indians and tourists flock to and pass through the Gateway of India, which holds court at the banks of the Arabian Sea. Africans, Asians, Arabs, Europeans, and Indians are all here, maintaining its cosmopolitan aura.

Near the Gateway of India stands the famous Taj Mahal Hotel, said to be Mumbai's classiest place to stay, with its red-carpeted floors, marble staircases, and elaborate dining rooms. The area is chock-full of magnificent restaurants and boutiques, and is a popular meeting spot surrounded by postcard vendors and snake charmers. Also located nearby are the famous Sassoon Docks, named after David Sassoon, whose businesses were so successful that it became known throughout Jewish Asia that any Jew in need of employment could find it in Sassoon's mills. Sassoon's eight sons spread throughout Asia and established the Sassoon empire, not only in Bombay and Calcutta, but also in Singapore, Hong Kong, Shanghai, Kobe, Nagasaki, Yokohama, the Moluccas, Baghdad, Saigon, Amsterdam, London, and New York.

Sassoon and his house are known as *Baghdadis*. They make up one of three groups that comprise Indian Jewry, all of whom have different traditions and customs, and all of whom are somewhat aloof from each other. The *Baghdadis,* who were the last group to arrive in India, also emigrated abroad, after India's independence and today number less than a hundred.

The *Bene Israel* and the Cochin Jews are the other two groups. Today, the *Bene Israel* is by far the predominant group in India, and account for nearly all of the 5,000 Indian Jews. They moved from the Konkan Coast in the second half of the eighteenth century, mostly to Mumbai.

We must remember that the early history of the Jews in India is obscure and remains shrouded in legend, myth, and folklore. Still, as the narrative goes, the *Bene Israel* trace themselves back to seven couples from ancient Israel who survived a shipwreck off Navgaon on the Konkan Coast in the unknown, distant past. (Some stories estimate the date at about 2,200 years ago.) As the years went on, the *Bene Israel* knew almost nothing about Judaism and didn't even know the word *Jew.* Somehow, nevertheless, they clung to vestigial Judaic observances despite centuries of isolation through their tenacity in maintaining the Sabbath, ritual circumcision, Jewish dietary codes, and the Hebrew prayer, *Shema*. Some historians believe their descendants became thoroughly Indian, except for observing Saturday as the Jewish Sabbath. The practice led them to be known as *Shanwar Teli,* Marathi for "Saturday oil pressers." Then, through a series of fortuitous encounters over the course of about 250 years, they transformed themselves into Jews, while their vocation remained oil pressing.

The *Bene Israel* were discovered by a Cochin merchant named David Rahabi who visited them in the eighteenth century, and believed they were lost Jews. He took three of them back to Cochin where he educated them in Hebrew and the rudiments of Judaism, and then had them sent them back as religious leaders. Thus began a long-standing relationship between *Bene Israel* and Cochin *Jews*. As *Bene Israel* prospered, they hired Cochin Jews to be their cantors, teachers, ritual slaughterers, and scribes. This learning "changed their ritual observance" and led to "the transformation of their identity and self-understanding," notes Professor Katz.

The third group of Indian Jews is known as the *Cochinis*. We shall meet them when I fly south to Kerala.

But while we are in Mumbai, we cannot and must not forget that in our own time, unfortunately, the city's notoriety spread with the brazen terrorist act of November 2008, which shook India, the world, and the Indian Jewish community, which had experienced hardly a drop of anti-Semitism throughout its long history. Yes, time stood still at 2120 hours on the night of November 26, 2008, in Mumbai. Assault rifles chattered. Time bombs exploded. Panic engulfed the city during a ten-gunman attack. Targeted was the Taj Mahal Palace Hotel, where thirty-two people died. Thirty-three were killed at the Oberoi-Trident Hotel. Fifty-eight were murdered at the city's busiest train station, Victoria Terminus. Attacks occurred at the popular Leopold Cafe and Nariman House, a five-story building in south Mumbai and home of Chabad. Those monsters murdered innocent people, Chabad Rabbi Berkowitz told an Indian TV interviewer a year after one of the worst terrorist attacks in history, in which 174 persons, including nine gunmen, lost their lives.

"Although more people have been killed in Mumbai in riots and bomb blasts then on that dreadful day, that attack had a lasting impact, heightening tensions between India and Pakistan, nuclear-armed neighbors that have fought several wars with each other since becoming independent from the British in 1947," wrote the *New York Times*. The terrorists apparently belonged to Lashkar-e-Taiba, a Pakistani terrorist group.

The 2008 battle brought the city to a standstill for three days. Included in the carnage were six Jews who were tied up and some say even tortured in Nariman House. Rabbi Gavriel Holtzberg and his pregnant wife, Rivka, were killed, along with four other Jews, two rabbis and two female tourists. An Indian nanny saved the Holtzbergs' then nearly-two-year-old son, Moishe, by spiriting him out of the building. Both now live with Moishe's grandparents in Israel.

The attack was "profoundly unsettling," and has focused eyes on the small Jewish community, which undoubtedly will never be the same again. The killings traumatized an entire country. The assault has left an "indelible imprint" on Jewish "minds and mind-sets," observed JDC's Elijah Jacob.

"This is a community which "never experienced an overt attack on a Jewish institution," explained Antony Korenstein, JDC country director who was in Mumbai at the time of the killings. "They are still digesting it all," he said, just after the attack.

Two years later, I talked to Antony, Elijah, and others; all agreed that despite the trauma of the murder, the community remains very strong. "Jewishness and unity of the community has been strengthened," Jacob said. "We no longer think of which synagogue we belong to; we belong to the Jewish community of Mumbai."

Attitudes have changed: "We cannot be complacent anymore. We can no longer keep the doors of our synagogues and institutions open to the public as before," Jacob pointed out, adding that the community has beefed up security in synagogues and Jewish centers. The local police are "providing protection to all Jewish institutions," reported Norman Elijah, president of the Reform Jewish Movement in India, known as JRU (Jewish Religious Union). "Security teams from Israel arrived on the scene to explain to Jewish community representatives security essentials."

These days in Mumbai, security in the metropolis is much tighter, in hotels, government buildings, and, of course, Jewish sites. One consequence of the attack was that the U.S. and India began to work together more closely to combat terrorism and to prevent future attacks in this city.

In this very resilient city, with its very resolute populace, lies the heart of an active Jewish community. Mumbai Jewry contains nine functioning synagogues, including a Reform Movement of Judaism congregation which meets at the Evelyn Peters Jewish Community Center (JCC), the anchor of Jewish community development. The JCC is sponsored by the American Jewish Joint Distribution Committee.

One Jewish house of worship, Shaar Hashomayim, is located in nearby Thane, a suburb of Mumbai, where many younger Jewish families are settling. Rabbi Avraham Benjamin is the spiritual leader. Even by 2010, however, Rabbi Benjamin was the only recognized rabbi.

Another typical synagogue is the wooden, Sephardic-style *Tifereth Israel Synagogue,* which contains pink Torah scrolls, a beautiful chandelier, and wooden benches.

The JCC includes a respected Judaic library, a youth corner, a computer room with three Internet stations, a classroom and activity rooms, a conference hall, and a huge community hall for socializing. Programs and meetings are held in the meeting rooms, and an active computer room draws many to attend computer classes. Basic Judaism is taught in classes for children every Sunday in Mumbai, and on alternative Sundays in Thane.

One year, forty-two Indian Jews participated in a ten-day tour of Israel through the sponsorship of Taglit-Birthright Israel. Summer camp is very popular, and is held at a rural retreat center. There, an intense infusion of Jewish spirit is inculcated into many of Mumbai's younger Jews.

Kosher meat and wine, ritual objects, books, and Indian Jewish calendars appear in Jewish homes. Other Judaica products are available in Mumbai.

A Jewish youth group meets in the center's youth lounge. JDC also supports JCC programs for the needy, including meals-on-wheels and cash assistance. The "Joint," as it is affectionately called, also sponsors the *senior citizens' home.*

Natasha Joseph, twenty, is an editor at the new magazine, *Kol India,* and is active in the Jewish community. She cites the myriad Jewish activities available in Mumbai during Passover, Israel Independence Day, and, of course, the Khai Fest, a Hanukkah festival sponsored by the Jewish Youth Pioneers.

Naturally, a Hanukkah candle-lighting ceremony conducted by Chabad in Mumbai is the same as those held all over the world, including in Bratislava, New York City, or Ho Chí Minh City. Every year, hundreds of Jews attend this ceremony at one of India's iconic and historic monuments, the Gateway of India. Chabad rabbis climb to the top of a huge crane, brought to the site each year, to light the menorah.

India's generally tolerant approach to religions and religious pluralism bodes well for the future of the Jewish community in Mumbai. One additional reason for India's acceptance, even encouragement of differences in various religious and cultural groups, is that "Hindus extend hospitality to the outside groups to the extent that the outsiders refrain from proselytizing Hindus," wrote C. J. S. Wallis, in *India Star.* Jews don't try to convert Indians.

Another story that I followed in India is the story of Jewish willpower, determination, and resiliency that is often spoken of, as with the congregations we met in Southeast Asia. A perfect example of that is the Reform Movement of Judaism group. We have spoken about India not being anti-Semitic, but that does not mean that Jews do not at times get caught in the crossfire of ethnic violence, such as occurred one dark night in January 1993, when a hand grenade was hurled into a four-story building in the Byculla district of Mumbai, the top floor of which was occupied by Rodef Shalom, the single Reform Movement of Judaism synagogue in India, supported by the JRU (Jewish Religious Union).

The incendiary device leveled the entire structure, including the prayer hall of the small congregation, with its decades-old membership records, lists of *brit milah,* bar and bat mitzvahs, death certificates, valuable possessions, prayer books, *sefer Torahs,* and the Holy Ark. The Reform Jewish Union group "very nearly lost its long heritage," wrote past president Sarah A. Samson.

It is important to stress that according to Jewish leaders, the fire-bombing was not directed against Jews or their house of worship, nor was it anti-Semitic in nature. It just happened to occur during that time of religious unrest in India, with bomb blasts and riots between Hindus and Muslims, as well as the political situation between December 1992 and January 1993. This attack on the building involved a "personal vendetta" between non-Jewish tenants, some of whom wanted to rid the building of a Muslim occupying an apartment there, said Jewish leaders.

Since that bleak night, the JRU congregation, which lost everything, has never given up. Services and functions were held in various residences, halls, and schools, and, for the last few years, in the JCC.

Though relatively young compared to the long history of Jews in this vast subcontinent of India, the JRU has grown from its very first days in Bombay in 1925, when it was introduced by Dr. Jerusha J. Jhirad, the first female physician in India. The new group was to be modeled along the lines of Liberal Judaism in England. Services follow Reform tradition. Mixed marriages are welcome, "so we can keep Judaism alive," said Norman Elijah, adding, "Ladies are called to the Torah."

Rabbi Leon Morris described the Yom Kippur Service in Mumbai's Reform congregation when he wrote in the 2000 issue of *Reform Judaism*:

> *On Yom Kippur the entire congregation dresses in white: the women draped in beautiful saris, and men, wearing white kurta pajamas, intone the melodious eastern Kol Nidre as the Sifrei Torah is removed from the ark. A visiting rabbi conducts High Holy Day services. At worship services, liturgy from the Liberal British prayer books is supplemented with traditional Bene Israel piyutim* [liturgical poems set to music].

As for the JRU in Mumbai, their prayers seem to have been answered. By 2013, the now 175-member group will be in their own quarters. The synagogue will be located on the top floor of a new, seven-story building at 23 Dadoji Konddev Marg, Byculla, Mumbai.

"We now have an opportunity," wrote Ms. Samson, "to make Rodef Shalom a truly Jewish center, catering not only to our local members, but also to visitors from abroad . . ."

"The history of India is a tale of incredible drama, of great inventions and phenomenal creativity, and of the biggest ideas," wrote author Michael Wood in his book, *India*.

Like most of the over 5 million yearly foreign tourists, I first embraced the northern "golden triangle" of India tourism: Delhi, Agra, and Jaipur. Every stone tells a story of an India that in the past came into contact with Persians, Egyptians, Greeks, Chinese, Arabs, Central Asians, the people of the Mediterranean, and the Jews. This area is an epitome of India, the seat of the old Hindu and Persian culture that arrived in Afghan and Mughal times, and later intermingled with the West.

Delhi, a city of civil servants, remains one of the world's most historic cities, as well as the capital of the world's largest democracy.

Several hundred years ago, Delhi was the most populous city in the world. It's almost there again, reaching 19 million in 2011. One hundred years ago, when it became India's capital—under the British, Calcutta (now Kolkata) was the capital from 1772 until 1911—the population was 238,000. Since it is a city that spans many millennia, from early historic times up to the present day, you cannot help but feel that you are walking comfortably in a living museum, even though this capital is rapidly transforming itself into a modern metropolis, with the skyline undergoing change as only the twenty-first century can bring.

Let's be clear: There are new and ancient cities of Asia that are the pulsating giants of the twenty-first century, and Delhi, as the capital of India, is one of them. This city, founded at least as far back as the sixth century BCE, is better known for its adventures in later periods in Indian history, particularly during the Mughal Empire, when it served as the capital from 1649 to 1857. But an Edict of Ashoka–period inscription shows that Delhi was already located on the trunk route connecting the main cities of Ancient India in the third century BCE.

Indians realize they have the obligation to preserve, protect, study, and document the rich legacy of one of the greatest cities on the planet.

There would never be enough days to observe and appreciate Delhi's many heritage sites of the Mughal Empire (1526–1857), whose architecture and art reached a high level of achievement. Marvel at the magnificent Red Fort (Lal Qila), the seat of Mughal power. These red sandstone battlements were erected on the banks of River Yamuna by Emperor Shah Jahan, a great Mughal emperor—the same Shah Jahan who supervised construction of the monumental Taj Mahal in Agra.

Jama Masjid, India's largest mosque, is also a monument to the vision and power of Shah Jahan (1592–1666), who takes his place in Indian history as a medieval Muslim ruler, as well as an active patron of palaces and mosques. The name "Shah Jahan" comes from the Persian language, and means "King of the World." This fascinating Delhi mosque took six years and 5,000 workers to construct, and features a water fountain in the middle of a huge court where worshippers wash their feet.

Wander over to the Qutub Minar Tower, a World Heritage site built in 1199 by the Turkish slave king Qutb-ud-din Aibak to celebrate his victory over the Hindu Rajputs. Though a strong and ferocious conqueror and ruler, he also possessed a fine sense of beauty, as evidenced by the five-story victory tower in this beautiful complex.

Riding through the Delhi market at *Chandni Chowk* on a bicycle-rickshaw, I realized that out of all the markets in the world, none can compare to this one. This market puts to shame most bazaars or *souqs* anywhere in the world. And oh, those pashmina shawls and Rajasthan jewelry! In this "mother of all markets," one has to maintain a positive attitude about crowds. Forgive the jostling in the teeming streets and enjoy the pungent smells of the fruits, vegetables, and spices. Bicycle-rickshaws carry passengers who either thrill at the powerful, unleashed energy of the market and the variety of goods and foods, or those who are scared out of their wits as trucks and motorbikes come so close that they grip the sides of their rickshaw, fearful that they are about to be run over. Tourists and natives alike walk through almost nonexistent passageways in a market that by and large is utter chaos. Deliveries are being made by carts, dollies, motorbikes, and mini-trucks. How one finds a specific store is beyond belief.

Modern New Delhi is a must-see. Admire India Gate (World War I memorial), the Presidential Palace, Parliament House, and the Secretariat buildings, home to the world's largest democracy—built by the British, who tried to hold on to their empire until the last minute. They managed to botch their departure, leaving in their wake at least a million casualties due to poor planning and bad timing, dividing a country where religious animosity depopulated regions and towns.

⌒

Stop off at the Judah Hyam Synagogue at 2 Humayun Road, opposite Taj Mahal Hotel, near the Christian cemetery, New Delhi, where attorney Ezekiel Isaac Malekar, honorary secretary of the synagogue, single-handedly keeps the ten-family Jewish community alive. "Israel is in my heart, India in my blood," Malekar declared.

"There is no *rabbi*, no *hazzan* [cantor], no *shochet* [ritual slaughterer], and usually no *minyan*," Malekar said, but there are always services held at 6:30 p.m. every Friday, in the winter (and at 7:00 p.m. in summer), and on Saturday mornings at 9:00 a.m. if there is a *minyan*.

Travelers always ask, "Why are there so few Jews in Delhi?" One would think that Delhi, the capital city, would have a large concentration of Jews, such as in London, Paris, or Rome. Not so!

First, the original sea craft carrying Jews from the Middle East naturally would have hit the southern coast of India, especially the area in and around Bombay. Having settled there initially, it's likely that many Jews grew accustomed to living in the cosmopolitan, business-oriented metropolis of Bombay.

Another contributing factor to the lack of Jews in Delhi could be the fact that they never really entered government service, even though they were encouraged to do so by the British. Indian Jews concentrated on business and agricultural trading pursuits. And if they did work for the British, they did so in Bombay and Kochi where the vast majority of the Jews resided. Attorney Malekar told an interviewer: "There are actually more Jews [in Delhi] these days because of all the embassies. There are about a hundred Jewish diplomats—not just Israeli, of course—and some do attend on the holidays."

Before World War II, a small Delhi Jewish community consisted of Afghan, French, Russian, and other businessmen exporting hides and skins. Prayer services were held in homes. During the war, more Indian Jews working in foreign embassies arrived in Delhi. A Jewish Welfare Association was formed in 1949, which raised funds for the prayer hall that opened in 1956. Today, besides functioning as a synagogue, the hall also serves as a center for Jewish and interfaith studies.

Because the community today is so small, members of the Israeli Embassy and Jewish diplomats from the U.S. and other embassies help to make up the bulk of attendance at services.

Ezekiel Isaac Malekar is truly "the one Jew that keeps the light of Judaism burning" at the Judah Hyam Synagogue, as he lives on the premises. He reminded me of Than Lwin (aka, Moses Samuels of Yangon, Myanmar), who carries the load of Jewish history on his shoulders in that city. Every day he walks a few blocks from his home to open the doors of *Musmeah Yeshua* synagogue to keep Judaism alive in Myanmar.

Before visiting it is wise to call or e-mail Mr. Malekar, a history buff, qualified attorney, and former deputy secretary of the National Human Rights Commission. He had the honor of participating in the national memorial services for Mahatma Gandhi and the country's first prime minister, Jawaharlal Nehru.

The day I visited Chabad House in Delhi, I felt I had truly entered into the sights and sounds of modern India, because Chabad is located in the General Market at T 305 Main Bazaar, Paharanj. Even though the night was chilly, the whole neighborhood seemed to be outside on the unpaved streets. The cacophony of languages—Hindi, Arabic, English, even Hebrew—made the street babel fascinating. The dim neon lights barely illuminated the street, giving the area a mystic feeling, which I somehow couldn't shake until I returned to the hotel later that night. The endless honking of car horns, as if each driver had fallen asleep and was lying flat on the horn, helped me to be alert when crossing the streets. In India, driving is mostly playing chicken with vehicles, pedestrians, or even the cows that roam freely along the urban concrete. I was in India!

When I reached Chabad House I was greeted by a poster that said WELCOME TO THE CHABAD OF INDIA—WE ARE YOUR JEWISH HOME AWAY FROM HOME. Only unlike Ho Chi Minh City, or even Bangkok, this headquarters is located on the top floor of a three-story building. It maintains its own entrance, with security. It used to be part of the Hare Rama guesthouse, but moved. Indeed, the neighborhood is an Israeli enclave, with Hebrew signs in store windows, and merchants knowing a few Hebrew words. A bookstore nearby sells some books from Israel. Many rooming houses in the area house young Israeli backpackers.

Chabad occupies a good location, as it's a short distance from the railway station. People don't stay long in Delhi, Chabad people say, as it is generally a short stopover for hikers and tourists.

On the wall behind the *bimah* hangs a huge picture of the Lubavitcher Rebbe and nearby the Holy Ark. A kitchen area with tables and chairs fills up the room, and Israeli papers and magazines are on hand. On Friday afternoons, the scene is hectic as a large crowd is expected for a delicious Sabbath meal, including traditional *matzah ball* soup. If the weather is suitable, dinner is served on the rooftop, with plenty of singing and joyous camaraderie.

On our visit we found some Israeli backpackers who had just returned from Kathmandu, Nepal, where a reported one thousand Israeli tourists attend the Passover *seder* during their trips to India, along with attending yoga classes, music courses, and talks by gurus. The Kathmandu *seder* is reportedly the largest in the world.

One must remember that Chabad House serves as a meeting place for Israelis and Americans, and lately, Australians and New Zealanders who travel to India alone or in pairs, hoping to link up with others along the way. The Chabad center also provides meals, advice, and prayer services. When travelers lose money or documents (as sometimes happens), Chabad offers a sympathetic ear—more than a cold embassy office. The rabbis of Chabad are known for their willingness to help practically and spiritually the often-troubled tourist.

At times, the Indian perception of Israeli backpackers and tourists is not positive, as they have little to spend and tend to bargain aggressively, the Eastern way. Yet people also know there is compulsory military service in Israel, and that these youngsters have come from a tense situation. It is reported that a higher percentage of Israelis have visited India than people from any other Western country.

The role of Chabad in maintaining far-flung diaspora communities, especially in Southeast Asia, is profound. Their work in ministering to traveling Israelis is significant. Chabad has done much to respond to this phenomenon of young Israelis in India.

Rabbi Menachem Mendel Sharf and his wife Debbi arrived at Chabad in Delhi in 1994. Under their leadership, Chabad in Delhi has become well-known to tourists, especially young people. They have made this Chabad center a warm and hospitable center and tourists in India who begin to miss their homeland can count on the Rabbi and Rebbetzin to give them a warm greeting. I believe the couple when they say, "Welcome to Chabad, your home in Delhi."

Delhi is only one of India's showcases.

After driving for several hours, directly out of the capital, along roads bustling with trucks, cars, tractors, and motorbikes, alongside horses, donkeys, and camels pulling carts and wagons, we arrived in Agra to visit the Taj Mahal. There's nothing like it anywhere else; indeed, it is the number-one "Wonder of the World."

Some people come to India just to see the Taj Mahal. Most tourists enter the grounds once, and move on. But if you have time, you should try to visit the site in the early morning and again in the late afternoon. Gaze at the Taj; each time the differences in morning and afternoon light will astonish you. The beautiful and well-kept gardens are astounding, too. No photos, movies, or television segments can do justice to this number-one wonder of the world, this memorial to love, this readily identifiable structure—perhaps the most beautiful building ever constructed.

Even this peripatetic traveler was relaxed. You don't push or rush on the grounds of this architectural marvel. The view and accompanying scenery of the Taj will last you a lifetime.

Despite the thousands of visitors, this faultless building, constructed on a bend in the River Yamuna at Shah Jahan's capital of Agra, does something else for the traveler: This famous Indian landmark puts one into a romantic trance.

We all try to sum up in words the awe we feel at first sight. The Indian poet Rabindranath Tagore called it "a teardrop on the face of eternity." Rudyard Kipling wrote that it was "the embodiment of all things pure." And it has been said that the Taj Mahal "requires neither moonlight nor sunset; it brings its own atmosphere, its own light, 'that was never yet on land or sea.'" Indeed, no artificial lighting is needed for the interior, for the dome is semitransparent, and there are several windows with perforated alabaster screens.

The story of the birth of this monument to love began in tragedy. Shah Jahan's thirty-eight-year-old wife, whom he loved very much, died during the birth of her fourteenth child, a daughter named Gauhara Begum. With her last breath, Mumtaz Mahal whispered to her distraught husband of their everlasting love, and begged him not to marry again. She wanted him to build her a mausoleum resembling paradise.

Mumtaz Mahal's death left the emperor heartbroken. It is said his hair turned gray overnight. The mausoleum, started in 1632, was built in her name (*Taj Mahal* is Persian for "crown of Mahal"). About 20,000 laborers participated in the building of this masterpiece, which took twenty-two years. After his wife died, Shah Jahan spent the rest of his life imprisoned by an evil son, Emperor Aurangzeb, in Agra Fort, looking out over the river to his wife's final resting place. One should visit the fort to appreciate how, from his prison quarters, Shah Jahan would gaze across the river toward the Taj Mahal, where his wife was buried. His remains were later laid to rest in the mausoleum.

The Taj Mahal is considered the finest example of Mughal architecture—a style that combines elements from Persian, Turkish, Indian, and Islamic architecture, including carved relief work and calligraphy. In 1983, the Taj became a UNESCO World Heritage Site.

Most visitors are photographed sitting on the marble bench at the Lotus Pool. Old and young couples alike pose for photos on this symbol of enduring love. Semiprecious stones are inlaid into the marble in beautiful patterns using a process known as *pietra dura*.

When Princess Diana visited India in February 1992, with her then husband, Prince Charles, "the power of the Taj Mahal's image was such that when she went to the Taj alone and allowed herself to be photographed—a single, disconsolate and melancholy figure seated on a white marble bench before a monument to an abiding royal romance—no words were needed," wrote Diana and Michael Preston, in their book, *Taj Mahal: Passion and Genius at the Heart of the Moghul Empire*.

About 3 million people visit India's most popular monument each year, including many American tourists. But as a sign of the economic times, this architectural masterpiece recently announced it would stop accepting U.S.

dollars (the greenback fell 12 percent against the rupee in 2011). Oh well, no matter; use whatever currency is necessary to see this wonder. In the words of Diana and Michael Preston: "The Taj Mahal is an expression not only of supreme love but also of confident power and opulent majesty."

If you are fortunate to have a loved one with you, and you are strolling on the grounds, sitting on the park benches, gazing at the monument or the enveloping minarets, you will agree again with the Prestons, that "at the heart of all the grandeur and magnificence lie two human beings who loved each other."

I had heard about another India—the one in the south, where tourists also feel the breath of history as they traverse a beautiful scenic region known as Kerala, "God's own country," or the "land of coconut." I was looking for the Cochin Jews, so I flew to Kochi (Cochin) in the southern state of Kerala. Like Mumbai, which was once called Bombay, like Kolkata, once known as Calcutta, Kochi was once named Cochin.

The Cochin Jews are the best-known of the Indian Jewish communities to the outside world; the other two, as we have seen, are the *Bene Israel* and *Baghdadi* Jews. The Cochinis, now numbering about a dozen in Kochi itself, are the smallest of the three groups in India today, though they claim to be the oldest. In the surrounding town of Ernakulam are the Black Jews, today numbering less than fifty.

This small Jewish community, with ancient roots and a sixteenth-century synagogue that can still be visited, stands in Cochin and attracts hundreds of visitors each day. Most Cochin Jews, who in the 1940s numbered about 2,500, emigrated to Israel in the 1950s and '60s. It was almost as if the whole city emigrated.

Legend has it that Cochin Jews arrived and were warmly received at the time of the destruction of the Second Temple in 70 CE. But the most significant physical evidence of the Jews' presence in medieval Malabar is kept to this day in the safe of the Cochin synagogue (Paradesi synagogue): three rectangular copper plates etched in Tamil language and given to Joseph Rabban, assumed to be the king of the Jewish settlement in Cranganore by King Cheraman Perumal. "While legend has the date of the plates to be 379 CE [fourth century], the eleventh century is a date much closer to contemporary scholarly assessment," says Professor Katz.

The Hindu king gave permission in perpetuity, or, in the more poetic expression of those days, "as long as the world and moon exist."

Cochin Jews had no contact with geographically isolated Jews near Bombay. Indeed, they were not aware of the existence of another Jewish community in India until the eighteenth century.

The "White Jews" (Paradesi) settled in the Cochin region in the latter half of the seventeenth century. They were exiles of the Spanish Inquisition and brought with them the Ladino language and Sephardic customs. They found the Black Malabari Jewish community quite different, and tensions between the two communities existed early on and lasted for centuries. It is true, however, that some of the European Jews intermarried with the older Jewish communities that had already been long settled in the region. But the majority of the Paradesi married within their community, a community divided by a color line into White Jews, Black Jews, and Brown Jews. The latter were also known as freed slaves, or freemen (*meshuhrarim* in Hebrew).

According to Edna Fernandes in *The Last Jews of Kerala: The Two Thousand Year History of India's Forgotten Jewish Community* the Black Jews "were denied entry to the synagogue, denied the right to perform rituals there, banned from chanting certain liturgical hymns, banned from reading the Torah or scriptures, and prohibited from marrying into White Jewish families."

⌒

One story goes that as late as 1550, the Raja of Cochin refused to fight a battle on Saturday because on that day his Jewish soldiers would not fight; and they were the best warriors he had. Probably India is the only country on earth so civilized that in war, out of deference to its Jewish soldiers, no battles were fought on the Sabbath.

⌒

My namesake, Benjamin of Tudela—like other Jewish travelers in the twelfth century—also visited India. Benjamin left extensive descriptions of the Jews of southwest India. His was the first extensive account of the

Jews of Malabar, though it must also be said that much of his writings were gleaned from other visitors.

Benjamin described the people as notably trustworthy. They "may even leave their goods in the open field without any guards." He discussed the cultivation of pepper, cinnamon, ginger, and many other kinds of spices. Like this writer, he also noted Kerala's "ferocious heat."

"All the cities and countries inhabited by these people contain only about 100 Jews, who are of black color as well as the other inhabitants," he wrote, adding that "the Jews are good men, observers of the law and possess the Pentateuch, the Prophets, and some little knowledge of the Talmud and its decisions."

That was the twelfth century. Now, in the twenty-first century, I, Benjamin of New York, find myself in a landscape replete with spices and exotic plants. Seeing men walking around in short-sleeved shirts, I quickly removed my jacket and enjoyed the sunshine in this city made up of a group of lagoons, islands, and inlets divided by narrow waterways.

More than 30 million people live in the densely populated state, a third of which is covered by forests. Driving in the city with my guide, Gopal, I learned that Kochi has a population of about 600,000, but an extended metro area includes 1.6 million. Visitors notice the economic boom taking place here—the high-rise apartment buildings and offices, the likes of which reflect the fact that India is on the move, with a 9 percent economic growth rate and the world's fastest-growing major economy after China.

Kochi is considered the commercial and industrial capital of Kerala, one of the most attractive states in India. The municipality was created in 1967, out of Fort Kochi, Mattanchery, Ernakulam, Willingdon Island, and a number of nearby villages.

Often called the "Queen of the Arabian Sea," and slightly smaller than Switzerland, Kochi is the epitome of long-ago India. A port-of-call for traders for thousands of years, the Arabs began trading way before Islam. The earliest mosque in India is said to be the old wooden prayer hall at Cranganore, north of Kochi.

Small kiosk-type shops dot the old part of Kochi town. Here, it's fun to bargain. Crowded, busy, and lively, but still relaxing; you can unwind here, and indulge yourself. Boat rides are very popular, especially the Kerala houseboats, or rice-boats as they are called. Kochi is an enchanting back-water destination, for it is made up of a string of picturesque and lovely islands, lagoons, inlets and of course, swaying palm trees to enrich your water cruise. I noticed that some companies mention that on your Kochi backwater tour, you can visit tourist attractions, including the synagogue which we shall visit soon.

Occupied by the Portuguese in 1503, Kochi was the site of the first European colonial settlement in the country, and remained the capital of Portuguese India until 1530, when explorer Vasco da Gama moved it to Goa. Kochi was later occupied by the Dutch and the British, and was the first princely state to willingly join the Indian Union when India gained independence in 1947.

The city is proud of the country's oldest European-built church, St. Francis, erected in 1503 and a popular tourist site. Vasco da Gama, the first European to reach India, was buried here for fourteen years before his remains were transferred to Portugal. The tombstone can be seen inside the church now used by the Church of South India.

Walking the streets, I see diversity in the faces of the people: Tamils, Gujaratis, Jews, Sikkimese, Anglo-Indians, Konkanis and Tuluvas. They speak Malayalam, the main language used to communicate and instruct, although nearly everyone I meet speaks English in this state, which my guide Gopal proudly tells me has a higher rate of literacy than any other.

In Kochi and outside the city, I marvel at traditional Kerala costumes, a marked contrast to Western clothing. Men wear colorful long, white, cotton *lungi*, a long piece of cloth wrapped around the waist, with typical batik patterns. South Indian women traditionally wear the *sari*. The streets are calm and the area remains a place where you can indulge yourself. Sailing around the islands in the backwaters and watching the city skyline from your slow-moving boat can bring about that peaceful interlude that one occasionally needs on this subcontinent.

I was heading to Mattancherry, a part of old Cochin City, specifically to Synagogue Lane in what is called "Jew Town," and one of the centers of the Kochi spice trade. I noticed that shopping was in full swing. Alongside small houses, small kiosk-type stores and booths dot the area. It's easy to bargain with the friendly salespeople in this crowded, lively market known for its precious antiques.

Tourists can spot the Jewish star on the lattice of many homes, and some even have Jewish names inscribed on them. If desired, tourists can obtain postage stamps with the Star of David at the post office.

But the outstanding Jewish site on Synagogue Lane is the whitewashed, rectangular Paradesi Synagogue, part of the "Living Heritage of India."

There is a long line of tourists from around the world waiting outside to enter. Finally a member of the congregation comes over, opens the doors, and we realize why the house of worship is a must for the visitor. First, the brass pulpit and hand porcelain floor tiles made in eighteenth century China are exquisite to the eye. No two tiles are alike.

Several torahs occupy the ark. Each has a crown of solid gold with precious stones, a gift of the Maharaja of Cochin, "the protector of the Jews." He lived next door in what is called the Dutch Palace, but is now a museum. The Maharaja wanted to live next to the synagogue so he could hear the Hebrew melodies wafting up from the Jewish house of worship. As noted, the copper plates, etched in Tamil, given to Joseph Rabban, the "Jewish king" of the Jewish principality in Cranganore, can be found in the safe of this synagogue.

I sat on the benches arranged in a horseshoe pattern around the main hall and marveled at the silk wall hangings as well as the chandeliers and glass lamps filled with coconut oil and admired this historical monument to Jewish life in India.

Upstairs, next to the woman's balcony is a room containing art work depicting the recent history of Indian Jews. The torah is read on Sabbath and festivals on this balcony.

Well worth a visit.

In 1968, the late Mrs. Indira Gandhi, prime minister of India, attended the 400th anniversary celebration, and a special commemorative postage stamp was issued. She ended her speech by congratulating the congregation with *Mazel tov!* Asked where she learned those words, she answered, "From *Fiddler on the Roof.*"

This prayer house is open Sunday to Friday, from 10:00 a.m. to noon and from 3:00 p.m. to 5:00 p.m.

All of the guides, tourist brochures, and maps highlight this synagogue. The original building erected in 1568 was destroyed by the Portuguese in 1662 and rebuilt by the Dutch two years later.

Outside this place of worship, which has the distinction of being the oldest-surviving synagogue in the Commonwealth of Nations, looms a graceful clock tower built in 1760 that displays dials in Hebrew, Malayalam, and Roman numerals.

As mentioned, about a dozen Jews live in Cochin, and another thirty-eight reside in Ernakulam, across the river. In search of the scattered tribe, I drove over to Emankulam to see Isaac Joshua, president of the Association of Kerala Jews. He told me he was very comfortable here. "India is my country," declared the eighty-six-year-old Jewish leader. Jews here are eager to refurbish the five empty synagogues still standing in area towns, badly in need of repair. The association is discussing obtaining funds for synagogue remodeling with the American Jewish Joint Distribution Committee (JDC), which aids Indian Jewry. The area's Jewish families engage in real estate infrastructure, security, and defense projects.

A few Indian Jewish families have returned from Israel, at least temporarily. Isaac Joshua's nephew, Anil Avraham, thirty-one, was born in Israel and is now a tour operator in Kochi. "I love this place," he says. Avraham prepares itineraries for tourists, speaks English and Hebrew, and handles many groups.

By the end of my trip, I have become friendly with Gopal and discover that he is very supportive of Israel, He is pessimistic about peace in the Middle East. "It will be a hundred years before you'll have peace with the Arabs," he tells me, adding, "It's a religious thing. Just like we here in India, with Pakistan—it's all about religion. It will also be a hundred years until there is peace between India and Pakistan, and for you, too."

My trip has convinced me that it is important for Americans, Israelis, and Europeans to learn more about India, its people and politics, and its future relationship with the U.S., China, and Israel. Robert Kaplan in his book, *Monsoon,* states "that the Indian Ocean will occupy the center of global change and international politics in the coming decades, especially with a rising China and India."

Already Israel sees the potential of establishing a logistical infrastructure in the Indian Ocean. With the cooperation of the Indian Navy, Israel Aircraft Industries is developing Barak-8 missiles for the Indian Navy and Air Force, which is capable of protecting sea vessels and ground facilities from aircraft and cruise missiles.

It is a positive move that Israel is seeking new friends and allies in a hostile world. India is definitely a good place to start. Actually, the process has already begun. In 2003, Yuval Steinitz, then head of the Israeli Knesset's Foreign Affairs and Security Committee, assessed the strategic alliance with India as a "very high priority, second only to relations with the U.S."

There is wide support for Israel today in the Indian government, although when it comes to Israel-India relations, it's important to remember that India has the third-largest Muslim population in the world—approximately 154 million Muslims—after Indonesia and Pakistan.

Israel and India are fast becoming friends, and have formed economic, military, and even political links. Bilateral trade, which was at $200 million in 2001, grew to $4.1 billion by 2009, excluding defense trade. And Israel has pulled ahead of Russia as India's largest arms supplier. Pakistan is seen as India's enemy, and that enmity is strong, especially after the Mumbai terrorist attack, which originated in Pakistan. In addition, Pakistan is known to have sheltered terrorists, including the late Osama bin Laden and his key lieutenants. How can Pakistan deny the allegation that the Army and intelligence services did not know that for years Osama bin Laden was, to use the words of Fareed Zakaria in an article in the *Washington Post,* "comfortably ensconced in an army town." Zakaria added "the evidence is now overwhelming that the army has been infiltrated at all levels by violent Islamists, including Taliban and al-Qaaeda sympathizers."

Pakistan maintains a significant nuclear capability, and its ongoing conflict with India has the potential to spark a regional conflagration. Islamabad also supports Jihadist groups used in a proxy war against India.

"For sixty years, Pakistan military has focused obsessively on its rivalry with India. Large elements within that military appear to be switching obsessions, and the United States is replacing India as the organizing principle around which Pakistan's military understands its national security interests. If that happens not only is the Afghan war lost but Pakistan itself is also lost." wrote Zakaria.

With Pakistan possibly drifting into a state of terrorism, the question is asked:

What does it mean for India and, in this case, perhaps for Israel, too?

Ponder the words of Martin Sherman, academic director of the Jerusalem Summit Lectures in Security Studies Program at Tel Aviv University, who writes: "In theory, at least, a strong Indo-Israel alliance would have the potential to create a formidable force for stability in a region threatened by radical fundamentalism and tyrannical theocracy."

The night my plane left from Mumbai, I realized that Gopal was prescient about how long it will take to achieve peace between Israelis and Palestinians, India and Pakistan. Over the TV news that night in December 2007 came the announcement that Mrs. Benazir Bhutto had been assassinated, many believed with the support of the Pakistani military or intelligence services. As a former prime minister, she could have brought hope to India-Pakistan relations, especially since both have nuclear capability. The murder case has never been properly investigated.

As my plane left "Incredible India," however, I began to recall the words that most Indian Jews use when they describe their life in that country: "generous mother," or "motherland." India has been "a generous mother, not only to the Jews who came to live here permanently . . . but to those who sought refuge with her temporarily," meaning Jewish refugees in World War II, according to Benjamin J. Israel in *The Jews of India*. Let us remember, too, that by their presence, the Jews have enriched India's multifaceted culture.

But if they were so happy in India, and were not oppressed, why did almost all of the Jews leave after 1947? True; India went through birth pangs after independence, causing a general restlessness to emigrate among large numbers of Indians. Also true was the fact that Jews, having believed they were protected by the British, might have felt that "in a free India they would suffer discrimination, a fear that has proved groundless." according to author Benjamin J. Israel.

This writer believes the real desire to emigrate was the fruition of the age-old dream of Jews returning to their ancient homeland, Israel, which after 1948 became a reality. As Noah Massil, formerly of Mumbai and now of Jerusalem, put it: "In the Torah, it is written, 'I will bring you to your land on the wings of the eagle.'"

When the opportunity came to join the Biblical "Ingathering of the Exiles," in the latter half of the twentieth century, Indian Jews began to emigrate: first, the young, followed by their parents, who left good jobs, sold their land and homes, and came to Israel in the 1950s and '60s, when Israel was struggling. By the 1970s and beyond, when life in the Jewish state had improved, most Jews had departed India. After 2,000 or more years, the Jews of India—like millions of Jews throughout the world—had returned to their ancestral home, *Eretz Yisra'el*, "the Land of Israel."

Still, this wonderful Indian Jewry, although meager in numbers in the twenty-first century, is empowered with a strong belief in Jewish continuity. And according to author Benjamin J. Israel, this diaspora community is "living evidence that, in at least one country in the world, Jews can exist with pride and honour and without any need for self-consciousness or protective withdrawal into a self-created ghetto."

Time Stops for Me in the Maghreb

Algeria and Morocco

> *The enemy of my enemy is my friend,*
> *The friend of my friend is my friend,*
> *The enemy of my friend is my enemy . . .*
> —*Arabic proverb*

Time often stops in the land of the Maghreb. It certainly halted for me that summer day in 1964, in Algiers, my first encounter with the Jews of North Africa in their native lands.

I found myself walking toward the *casbah* (fortress) on my way to meet the last remaining Jews in that war-torn country. During the Algerian War (1954–62), the *casbah* was a hostile enclave, all but impenetrable to French forces trying to crush the uprising. The *casbah* was the old Turkish quarter, occupied mostly by a large Muslim population bursting at the seams. One square kilometer housed a teeming population of 100,000.

Squalid, labyrinthine alleys concealed ancient houses built around open courtyards. The tortuous passageways of the *casbah* were so narrow that one could jump from one rooftop to another. Despite being independent for two years, an uneasy calm still hung over this hauntingly beautiful port city and capital, Algiers, once the jewel of France's colonial empire. "Algiers the White" aptly describes this city awash with white buildings.

Algeria, sandwiched between Morocco and Tunisia, known (and often feared) as the Barbary Coast, was the first Arab country I had ever set foot in. A little scary for someone who had lived in Israel and had traveled extensively through France and who had become somewhat of a Francophile.

As a reporter and an individual consumed by world news, I had followed the gory details of the French-Algerian War, or, as the Algerians called it, the Algerian Revolution. That revolt ended French rule in a country that France had occupied since 1830. The battle lasted nearly eight years, almost twice as long as the Great War of 1914–18, and toppled six French prime ministers and the French Fourth Republic as well.

As I wound my way to the Jewish community synagogues in the *casbah*, I mumbled, way down deep under my breath, *Algérie française,* even though the French had departed. Three-quarters of a million French settlers—*colons,* as they were called, or *Pieds-Noirs* ("Black-Feet"), had sailed away, along with nearly all of the approximate 140,000 Jews.

Just a few years ago, the city was racked with plastic bombs, hurled with expertise into crowded cafes. *"Comme Chicago,"* the Algerians explained.

I began the long walk up the hill to the north of the city where the *casbah* is located. There I would find my people. Broken sidewalks, however, slowed my pace, so much so that it reminded me of my walk a few years back to the Jewish community center in Istanbul, another exotic city steeped in Islam. There, too, dozens of cracked sidewalks had slowed my steps.

I felt as if I were an intruder even as the refreshing aroma of spices filled my nostrils. The air was balmy, creating for me an atmosphere redolent of the past.

For a journalist, this was a challenging day for a first visit to Algiers. The very last of the French troops were leaving; the border war with Morocco had erupted; and gunmen had fired a few submachine-gun bursts at the residence of the former president, Ahmed Ben Bella.

The *casbah* is situated in the oldest part of the city.

Arriving at the community center and synagogue, the first Algerian Jews I met consisted of a group of old men seated on half-broken chairs around a table in an otherwise-empty office. Their deeply lined faces showed the fear and uncertainty of a country just ending a bloody eight-year civil war.

It was then that they told me an expression I was to remember all my life: "We are *le dernier carré,*" they said, "the last infantry square," which was used by Napoleon as protection from enemy cavalry charges. The carré, which usually contained a four- to six-row formation in depth, could move in a square in any direction—the idea being not to expose the rear or sides of the soldiers to the cavalry.

After the 1962 Evian Accords peace treaty between the Algerian revolutionaries and France, the Jewish square, like Napoleon's last square at Waterloo, had vanished. As history so aptly informs us, Napoleon went down in defeat; so, too, did France, in Algeria.

Looking back on it, it was inconceivable that France would ever give up Algeria—that is, until November 1, 1954, All Saints' Day, when the FLN (*Front de Libération Nationale)* revolted. Within a year, the FLN was waging total war against the French. Rebel atrocities increased, and French military repression erupted. Soon, the French army would regard every Muslim as a potential killer. A full-blooded war existed to the end.

The vast majority of Jews in Algeria, as well as Morocco, "remained passive in the struggle, as if petrified by the imminent events which they knew would mean the end of their existence in the Maghreb," noted Andre N. Chouraqui in his book, *Between East and West: A History of the Jews of North Africa,* adding that "the Jews proudly considered themselves French in every respect."

Despite their fears, Algerian Jews had discreetly supported the action adopted by the French against the rebels. As Alistair Horne, historian, scholar, and author of *A Savage War of Peace: Algeria 1954–1962,* put it: "[T]he Jews tended to find themselves in the tragic position of being caught between two fires: between the European and Muslim world."

In 1962, when France turned over the country to the Algerians, the Jews—sensing overwhelming danger from the Muslim population—left a country they had lived in for twelve centuries for the French mainland. Their fellow Jews in Morocco, the Maghreb neighbor to the West, had already begun to leave for Israel.

I realized that with this exodus of Jews from North Africa, Jewish history would radically change course, although at that time, Jews—including this writer, sitting in the Algiers synagogue—could not yet see the full picture.

All of these thoughts were running through my mind as I sat with Jewish leaders in the synagogue, in the *casbah,* when the guttural sobs of an old man in a dirty Arab dressing gown interrupted our conversation.

I was taken aback, but sat in silence.

The old man repeated his demands to the office clerk behind the desk, through his tears. It was a diatribe which had begun when he had first burst into the community center. The group of senior men seated around me knew him, these leaders from the remnants of the community. He had come every day since his arrival a month before. He was a seventy-year-old rabbi from Morocco who had walked with his flock of three hundred Jews across the desert to Algiers. He had no maps, no compass—only his sense of direction.

As the men listened, one of the leaders who had remained in Algeria got up, brought over a chair, and sat down. He began comforting the old man, who continued his pleading as if it had been pent up within him all his life. "I demand my papers to go to to Israel," the man declared in Arabic.

The Moroccan rabbi was nearly six feet tall. Age had bent him over only slightly. His face, though worn, still projected hope. His soiled garments flowed loosely about him. His feet were caked in dust. Like thousands of Moroccan Jews, he was in flight. Somehow, they were getting out, despite the Moroccan government's closing the borders from time to time to Jewish emigration headed for Israel. From ports along the northern shore of the Mediterranean, Jews were making it to Israel despite the ban. Most of the Moroccan Jews, especially those from former Spanish Morocco, had already set out for Israel. With them, it was a combination of desperation and little choice.

In the room with the Jewish leaders, I could see that the local rabbi had succeeded in getting the Moroccan rabbi to sit down and rest, freeing him up to give me a tour of the synagogue.

The younger, local rabbi had been born in Algeria. He wore a neat, Western suit and a small yarmulke on the back of his head. He didn't smile much these days. He traveled from Algiers to Bone, to Constantine, supervising *kashrut* and conducting services. He proceeded to show me the prayer hall and the community center, which had been attacked by an Arab mob a few years earlier. On December 12, 1960, an FLN mob had sacked this great synagogue. They had gutted the building, ripped the Torah scrolls, and desecrated the walls with swastikas and slogans, including "Death to the Jews," according to author Andre Chouraqui. Several Jewish officials had been kidnapped and assassinated in a series of violent acts within the Jewish community, noted author Horne.

Now in 1964, this *Beth Hamedrash* (house of study) remained empty and dusty, with a *minyan* only on Saturdays, and not every Saturday. We toured the dreary library, the conference room, and the unused classrooms before returning back to the main room, where the older Moroccan rabbi talked on.

While we were gone from the room, a telphone call had come through that the Moroccan rabbi's papers were now in order. The Algerian Jewish leaders explained that to get the proper documents to permit the rabbi to fly to France and then on to Israel took time. Algeria and Israel did not have diplomatic relations, so preparations had to be done carefully.

They told him that in a few hours he would be out of North Africa and on his way to *Eretz Yisra'el* (The Land of Israel). His plane would leave that very afternoon for France.

The older rabbi smiled at the mention of the Promised Land, and began to chant a prayer in Hebrew. No one except the local rabbi joined in response. The younger rabbi helped the old man up from his chair. They left the room, and walked down the hallway. They walked slowly, arm in arm, their backs straight. The two rabbis—one, the last representative of a once-thriving North African Jewish community life, and the other, about to fulfill the promise, "Next Year in Jerusalem"—departed from the synagogue together. The younger rabbi wanted to bid his colleague a good journey as well as bring him to the waiting escort outside who would take the rabbi from Morocco back to his temporary room in a Jewish family's residence to prepare for his flight.

As I walked back to the hotel later that day, the afternoon flight to Paris rose out of the city and headed over the beckoning, blue bay. The older rabbi was on it. The other remained in Algeria, temporarily, to save

Jews. When the aircraft landed in France, the rabbi would leave the plane, board another, and eventually arrive in a small country, Israel, and as one of the "forgotten million," he would spend his remaining days on the soil of the Jewish state. Over the years, I was to learn that the synagogue I had visited as well as all the synagogues in Algeria were converted into mosques.

⁓

Nearly all the Algerian Jews left in 1962. But how in such a short time could such a huge number of Algerian—and some Moroccan—Jews, estimated between 150,000 to 200,000, pick themselves up, go to France, be welcomed by that country, receive benefits and aid, and even regain their jobs?

Answer: Because the Crémieux Decree of 1870 stated clearly and unequivocally, "All Algerian Jews are French citizens." So, when they arrived in France, they were entitled to retrieve their jobs in the civil service, postal department, and other government services, as well as obtain all benefits entitled to citizens of France and to the *Pieds-Noirs* ("Black Feet")—those French men and women who had lived in Algeria before the country achieved independence and had returned to France.

Ever since the French entered Algeria in 1830, Jews had benefited immensely. Most went to French schools; their acculturation had pushed them into the orbit of French civilization, and they were almost completely integrated into French culture.

Like the three-quarters of a million *colons*, the Jews never imagined France would give up Algeria, which it claimed until the very end was part of France. During the last few weeks before the granting of Algerian independence in July 1962, Jews—seeing the chaos and pandemonium in which Algeria had plunged—suddenly pulled up roots and disappeared from a land where they had lived for twelve centuries. "Its suddenness resembled a flash flood in a Saharan wadi," wrote Chouraqui, adding that both the *colons* and the Jews had "vanished from the country as if by magic." They had abandoned everything.

The altered circumstances in Algeria and Morocco changed world Jewry, a transformation that is still evident today in the twenty-first century. "Had it not been for the conflict with the French that brought upheaval to the area, and overthrew its social and economic system, the Jews might well have remained in North Africa for centuries in comparative harmony," declared Chouraqui.

Most of the nearly 140,000 Algerian Jews, as well as those from Morocco who did not go to Israel, left for France, not only revitalizing the French Jewish community, but also making it one of the strongest in world Jewry, as well as the third-largest Jewish community in the diaspora after the U.S. and Russia. Indeed, this massive North African Sephardic immigration to France was one of the few times in Jewish history when a community was transformed from Ashkenazi to Sephardic.

The new Sephardic immigrants brought with them their language, customs, and culture, along with the memories of the poets and philosophers who had raised the genius of Israel to towering heights. They moved into French towns and cities where very few Jews—or none at all—had resided before, such as Avignon, Aix, Cannes, Antibes, Rennes, and Biarritz. The French Jewish community was rejuvenated. Some Algerian Jews, as we have seen in chapter 3, would eventually settle in Tahiti, where I had the pleasure of meeting them.

I left Algeria and flew to Marseilles, where I witnessed the newcomers being met by the Jews of France at the port. French Jews were overwhelmed by the massive immigration.

I met the Algerian Jews in the Place de la Bourse in Marseilles. They were inconsolable; after all, they had lost everything. Still, they were determined to make a new life.

To Ashkenazi French Jews, the absorption of these Sephardic newcomers was their duty, and with the aid of organizations such as the American Jewish Joint Distribution Committee, they openly welcomed the newcomers.

The massive influx of North African Sephardic Jews in the 1960s was one of the most exciting movements of immigration in contemporary Jewish history. Nearly 300,000 Sephardic Jews came to France in the 1960s, revitalizing French Jewry to such an extent that some have called the present Jewish community of France "the Second French Jewry."

The Sephardim brought activity and momentum, an infusion of new blood. They set up community institutions, synagogues, and Talmud Torahs.

They were proud of their Jewishness and were not as reserved as French Jews when it came to demonstrating against a government action or a policy against Israel. Not only was their arrival welcome, their integration into Jewish and French society was also very successful. They launched themselves into key positions in French government, education, art, medicine, and science.

When I left Marseilles I knew that my involvement with Algerian Jews would never end, and it has not!

Several decades later, I am once again traveling in France—Marseilles, Toulon, Toulouse—and I realize that I could have met Dr. Poul's father, Eric Abraham Poul whose story I began telling the reader in chapters 3 and 4. Writing these pages on Algeria and Morocco, the name "Poul " constantly reenters my mind, because of his combat time with the French Foreign Legion at Dien Bien Phu, and then his service in Algeria.

Dear reader, you know from chapters 3 and 4 that I never actually met Eric Abraham ben Yosef Poul personally. But his son, Dr. Poul, told me of his father's fascinating life in the French Foreign Legion and his time in Algeria.

"Algeria was very hard for my father," explained Dr. Poul. "He never liked Algeria. At that time, he was married and had a daughter back in France. I think my father didn't have any political opinions on the Algerian problem, but he felt that as a Legionnaire, one always had to obey his superiors."

During the last few years of the eight-year, French-Algerian War, Algeria entered a twilight zone of more and more bloodshed and hatred, brother against brother, Frenchman against Frenchman, Arab against Arab. Not only was there a war between the French Army and the FLN and its terrorists groups, but at the end, a near civil war broke out between the *colons* and the army, and between the *colons,* the Algerians, and the French Army.

Sgt. Poul got caught up in the quagmire. He was a member of the "1er REP," the tough 1st Foreign Parachutist Regiment, which remained very close to the secret *Organisation de l'Armée Secrète* (OAS), the colonist terrorist army group composed of civilians and military deserters who had pledged to continue to fight for *Algérie française using* underground techniques of terrorism.

Poul's regiment was involved in the Generals' Putsch in 1961, a movement of a half-dozen generals, colonels, and civilians who were angered at what they saw as the French government's treason and lies toward French Algerian colonists and the loyalist Muslims who trusted it. The *putsch* aimed to seize control of Algeria as well as topple President Charles de Gaulle and the French government in Paris. Units of the Foreign Legion offered prominent support, as did the well-armed OAS.

Tanks on the Place de la Concorde? Yes, there were!

Assassination attempts on President de Gaulle? Yes, there were!

Explosions in cafes and killings in Paris? Yes, there were!

Although a brief fear of invasion swept through Paris, the revolt collapsed in four days largely due to cooperation from the French air force and army, which remained loyal to General de Gaulle. Poul's paratroop regiment was broken up after the failed *putsch* and Poul apparently lost rank when he was retired to France because he had been in the 1er REP.

After his discharge from the Legion, Eric Abraham Poul frequently went to Morocco on family vacations.

But the story does not end there. In April 1987, my friend, Dr. Poul, son of Eric Abraham Poul, moved to Tahiti, and like his father, he, too, served in the French Foreign Legion as a doctor.

Still, despite his connection to Morocco, and after serving in various countries, Dr. Poul said his father possessed a deep, lifelong nostalgia for Vietnam, above all. Dr. Poul explained that he had sent letters containing pictures of Polynesia to his father. The last letter his father sent to him, before he passed away in April, 1987, said that he wanted to come and visit his son in Tahiti because his son's letter and photos had reminded him of Vietnam. Unfortunately, Eric Abraham Poul died a few days later.

<hr />

And now with Algeria behind me, I was headed for Morocco.

I discovered the joys of Morocco because I am constantly inundated with tourist information, telling me that new resort communities are springing up and infrastructure improvements are occurring throughout the country. And with good reason: About 10 million visitors arrived in 2010; a decade ago, it was only 4 million.

Morocco boasts desert trails and ski slopes, beaches and golf courses, leading to its fond label as "Europe's playground." It's only a several-hour flight from most of the continent. No wonder tourists flock here, especially from France and Spain; it's close by—so near, in fact, that many Europeans immerse themselves in the history of this kingdom, whose ruler is now Mohammed VI, son of Hassan II. Many in world Jewry consider him and his late father to be their friends.

The twists and turns of Jewish history can sometimes cloud our vision before setting foot in this and any other exotic land. Once there, however, many frequent signposts pop up—the small synagogues and the meager Jewish congregations—reminding us of the once-great, large Jewish community that thrived here. Morocco is such a destination.

For Jews, the road to Morocco has often appeared to be narrower and harder to navigate, full of potholes, yet it's still a wonderfully rewarding pathway to pursue. Nothing is perfect in the Jewish diaspora. The Jewish experience in Morocco, as in many countries I have traveled, was cyclical, with favorable times followed by anti-Semitic attacks.

After meeting the Jews of Algeria, I was now about to come in contact with more of the forgotten Jews of the Maghreb—in this case, the Jews of Morocco, who lived an isolated life until they arrived in Israel in the mid-twentieth century.

For all intents and purposes, all Jews could have departed from Morocco, but they did not; Morocco was, and is not, Algeria where only a few Jewish seniors still reside. I never met any Algerian Jew living abroad who even thought of ever returning to Algeria which, since independence, has joined much of the Arab world in expressing hostility to Israel.

⌒

Morocco can play havoc with your imagination; a mirage can appear in front of you as it often does before a camel driver. Several so-called mirages occurred to this traveler.

One day, I found myself in the Atlas Mountains on my way from Fez to Marrakech, via a shortcut through the mountains, a drive which would save several hours of travel. The shortcut is well worth the trip, not only because it saves time, but also because the views are magnificent. I would observe great cedar forests, caves, and gorges, my guide told me.

A cold morning greeted me, a little too cold even for Morocco, which supports a cultivated country of fields, farms, orchards, and gardens, along with deserts, oases, even sandstorms. In winter, though, some guidebooks mention often-impassable roads through the snowcapped Atlas Mountains. So we set off, accompanied by our guide, El Kherchi Abdllatif of Heritage Tours Private Travel.

Surprise, surprise—snow began to fall. Not heavy, but enough to blanket the road up ahead. A thin, wooden barrier pole came down at the checkpoint. We stopped.

The snow kept falling. We sat on the road for over an hour, the heater barely warming us in the backseat. I recalled reading about tragedy befalling people who get caught in severe snowstorms; they die.

Dressed in a *djellaba,* the long, loose-fitting outer robe blowing away from his body and limbs like the windblown flaps of a tent, the guide exited the vehicle. His monk-like hood covered his head, and his sandals made huge footprints in the snow. Running out to the checkpoint ahead, he came back shivering. Warming up in the car, he told us that they had closed the road, but would open it in twenty minutes. Of course, twenty minutes came and went; thirty minutes came and went, and then an hour. The snow kept falling.

"We are going to be here a while," the guide said, still insisting that this was the shortest route. Otherwise, we would have had to return to Fez to connect with the main highway that runs along the shoreline, and that would have taken a few hours longer.

There was no letup; the snowflakes didn't stop, and officials at the checkpoint prevented us from proceeding onto the mountain road to Marrakech. We detoured to the coastal road, and reached our destination many hours later.

When I returned to the U.S. and met up with some of my colleagues, my first words were: "I got caught in a snowstorm!" They were astonished. It's the unusual, the exotic, that makes a good story of a travel vacation.

Obviously, I could have done without the snow. I wanted to meet the Moroccan Jewry, once part of the forgotten Jews of the Maghreb.

The Maghreb Jewish refugees who came to Israel were lineal descendants of one of the most ancient pre-Carthaginian and productive civilizations in Jewish history. Historians tell us that in days past, Jews spoke Arabic if they lived among Arabs, and a mixture of Berber and Hebrew if they resided among the Berbers. Some reported that Jews regarded themselves as French and were treated as such. They added that Jews were not popular with Arabs, and did not socialize with them.

During the Islamic renaissance between the ninth and thirteenth centuries, the Moroccan Jewish community fully rivaled Spanish Jewry in its affluence and literacy. After the fifteenth century, Maghreb Jewish ranks were augmented by some 40,000 Sephardic newcomers, including 20,000 who settled in Fez, all fugitives of the Inquisition and the Spanish expulsion. From the medieval to the early modern era, the galaxy of Maghreb Jews included poet Yehuda Ibn Abbas, religious philosopher Moses Maimonides, mathematician Yusuf Ibn Aknin, and others who were renowned for their scholarship in science and literature.

We must remember that Jews in North Africa lived under Islamic jurisdiction and were classified as a *"protected people,"* or *dhimmi:* Christian and Jewish subjects of a Muslim ruler. "The Muslim ruler was supposed to guarantee their lives, liberty and property, and was responsible for their freedom of religious practice," writes author Michael M. Laskier in his book, *North African Jewry in the Twentieth Century: The Jews of Morocco, Tunisia, and Algeria.* Even though *dhimmi* paid a special poll tax, they were kept at a disadvantage legally and judicially.

⌐

About 30 million people live in Morocco, which is located in the northwest corner of Africa and has been inhabited through the centuries by Carthaginians, Romans, Christians, Berbers, and Arabs, as well as Jews.

"It would be futile to try to fix a precise date for the establishment of the first Jewish settlements in North Africa, but it is generally accepted that the first communities of any importance date from about the time of the destruction of the Temple in Jerusalem by Nebuchadnezzar in 586 BCE," notes author Andre Chouraqui. Moreover, as far back as the first century CE, arriving Jews converted many North African Berber tribes to Judaism.

Berbers, as defined by Fergus Fleming in his book, *The Sword and the Cross: Two Men and an Empire of Sand,* are a "race of semi-pastoralists who claim priority as the first inhabitants of North Africa." Having converted to Judaism, they resisted Arab incursion into North Africa until they were conquered and forced to convert to Islam.

Chouraqui points out that a fighting Jewish army put an end to Greek Cyrenaica at the beginning of the second century CE. The initial military successes of the Jews indicate an effective organization and an intensive penetration among the Berber masses.

Encyclopaedia Judaica notes that even the Arab conquest of Morocco and its conversion to Islam did not bring about the elimination of the Jews or those Berbers who had converted to Judaism.

Berbers played a substantial role in the development of the Maghreb. For instance, several Islamic dynasties, both Arab and Berber, controlled North Africa between the seventh and sixteenth centuries, though after the 1500s, Morocco was controlled by the Sharifian dynasty, which is still in power today.

Even into the middle of the twentieth century, half of the Jews of North Africa were descendants of Berber converts. At one time, many of the Berbers of Morocco were Jewish.

I kept hearing stories about Berber bravery—that they make the best soldiers, and that their women stand as true fighters. Often cited was one woman who remains a legend in Moroccan history. She was said to have been born to a poor Jewish family of cave dwellers. This female Berber military leader was known as the Jewish Berber priestess, Kahena, queen of the Berbers.

Kahena dwelt in the Aurès Mountains and led Berber tribes. In 688 CE, Kahena threw her Berber forces against the Arabs and routed them. The victory made her Queen of the Maghreb. A later defeat led to the Berber tribes surrendering and converting to Islam, although the Berbers who had accepted Judaism stayed loyal, according to Chouraqui.

⁓

Berbers love to bargain, and here are some of their pointers: Make sure you start low and bargain hard. After the merchant offers you the opening price, come in with one-quarter to one-third less. Then the true fun begins, the price going back and forth like a yo-yo, especially in the *souk,* where bargaining is accepted.

As mentioned, you know you have succeeded if merchants call you a "Berber." They are complimenting your acumen and perhaps your longevity.

Upon my return to the U.S, I asked an Arab lady from Morocco by the name of Fatima what languages she spoke, and when she said Berber, I asked her what that language sounded like. "Like Hebrew," she replied, "with all the guttural, deep *Het* letter sounds."

Before I leave our discussion of Berbers, a note from tour guide, Chaim Mizrachi, in Israel, told me that many Moroccan Jewish families now living in Israel have Berber names. Some Jews still speak Berber, both in Israel and Morocco.

To this day, the image of the Berbers as strong desert horsemen is kept alive. It may be touristy, but no more so than American Wild West shows or rodeos. At programs and shows geared to visitors, Berber tribes perform and entertain; they gallop about and shoot antique rifles as if in a real skirmish. With Arabic melodies floating through the air, and men and women resplendent in traditional wedding dress, they make a *spectacle magnifique*.

Another mirage occurred in Casablanca, where I began my journey.

At Mohammed V International Airport, I began searching for the little airport hangar that I had seen a million times. There, out on the tarmac, Bogey, Ingrid, Paul, and Claude Rains, who, as Captain Louis Renault, gave orders to his police: "Major Strasser has been shot. Round up the usual suspects."

And there he is—Rick, telling Captain Renault, "Louis, I think this is the beginning of a beautiful friendship."

Casablanca should be the beginning of any trip to Morocco. But I don't want to linger too long in this city on the Atlantic Ocean. Better to head to Fez or Marrakech and beyond to the Atlas Mountains, where it snows in winter. Or travel south to the fortified towns built by the Portuguese, especially Essaouira, now a very "in-place," also located on the Atlantic Ocean.

Still, one of the joys of visiting Morocco is Casablanca, a busy city, port, airport, with busy hotels and very busy restaurants. On a Sunday afternoon, it's hard to get a table at the crowded Restaurant de Peche in the port frequented by middle-class families speaking French and Arabic, and ordering up excellent fish dinners.

Other cities may be more attractive, such as Marrakech and Essaouira, but let's face it—none can compare to the social, entertainment, and cultural life of this city. "It's the movies and cafes—that's why I live in Casablanca," said our driver.

Casablanca, with its broad avenues, skyscrapers, and luxury hotels in the "new city," and traditional, much smaller whitish-gray blockhouses in many of the "old city" quarters, make this a city of contrasts and certainly not the roguish city of Bogey and Ingrid.

Five million people reside in Casablanca, one of the four largest municipalities on the African continent. And while there are small pockets of Jews living throughout the country's major cities, the bulk of them remaining in this kingdom reside in this metropolis.

Casablanca means "white house," a name given to this urban center first by the Portuguese, and then by the Spanish, who plied the waters of the Atlantic and established fortresses and harbor towns along the coast. Until the eighteenth century, Casablanca was a mere fishing village. Then, it began to boom as the principal port of North Africa. It held a major role in the trading of sugar, tea, wool, and corn products to the Western world.

In 1943, the Casablanca Conference was held at the Anfa Hotel and was attended by President Franklin D. Roosevelt, Winston Churchill, and Charles de Gaulle. They planned the Allies' European strategy.

To make a city great in the eyes of the world, rulers and governments erect a monument, a statue, a building, or a house of worship. In Casablanca's case, I marveled at the Hasan II mosque, a must-see for every tourist. The minaret is the highest in the world and is said to symbolize tolerance and peace. Touring this monument rising out of the ocean, I admire the facades encrusted with mosaics. The flagstone, marble, and granite make up a massive structure that can hold 25,000 persons, plus 80,000 in the courtyards and surrounding squares.

Between 1948 and 1968, tens of thousands of Moroccan Jews moved to Casablanca either to settle permanently or to await emigration. Eventually, most went to Israel, France, Canada, and the U.S.

Since most of the approximate 4,000 Jews in Morocco today live in Casablanca, we must stress at the outset that this is one Jewish community with hardly any assimilation or intermarriage. While few in numbers, this is neither an already-dead community nor even a dying one, despite all the headlines which for years have reported the demise of Moroccan Jewry.

Serge Berdugo, ambassador at large to the kingdom of Morocco, general secretary of the Council of Jewish Communities of Morocco, and a former minister of tourism, has pointed out that in Casablanca, there are twenty functioning synagogues, four Jewish caterers, ten kosher butchers, five kosher restaurants, a Jewish sports club, two Jewish social centers, a Jewish youth center, a Jewish museum, a senior citizens home, and three Jewish school networks.

Still, Jacky Kadoch, president of the Jewish Community of Marrakech-Essaouira, is not so sure Jews will still be here in twenty-five years. "It's the demographics," he declared, repeating what I would hear over and over again—that most of the young people leave. Kadoch and other Jewish leaders have noted that not only do these young adults depart to study abroad, but also, while they are in foreign lands, they often marry, never to return. Demographics are not in their favor.

But others, such as Ambassador Berdugo, have noted that several families do return each year to Morocco, and that this could balance out the loss in emigration of the young. He also noted that this is not only a Jewish concern, adding, "There are 4 million Moroccans abroad."

Along with his comments about the return of Jewish families to the country, the ambassador also voiced hope for peace in the Middle East. "Morocco," he declared, "is a living example of Jews and Arabs living in a normal relationship. With peace, more Jews would want to come back."

I also asked tour guide Raphael Elmaleh in Casablanca if the Jewish community of Morocco will survive. "Everybody has been asking that question for two thousand years when there were Jews here," he answered. "While the community is reducing in numbers, there'll always be Jews here."

Mrs. Joelle Bensimon, an American investor who travels frequently to Morocco and was herself born in Fez, insists that as long as the king is in power, the Jews will live in peace. She left Morocco as a teenager, and recalled her father telling her that when one Moroccan king was on his deathbed, he told his son—the next monarch—to treat the Jews well and everything would be all right.

In the wake of the riots sweeping North Africa in the spring of 2011, Moroccan protestors marching in largely peaceful demonstrations called for some of the king's powers to be handed over to a newly elected government. The king has promised "comprehensive constitutional reform." Morocco, more than Algeria, does allow limited freedom of expression and has remained relatively peaceful. And on June 30, 2011, Moroccans approved constitutional changes proposed by King Mohammed VI which would introduce greater political openness and according to the *New York Times*, "ward off the unrest that has swept the Arab world." Under the proposals, the prime minister would no longer be appointed by the king, but would be selected by the majority party in parliament. Mohammed VI "is considered to be a less rigid ruler than his father, King Hassan II," added the newspaper.

Jacky Kadoch said the Jews in Morocco find themselves in a good situation and that the present king, Mohammed VI, remains serious about democracy, women's rights programs, and other issues.

A Moroccan government release noted that the nation remains the largest single Jewish community in the Arab world, and has enjoyed the protection of its monarchs since the eighteenth century. Jews agree: that Moroccan kings have been very good for the community.

Indeed, Mohammed V protected the Jewish community during World War II, as did the timely arrival of the Allied forces, which landed in North Africa in 1942 and overthrew the Vichy government. The latter caused incessant humiliation for the Jews. The story is that when the Germans demanded lists of Jews to prepare for deportations, Mohammed V reportedly answered: "There are no Jews here, only Moroccans." He refused to turn over lists of his Jewish subjects to the Nazis.

Considering all that is happening today across North Africa, the Middle East, and beyond, to Iran, why would several thousand Jews live in an Arab country? The simplistic answer, but with an element of truth in it, is "business." Most of the Jewish community is middle-class, comfortable but not wealthy. Since they manage successful businesses they are reluctant to leave. As for seniors, they, too, are staying put in their communities, in familiar surroundings, with their families, clubs, and institutions that help them, especially since Moroccan Jewish tradition calls for helping the poor with food and clothing.

According to the American Jewish Joint Distribution Committee (JDC), "Moroccan Jewry is largely self-sufficient, but still needs help maintaining the medical, educational, and other welfare programs and services it has established." JDC also helps provide Jewish and secular education for all Jewish children through the components of the Jewish school system: Ozar Hatorah, Chabad, and Alliance Israelite Universelle.

According to Berdugo, each year more than 40,000 Jews of Moroccan origin return to the country to vacation, to celebrate religious ceremonies, or to pray at holy sites. As in Cuba, visitors are helping to sustain this Jewish community through tourism and investment. Tour guide Chaim Mizrachi in Tel Aviv says his agency sends about 15,000 Israeli-Moroccan Jewish tourists a year to Morocco.

Like the other countries I visited in traveling the diaspora, such as Russia and India, Moroccan Jewry is benefiting from some Jews returning and settling here again. Small numbers of professionals and businesspeople from France, Israel, and the U.S. are opening up offices and businesses. Some observers put the number of new arrivals at about fifty to seventy-five a year, including Jews from France, some of whom are moving their families to Morocco—especially since the French Republic has seen a marked rise in anti-Semitism and anti-Jewish violence by radical elements in the large Muslim community in France.

Avi Dayan, a jeweler from Canada who takes a group of Moroccan Jews every year from North America to Morocco, pointed out that many of the students who go abroad open up branches of their parents' businesses.

One way to tell that newcomers are entering the country is the fact that the JDC is sponsoring a tutorial class at the Ozar Hatorah school for children of families who have returned to Morocco, many of whom need language skills.

According to author and journalist Raphael Rothstein, writing in the *National Jewish News* in 2007, there's a joke circulating in Europe: "[I]n view of the rise of anti-Semitism in France and the Arab-Islamic threat to Israel, the safest place for a French Jew is Morocco."

Meanwhile, Moroccan Jewish youth remain very committed to Judaism. Many keep kosher and attend synagogue services. Jews in Casablanca are proud of their Jewish school system, which includes a half-dozen schools. Educational networks Ozar Hatorah and the Alliance Israelite Universelle schools are prominent.

About 700 Jewish students—a remarkable figure—attend Jewish schools, where the education is quite good, I was told. The problem arises when the young Jewish high school graduate obtains this solid educational foundation in Morocco and then heads to France, Canada, Great Britain, and the U.S. for higher education and doesn't return.

Guide Raphael Elmaleh pointed out that while it's true many students go abroad after graduation in Morocco, "a portion do return to Morocco to take over the father's business."

Neveh Shalom is the Ozar Hatorah school located at 140 Taha Hussein, ex-rue Galilee. This is a girls and boys primary school, and the same building houses the Rashi community high school for girls and boys.

Alliance Israelite schools in Casablanca include a kindergarten and primary school at 83 Boulevard, Moulay Youssef; Ecole Maimonides High School, on 8 rue d'Indochine; and Ecole Normale Hebraique at 28 rue du Chasseur Jules Gros. A number of Muslim students attend Alliance high schools, but not Ecole Normale.

Ohalie Yosef Yitzhak Lubavitch, at 174 Boulevard Ziraoui is about to close, it was reported. I met and talked with Mrs. Raizel Raskin before the proposed closure. She told me that attendance came to about a hundred students in the well-kept classrooms. Mrs. Raskin and her late husband, Rabbi Yehuda Leib Raskin, served the Jewish community of Morocco for many years. She stayed on to help educate and inspire. A *mikveh* is located here, as is a Chabad synagogue.

About 120 primary and secondary students benefit from JDC-supported special education and tutorial classes, as do 30 Ozar Hatorah students; some of the latter have learning difficulties, and attend tutorial classes if they need additional academic assistance.

Bet Chabad is located at rue al Khaouarizmi, ex, J.J. Rousseau, corner 10 rue Washington, Casablanca, 20000.

For such a small community, I am amazed that there are twenty-three synagogues, eighteen of them holding a daily *minyan,* the rest, weekend *minyanim.*

Most tourists visit and pray at Temple Beth El, 61 rue Jaber Ben Hayane (ex rue Verlel-Hanus), Casablanca. A *minyan* is held every morning and every evening. Beth El, one of the largest congregations, is the main synagogue, and American and Israeli tourists attend services here. Seeing the stained-glass windows, done in the Marc Chagall style, is a moving experience. One marvels at the hall's beautiful chandelier, as well as two menorahs that grace the *bimah.* Moreover, the paintings and handmade decorations add to the structure's attractiveness.

The affluent neighborhood of Anfa boasts many handsome villas. A beautifully designed synagogue, Migdal David, was built here about ten years ago because the Jews of that neighborhood wanted their house of prayer nearby so they would not have to drive on the Sabbath. If you would like to attend this synagogue, ask someone in the community to direct you, as it can be difficult to find. This house of worship also contains a *mikveh.*

A highlight of any visit to Morocco is a trip to the lovely Museum of Moroccan Judaism, Le Musée du Judaïsme Marocain—the only Jewish Museum in a Muslim country, according to Dr. Simon Levy, the president of the museum foundation. The museum is located at 81, rue Chasseur Jules Gros, Casablanca, in the suburb of Oasis, fifteen minutes from the city center.

Architecturally, the museum is a gem, housed in a lovely villa and surrounded by lush gardens, palm trees, and a lovely patio. But inside is the real treasure: the artifacts of a once-great Jewish community, gathered from hundreds of Moroccan Jewish communities. Even though the collection is still a work in progress, a vast array of Judaica is professionally and carefully placed in glass enclosures, revealing the history of the Jewish community and its influence on modern Moroccan society.

The exhibits include historic artifacts such as documents, traditional clothing, and ceremonial objects, a vast collection of photographs featuring synagogues, the *mellah* (Jewish quarter), and other landmarks that remain from 2,000 years of Jewish civilization in this region.

Unlike Algeria, the exodus of Jews from Morocco took time. Jews departed first in 1947 and 1948, with the birth of Israel, and then again in 1955 and 1956, the years Morocco gained independence. When Arab governments assumed power in the Maghreb and beyond, "emigration soared to record figures," according to author Chouraqui. A sudden switch in the attitude of Morocco regarding its Jewish citizens occurred when that country refused to allow Jews to leave. "Nevertheless, thousands of Moroccan Jews braved the hazards of clandestine immigration, an operation which displayed great courage and heroism as well as remarkable efficiency," wrote Chouraqui. "In 1961 and 1962, the rate of emigration swelled anew and brought about the final liquidation of many Jewish communities in the Maghreb." Chouraqui added that by 1972, only 80,000 Jews lived in Morocco. By 2011, only 4,000 remained.

One emigration incident turned out badly. In January 1961, a 65-foot boat called the *Pisces,* secretly transporting forty-three Jews from Morocco to Gibraltar, sank. Only the Spanish captain and his brother-in-law survived, Laskier noted.

Perhaps long forgotten because of their role in secretly rescuing Jews from Europe and Ethiopia, for instance, is "the fact that the task of organizing the emigration fell to the Mossad Le-Aliah Bet, Mossad [Israel's secret service apparatus], and the Immigration Department of the Jewish Agency," pointed out Laskier.

According to Laskier, many factors came together to hasten the need for Jews to leave North Africa from 1948 on: political instability in the region; Jewish anxiety about living among Muslims without French protection; the birth of Israel and North African Muslim solidarity with the Arab states; as well as the desire of many to emigrate to the new Jewish homeland. In the end, they fled, leaving everything behind.

To observe relics from centuries-old Jewish communities in the museum, including Torah scrolls, Kiddush cups from Fez, Hanukkah menorahs, *tefillin* bags from Casablanca, kaftans beautifully designed and embroidered, and *mezuzahs* from Essaouira, visit Tuesday through Friday, 10:00 a.m. to 6:00 p.m., and by appointment on Sundays. Website: www.casajewish museum.com.

"O Fez, all the beauties of the Earth are united in thee!" a historian once wrote about one of the oldest spiritual and intellectual centers of Morocco, once the home of a large Jewish community of personalities whose names live on, and of famous *yeshivas* and at least forty synagogues.

The same historian is said to have declared: "O Fez! May God preserve thy land and thy gardens, and give thee to drink of the water of snows!"

I thought it was a dream; it wasn't! One morning, I was startled awake by the sound of the *muezzin* calling the faithful to prayer before dawn. This before-sunrise call was deafening, just about shattering my eardrums. The mosque and the top of a minaret must have abutted the hotel. In most modern mosques these days, electronics amplify the *muezzin* during his task.

The enormous sound of the prayer call arrived between four or five o'clock in the morning, destroying my sleep. For over a thousand years, Fez Jews have heard the five-times-a-day call of the *muezzin,* so they were used to it. Not I.

The Fez market *is* the mother of all markets. It is synonymous with Morocco, wrote author Paul Bowles. Some people never go out of the medina, which contains cafes, apartments, household items, jewelry, tanneries, antiques shops, rugs, and food. The Fez medina is believed to be the world's largest contiguous car-free urban area.

Nothing can compare with the throbbing *souk* in Fez. That's why many female travelers know that besides sightseeing, entertainment, and touring, Morocco is a shopper's paradise. It helps having a male—husband or significant other, son, nephew, or cousin—along in the *souks.* Males often enjoy the bargaining that goes along with a trip to the market. Take in the brassware, jewelry, carpets, leather goods, clothes, kaftans, pottery, and on and on.

More important, one must watch out for donkeys. Yes, donkeys! When you hear shouts of the word *balek* in Arabic, or *Attention!* in French, get out of the way; you don't want to be smacked by a donkey laden with crates or sacks rumbling past with only inches to spare on either side.

By a miracle of history and geography, Fez, located in the north-central part of Morocco, is a city where the Middle Ages can be seen and studied firsthand. Walking in this complex, fascinating *souk,* with its dark shadows and evocations of the past, travelers begin to understand those past centuries. The walls of the houses press so tightly upon each other that only donkeys and pedestrians can thread their way through these medieval passageways.

Fez's climate is said to be warmer because it was built in a wide crevasse below the plateau of the plain, and is thus sheltered from icy winds. Not so during the winter I traveled to Morocco; I learned from my snow experience that the weather can be unpredictable.

In these crowded markets, it's easy to get lost. My guide wore his *djellaba* with a sharply peaked hood. He looked like the grim reaper. Maybe that's why I felt secure as we walked and walked, seeing only a small portion of the four thousand tiny cubicles that serve as shops.

It was Idris I who seized control of Morocco in the late eighth century from the Muslim Abbasid caliphate of Baghdad. He founded Fez on the right bank of the River Fez in 789 CE. His son Idris II was instrumental in unifying the Maghreb from his base in Fez which he refounded on the left bank of the River Fez in 808 CE.

When Idris II opened Fez to Jewish settlers, he began a glorious period of Moroccan Jewry. Despite often suffering under Muslim attacks, Jews maintained a profound sense of their distinctive culture.

Years ago, I attended a banquet hosted by Moroccan Jews in New York, many of them young men and women who were born in that North African country. I admired their spirit in keeping Moroccan Jewish customs alive and in getting the message out about the Sephardic contributions to Judaism. I also marveled at the lavishly colored kaftans and jewels. The reputation of Moroccan Jewish craftsmen for gold and silver making, jewelry design, as well as leatherwork and cloth embroidery, reaches worldwide proportions.

As a former capital of Morocco and a holy city, Fez grew to about 200,000 persons by the fourteenth century. Today it boasts 800,000 residents and draws tourists from all over the world.

Fez is shrouded in mystery. Each traveler will find something unique behind its high walls.

I felt as if I had taken a step backward into past centuries.

~

Even in the twelfth century, Fez was a major spiritual and intellectual centers of Morocco, even though Jews often had to hide their Judaism. More than forty synagogues, a Bet Din, communal ovens, ritual baths, and schools—all were located in the Jewish quarter, known as the *mellah*.

Many traditions and stories abound as to the origin of the word *mellah*. The word stems from the Arabic word for salt, and refers to the area of Fes el Jedid, the location where the Merenids had transferred the entire Jewish population of Fez in 1438. Jews were restricted to and lived in this ghetto, a city within a city. No two were alike, says Chouraqui, who adds, "[T]he worst misery in the European ghetto [is] not comparable to the moral and material degradation that existed in the *mellahs* of the foothills of the Atlas or the remote Sahara until they emptied with the migration of their inhabitants to Israel."

The sultan knew what he was doing; he gave Jews the nonproductive land near the city on which to build their quarter, with airless alleyways and dark, narrow streets.

Some say the name *mellah* was derived from a job that Muslim city authorities assigned to Jews: salting the decapitated heads of criminals and the like before they were hung up to adorn the town's gates and walls.

Guides tell you that Jews under the sultans lived in the *mellah,* and they usually go on to explain the significance of the word. They may or may not tell you it was a "social prison," according to author Chouraqui.

In Marrakech and other *mellahs* of southern Morocco, Jewish life was difficult to say the least. In Meknes where 6,000 Jews resided in 1900, Jews lived better, with just over 1,000 living in 260 homes located next to the palace. Crowded conditions certainly existed from the nineteenth century up until the mid-twentieth century. In today's Morocco, however, Jews are not forced to live in a *mellah*.

"Feverish activity could not hide the underlying despair. The windowless houses, the poor construction, the misery which oozed from the very stones, and the expression on the faces of the *mellah's* inhabitants attested by their ugliness and their vulgarity to the fact that happiness, security, and living itself were rare pleasures in these surroundings. Rot and decay infested the houses in time; only the wooden or iron beams which shored them up kept them standing," notes Chouraqui.

"The splendor, the colors, the rich aromas, the Arabian Nights world that existed in even the poorest medina of North Africa was absent from the Jewish *mellah*," adds Chouraqui. There was no running water in the homes of the *mellah,* only a vat at the entrance of each street that served as a communal source of water.

In the *mellah,* "with a few exceptions, [Jews] . . . were not allowed to ride horses at all, according to Budgett Meakin, in *The Land of the Moors.*

Since the Fez *mellah* remained close to the sultan's palace, he allegedly protected them. The exterior walls of the *mellah* houses kept out the world, and "the narrow alleys climbed and twisted haphazardly. Street surfaces often flooded under the slightest rain, and a horrible stench arose from the rubbish strewn about them," writes Chouraqui.

While Jews were allotted a quarter of their own, they were forced to pay high taxes.

Even so, the affluence of Fez "gave rise to a level of activity which tore through the atmosphere of stagnation," according to Chouraqui. The area was a beehive of activity, with Jewish merchants, craftsmen, and day laborers working hard to meet their needs. Those that failed, begged.

Jews helped make Fez a commercial center because they traveled widely and traded. Though they lived in a closed society, violence often struck the community. Even as late as 1912, two weeks after the establishment of the French Protectorate over Morocco, a revolt broke out in the *mellah* against 12,000 Jews. Their homes were attacked and ransacked and set on fire by an Arab mob. About 60 Jews lost their lives, says the *Encyclopaedia Judaica.* In 1947 there were 22,484 Jews living in Fez and its surroundings; by 1969, there were only 1,000 Jews left in the area.

I especially wanted to visit the home of Maimonides (1135–1204), who remains the most illustrious figure in Judaism in the post-Talmudic era. A doctor, he stands as the most significant Jewish intellect and teacher from the time of the Prophets until Spinoza.

According to the *Encyclopaedia Judaica*, "The influence of Maimonides on the future development of Judaism is incalculable. No spiritual leader of the Jewish people in the post-Talmudic period has exercised such an influence both in his own and subsequent generations."

Born in Cordoba as Moses Ben Maimon, and known in rabbinical literature as the *Rambam,* from the acronym Rabbi Moshe ben Maimon, he is better known by the Hellenized version of his name, Maimonides.

Fez may be old, but I felt I could hear the footsteps of Jews echoing in the street, especially those of Maimonides, "the greatest rationalistic philosopher of Judaism, and author of the *Guide for the Perplexed,* according to H. H. Ben-Sasson, editor of *A History of the Jewish People.*

Maimonides's family arrived in Fez in 1160 and left in 1165 due to the martyrdom of the leading rabbi of the city, Judah ibn Shoshan. Maimonides fled the tyranny of the Almohads, a violent fundamentalist Muslim sect originating among the Berbers. In the years when the family lived in Fez, many Jews had adopted Islam, "and their consciences were troubling them," according to the *Encyclopaedia Judaica.* Maimonides wrote that "a Jew must leave the country where he is forced to transgress the divine law," and not remain in a kingdom of forced conversion. So, the family left Fez in 1165. A month after their departure, they landed at Acre where he remained for about five months. After a tour of the Holy Land, he took up residence in Fostat, where for eight years he devoted himself to study. Only after 1185, when he was appointed one of the physicians to al-Fadil, virtual ruler of Egypt, did Maimonides receive fame, according to the *Encyclopaedia Judaica.* In the years between 1185 and 1193, he wrote the *Guide for the Perplexed.* He died in 1204 in Fostat, Egypt. His remains were taken to Tiberias for burial, and his grave remains an object of pilgrimage. I am happy to say I have visited most of the cities where the *Rambam* made his home, including his birthplace in Cordoba, his home in Fez, then Cairo and Jerusalem, and his burial site in Tiberias.

So I made my way to the *medina* where the guide and I found the *Street of the Jews* where Maimonides may have lived. A single ray of sunlight allowed me to see down the narrow, dark alley in this medieval section in Fez. In this claustrophobic passageway stands the building that supposedly housed Maimonides and his family, then refugees from Spain.

No one is sure, I am told, if this is the correct house. Possibly, Maimonides walked in this sunless alleyway, with so little space that it did not constitute a street. It was an experience to touch the doorway and recall that even in the poverty-stricken ghetto, Jewish doors were always open, and a warm welcome offered to the weary traveler.

"Thank you, Rabbi," I fantasized saying to him, "for allowing me and thousands of others to come to your home."

Today, two synagogues in Fez serve about a hundred Jews, mostly senior citizens. Em Habanim, similar to a community center, with a small restaurant and a *mikveh,* is one. Avi Dayan told me that one of the donors of the building was his grandfather, Eli Tobali. "It was common in Morocco," he added, for the synagogue to bear the name of the person who financed it. The second synagogue in Fez is the Ben Saddoun congregation.

One can visit another house of worship, the restored ibn Danan, said to be the oldest extant synagogue in Fez. Its restoration in the Old City was part of a comprehensive UNESCO project to preserve the monuments and fabric of this medieval city. Its rededication in February 1999 was attended by more than 400 persons.

After the independence of Israel, the Jews in Morocco, as in other Muslim lands, often suffered from severe attacks by Muslims. For 2,000 years, Jews were a large part of the Moroccan economy, and they certainly were part of the Fez market. One guide told me, "We were sad when the Jews left; they had economic power."

Entering Marrakech I recalled a line from Paul Bowles's novel, *Let It Come Down:* "Do you know Marrakech? Ah, you must go. In the winter, it is beautiful."

We checked into La Mamounia, the grande dame hotel in Marrakech. The establishment takes its name from the surrounding gardens, which were once called the "Arset El Mamoun." The park covers nearly twenty acres.

Hotel La Mamounia is located on Avenue Bab Jdid, in the heart of Marrakech, within an idyllic seventeen-acre garden surrounded by twelfth-century ramparts. Described as a palace, the hotel has 171 rooms and 56 suites. The hotel stands as a legend, a fable unfolding timeless Marrakech.

An ambitious renovation by French designer Jacques Garcia, unveiled in 2009, has turned the original deco complex into a lavish, distinctly Moroccan landmark, decked out with a spa, a fitness center, and a quartet of restaurants.

Marrakech has served as one of the greatest trading centers of the Sahara and is described as the last large outpost this side of the snowcapped High Atlas Mountains and the desert beyond.

Some believe you don't need a guide in Marrakech. The only itinerary to follow is to find the next great meal, museum, outdoor market, or cafe in this adventurous and exotic destination. Still, at least you should have a guide in the *souk*.

As I sat in this luxurious hotel surrounded by Marrakech's twelfth-century ramparts, sumptuous palaces, and gardens, I thought of the illustrious names of those who had stayed here before me. Shall I start with Winston S. Churchill?

Mirage again! There he is! Winnie—a photo of Churchill standing in the garden of La Mamounia. The great statesman's left hand is in his suit jacket pocket, his right hand holding a long cigar. Another photo with no hat on; but next to it, the famous shot of Churchill sitting in a patch of desert, painting the landscape. He is wearing a white suit and a brown hat, a cigar held tight in his mouth, with paintbrush in hand.

Historic La Mamounia Hotel has been visited by hundreds of dignitaries. Churchill himself took President Franklin D. Roosevelt to the hotel after the Casablanca conference in 1943. Churchill, the consummate artist, stayed at this wonderful establishment and is reported to have said that the view from the roof was *paintaceous*.

Other stars, artists, and government people who have stopped at La Mamounia include Isaac Stern, Yoko Ono, Sharon Stone, Tom Cruise, Elton John, Joan Collins, and Catherine Deneuve, as well as Hillary and Chelsea Clinton, Margaret Thatcher, Queen Elizabeth II, and Ronald Reagan. Also, Enrico Macias, the famous and still-popular French Jewish international singer and musician, who was from Constantine, Algeria.

Churchill had his own suite at La Mamounia, and this writer was priv-ileged to see it. Brightly colored furniture fills the room. I stood by his desk, which remains untouched, and even spy one of his old hats hanging from a coat rack. The suite is preserved exactly as it was when he last stayed here.

I went up to the rooftop of La Mamounia at dusk and watched the sun set. Churchill was right; it is *paintaceous.*

"Wait until five o'clock," El Kherchi Abdellatif, our guide in Marrakech, said. "I have something magnificent to show you."

I was standing in the huge Djemaa el-Fna Square, the cultural and entertainment crossroads for all of Morocco. No wonder the tour buses were lined up around the square.

The city's main square comes to life each evening with acrobats and storytellers and food stalls. *Djemaa el-Fna* means "Square of Execution." A century ago, the heads of people executed for conspiracy against the sul-tan were publicly exhibited in this square. But today, it is a huge stage for performers, outdoor stalls, and cafes. This frenetic square—said to be the greatest in all of Africa—is a sight not to be missed. First, go up to one of the rooftop cafe terraces for a grandstand seat. Here, you can observe the spectacle below: costumed musicians, acrobats, snake charmers, fortunetell-ers, all practicing their crafts. And in the square itself, for a few coins, you can take a photo of these exhibitions.

Brassware, jewelry, carpets, leather goods, and pottery can be obtained here, in and around the square. Of course, if you miss these items in Mar-rakech, you will have every opportunity to buy similar goods in other cities.

As dusk fell on the square, the mystique of North Africa enveloped me.

After I returned to the U.S., I heard about the terrorist attack in the Djemaa el-Fna Square on April 28, 2011. A bomb tore through a busy cafe known as the Argana, which is frequented by foreigners. Fourteen of the sixteen killed were foreigners, including an Israeli couple and Peter Moss, from London, who had worked for *The Jewish Chronicle,* according to BBC news. The method used in the attack pointed to al-Qaeda in the Islamic Maghreb.

Regarding terrorism, Morocco generally has been quiet over the years. In May 2003, 45 people including suicide bombers were killed, and more than 100 people were injured in Casablanca when that city was hit by terrorists. The heinous act was linked to al-Qaeda. At least three of the five targets in the terrorist operation were Jewish: a Jewish social club and restaurant, a Jewish cemetery in the old city, and a Jewish-owned Italian restaurant. The blasts occurred on a Friday night, but obviously Jews were not in the Jewish locations, nor were Jews among the victims. Since Jews were the target of the terrorists, the community was shaken.

There are so many wonderful sights in this city, where even in winter it feels comfortable temperature-wise—much warmer than the cities in the north. Palaces, pavilions, and gardens make up the Marrakech scene.

Dominating the city is the twelfth-century Koutoubia Mosque designed by medieval architects; its minaret not only dominates the city but can also be seen for quite a distance outside of the municipality.

Don't miss the tannery, still in its medieval state: Huge vats with dyes and muddied waters, and the skins basking in the sun. Do not fret. You will have a chance to buy leather products, if the repugnant smell doesn't get you first.

I found the visit to the tannery memorable; believe me, the sights and smells will last you a lifetime. Nowhere else in the *medina* do you get a stronger sense of suddenly being transported back to the Middle Ages than you do at this tannery. From the surrounding roof terraces, you can spot the vats that are used for soaking skins after the hair and flesh have been removed from the sheep, goats, cows, and camels. Keep your distance from the vats because the decaying skins and the animal urine—used for centuries to cure the leather—will cause you to hold your nose. Just watch the soaking and drying, and then witness the end product: leather jackets and bags on display, for purchase, of course. It's definitely a worthwhile travel experience. While travelers have sung the praises of Moroccan leather goods for ages, I am surprised to learn that these men form a venerable guild in which jobs are passed down from father to son.

In contrast to the white houses of Casablanca, the walls of the houses here in Marrakech are pink, the color of the desert. If you like wintry scenes (without being in one), you can gaze at the snowcapped peaks of the Atlas Mountains in the distance.

"The city itself is expanding," said Jacky Kadoch, president of the Jewish Community of Marrakech, a small Jewish community—about 250 persons—with two synagogues. The newer, modern house of worship is located in the New Town at Boulevard Zerktouni, Impasse des Moulins, des Moulins (Gueliz), and is visited by most Jewish tourists on Friday night and Saturday morning, when services are held. Men and women sit separately in this Orthodox synagogue, which contains 200 seats.

Another synagogue is located in the Old Town, at rue Talmud Torah. The *shamash* blesses all visitors. Most tourists do not mind his asking for a donation. As two British tourists told me, "He's looking after our heritage; it's the least we can do."

Jacky Kadoch indicated that tourism is expanding, and many Europeans, including Jewish businesspeople, are investing in this commercial city. After all, it is a former capital, a tourist center, and a metropolis for the High Atlas Mountains and the northwest Sahara. You can still observe mountain and desert people visiting the city markets to exchange skins, hides, dates, and animals for cereals and imported goods.

Once the capital of Morocco, the city has always retained its economic importance. Indeed, it is said that from 1745, Jews lived in Marrakech in better conditions than anywhere else in Morocco. Since *yeshivot* (religious houses of study) flourished in the city, many Jews from throughout North Africa came to study with the *kabbalists*. The guides and Jewish leaders taught me that when a vast Jewish population existed here, many of Morocco's educated Jewish elite inclined toward mysticism and studied *kabbalah*.

The *souks* (markets) in Marrakech are picturesque, though not quite as crowded or medieval as those in Fez. I found bargains galore. In these markets, one is obliged to bargain. Indeed, it seems bargaining is the most popular sport in the country. Whether in busy old markets, boutiques, hotels, or airports, the reduce-the-price discourse comes into play.

Before 1948, the year Israel achieved independence, about 30,000 Jews lived in Marrakech. In 1951, the Jewish population dropped to just 17,000, and by 1960, to only 10,000. In 1970, only a few hundred Jews remained. In 2011, about 250 Jews live in the city.

As I departed this "oasis city," I realized why Moroccan Jews have a special place in their hearts for Marrakech.

⌒

Even stylish travelers from all over Europe and North Africa, as well as the expatriates of Marrakech, think nothing of driving two hours from Marrakech to Essaouira to unwind, even for a few days.

Ah, Essaouira, Morocco's easiest and most-relaxed seaside-resort town.

A French architect, Theodore Cornut, laid out the town, which was actually built by European captives under the Frenchman's supervision. We find this *medina* attractive and clean, with wider streets and more open spaces, and while not what one experiences in Marrakech, the town does hum all day, and it's easy to navigate without any hassle, especially since vehicles are barred from *medina* streets.

"A northeast wind, a cloudless sky, a glowing sun." That's what a British consul wrote about Essaouira, a hundred years ago. His description of this Moroccan city, formerly called Mogador, was a Berber word meaning "safe anchorage." And he was right, for Essaouira is a good escape for the soul; it's quiet and calm.

Seagulls are continuously wheeling overhead, their cries occasionally silenced by the *muezzin's* call. The backdrop of the azure sky contrasts appealingly with the white buildings and sand-colored fortifications.

This white-walled port city on the Atlantic coast, considered also as a health resort, has captured the hearts of tourists. Midway between Safi and Agadir, its land was once inhabited by the Phoenicians and Carthaginians. Known for tourists wandering along its picturesque walls, *Essaouira* is thought to be derived from the Arabic word for "ramparts," but translates as "little image." The walls give the city its charm, as well as the blue-and-white *medina,* a "sweet retreat," especially if you have been in big-city Casablanca, or the frantic town of Fez.

In 1949, film director and actor Orson Welles stayed in Essaouira, where he filmed the classic version of *Othello* that contains several memorable scenes shot in the labyrinthine streets and alleys of the town's *medina.*

I sat in one of the cafes on the Place Mouley Hassan and watched the world go by, later dining on delicious, grilled fish, caught fresh that morning for lunch or dinner and displayed at stalls alongside cafes by the harbor. Actually, I walked with my guide to the stalls and watched as he carefully examined each fish, choosing the best one to be grilled for our lunch.

Travelers still find Essaouira exotic. It is quiet and calming, without the rush of the major cities, and somewhat off the beaten track. Its market is not old and overcrowded with visitors, and its passageways are wider than other *souks*. I relaxed while walking the seashore and seeing the fishermen mending their nets.

This city, like every city in Morocco, remains a good place to shop. For instance, to find quality woodwork in Essaouira, like cedar boxes, try Afalkay Art, 9 Place My Hassan.

In 1760, Sultan Mohammed Ben Abdallah founded the city and named the fortified port Essaouira to serve as a rival to Agadir by order of the sultan. Interestingly, *Encyclopedia Britannica* says "a colony of Moroccan Jews was installed to extend commerce." Sultan Mohammed Ben Abdallah chose ten important families and conferred upon them the title of "Merchant of the King." They received luxury housing, and were entrusted with missions to the European courts. For a century and a half they dominated Moroccan trade. These privileged personalities became the nucleus of a dynamic community which lasted until just after World War II, and gave the town a distinctly Jewish character. *Encyclopaedia Judaica* notes that everyone rested on the Sabbath and Jewish holidays.

Under the 1912 French protectorate, the city lost some of its economic importance, and only a small community of 5,000 Jews remained. Many of them left in the 1950s and '60s. By 1970 most lived in Europe, North America, and Israel, and only a few hundred Jews continued to live in Essaouira.

In 1844, the French bombarded the city to force Morocco to stop supporting Abd al Qadir, the leader of an Algerian resistance movement. The city went into a decline when the French turned Casablanca into the commercial capital, and when Agadir to the south opened to foreign trade.

There are only two Jews remaining in the somnolent town of Essaouira; one is Joseph Sebag, who operates a fine bookstore known as Galerie Aida, 2 Rue de la Skala. I bought Paul Bowles's book, *The Sheltering Sky*, from him.

In a way, Joseph Sebag's store is located in a historic spot. Several doors down stands a gutted-out synagogue, Synagogue Attias, which is literally falling apart. Once a popular house of worship, guides will show you the indentation where the Holy Ark once stood. According to Joseph Sebag, no restoration is planned for this house of worship, which closed in 1988.

Wherever I am in Morocco, especially in the Essaouira-Marrakech area, I know that behind the mountains lies the sun-baked Sahara Desert. Some Jews still remain there and practice the religious traditions that are shared by Moroccan Jews throughout the world, such as the North African Jewish custom of the veneration of *tzadikim* (righteous ones), or, in the case of Morocco, "saints," generally repudiated by Judaism.

This custom of the veneration of saints came about because the Jews lived among the Berbers. Saint veneration is virtually unknown among Jews elsewhere, according to author Chouraqui, who points out that while *Hasidim* hold their *tzadik* (righteous one) in veneration and gather around his grave, the practice was never as widespread as it was in North Africa.

At times, Arabs, Berbers, and Jews shared the same saints and traditions, such as a *hamsa* worn as a defense against evil. The *hamsa,* which in Arabic means "five," is also called the "hand of Fatima." Jews call this palm-shaped amulet, popular throughout the Middle East and North Africa, "the hand of Miriam." The *hamsa* is often incorporated into jewelry and/or hangs in homes as a superstitious defense against the evil eye.

At the anniversary of the death of a famous rabbi and scholar, a *hillula* (pilgrimage celebration) is held and attended sometimes by thousands. Singing and prayers are heard far into the night, and participants share toasts of wine and whiskey. Homilies are delivered by visiting rabbis. A lavish dinner of lamb and fish is prepared—all in the spirit of the revered rabbi. Tradition has it that people pray at the tomb of the righteous one so that they will utilize their abilities to help bring about salvation.

Not far from Joseph Sebag's bookstore stands Synagogue Rabbi Haim Pinto at 9 Impasse Tafilalet, Essaouira, which has been preserved as a historic site of Rabbi Pinto (1748–1845), who was born into a distinguished rabbinic family in Essaouira, then called Mogador, and who became the leading rabbi in the city. On the anniversary of his death (26 *elul*, 5605, in the Hebrew calendar, just before *Rosh Hashanah*), Moroccan Jews come from all over the world to pray at his tomb in the large Jewish cemetery here. Rabbi Pinto is remembered as a man whose prayers were received in heaven in such a way that miracles resulted.

In discussing this practice of veneration of saints, I must mention Rabbi Amram Ben Diwan, who was born in Jerusalem but later settled in Hebron, where he was asked to be an emissary to Morocco. He moved to the town of Wazan where he was known for his miracles.

In this case also, each year on the Jewish holiday of Lag B'Omer, Moroccan Jews travel to Wazan, north of Fez, to make the pilgrimage to the grave of their saint. Numerous miracles are said to have occurred on his tomb: illnesses healed; the blind regaining their sight; the mute finding their voice; the paralyzed returning home on their own; and infertile women giving birth after having prayed there.

Regarding Rabbi Ben Diwan, the tale is told of a French army sergeant with a paralyzed son. This soldier had a Jewish friend who told him to take his son to the tomb of Rabbi Amram Ben Diwan in Wazan. At first the sergeant was skeptical and refused. However, he promised that if a miracle occurred and his son was healed, he himself would finance the construction of a road so that people would have easy access to the rabbi's tomb. The miracle occurred; as the son approached the tomb, he began to walk. The father built the road.

Another revered rabbi is Rabbi Shlomo Bel Henes, who is buried in the Ourika valley in the High Atlas Mountains, two hours by bus from Marrakech. Tour guide Rafi Elmaleh tells me the last Berber Jew there watches over the tomb of Rabbi Bel Henes. Rafi takes groups there to see the tomb, though all the Jews have left the town. Once Ourika contained 300 Jewish families, two synagogues, and Jewish schools. The town provided kosher food as well as *matzah* for Passover.

Jews have left Algeria, but they have never completely departed from Morocco. Even so, there is much nostalgia for the days when Moroccan Jews lived in what some call a "Golden Age"—when Jewish and Muslim children played side by side—when in some cases in the nineteenth and twentieth centuries, it was an easy life, slow, calm, and simple. "It was a good life," says Mrs. Joelle Bensimon, who left Morocco with her family in 1967. "We had a beautiful heritage," she added, noting that she has returned to visit Morocco several times.

Jews from Israel and the diaspora will continue to enrich this community. Moroccan Jewish culture will be kept alive in Morocco itself—of that I am sure—although much will depend on former Moroccan Jews.

In a speech before the American Sephardi Federation in 2010, Ambassador Berdugo quoted King Hassan II as saying, "When a Moroccan Jewish citizen leaves, we lose a resident, but we gain an ambassador."

As Berdugo pointed out, "Today we have around 1 million Jewish ambassadors all over the world, including 600,000 in Israel, deeply attached to their Moroccan identity." While no man or woman can predict the future, it must be noted that for over 2,000 years, Jews have had a historical presence in Morocco. Chances are at least for the short term, Moroccan Jews will remain here.

A Jewish Community is Saved in Cuba

Adventures in Havana

"The Cuban Model Doesn't Even Work for Us Anymore."
—*Fidel Castro,* Atlantic *magazine, September 8, 2010*

Cubans are not free. Cubans live under a dictatorship. Cubans tell jokes about their regime:

A man and his parrot are standing on the balcony in old Havana, Cuba.
Two policemen walk by and look up at the man and his pet.
Suddenly, the parrot shrieks: "Down with Castro. Down with Castro."
The astounded cops wave their fists at the man and yell up to him: "You'd better
fix that parrot or we'll be back tomorrow and take you and him al paradon
[to the wall]."
"Yes, officers. Of course. Will do."
Sure enough, within minutes, the frightened Cuban and his parrot are meeting
with his priest.
Next morning, the man and parrot once again are on his balcony when the two
policemen saunter by. "Comrade! There's that man and his parrot. Let's get him,"
says one of the cops.
"Watch this," adds the policeman as he shouts up to the balcony: "Down with
Castro. Down with Castro."
To which the parrot replies: "Bless you, my son. Bless you."

Except for a lottery or limited opportunities, Cubans are not free to emigrate. Another story making the rounds indicates their deep desire to do so.

"Fidel," says Raul, "I have an idea. Why don't we build a bridge from Havana to Miami and anyone who wants to leave can do so freely?"

"Raul, that's crazy," Fidel replies sharply. "There'd be only the two of us left."

"Two?" answers Raul his voice emphasizing the word. "Two?"

Obviously younger brother Raul changed his mind later on, when Fidel turned the government over to him because of illness in 2006.

⌒

I consider myself lucky. I have a license to visit the Jewish community of Cuba on a humanitarian mission. Not too many Americans are allowed to catch a glimpse of this Marxist island off the coast of Florida. It's still illegal for U.S. citizens to travel to this beautiful Caribbean island unless you have permission from the State Department, or are part of a humanitarian/ religious and educational mission—missions, incidentally, which recently became more available. Like other travel destinations, Cuba conjures up a "forbidden place," and that in itself creates excitement.

Slightly more than 40 years after Fidel Castro overthrew the corrupt government of Fulgencio Batista, we found ourselves on a forty-three-minute flight from Miami to Havana's José Marti International Airport for my first trip to Havana. Not a busy airport, to say the least; only one other plane stood on the tarmac.

The year was 2004. On this trip, we were quickly rushed through customs. The officials don't stamp American passports if you ask them not to. We exited the terminal and found ourselves among hundreds of locals, shouting, waving their hands wildly in the air—not unruly, but excited, patiently waiting for their Cuban American relatives to disembark. Those cousins, sisters, brothers, aunts, and uncles were bringing in huge cartons filled with clothes, electrical appliances, and medical supplies. I soon learned that these gifts, including cash, help keep Cuba afloat financially—more than $1 billion a year. If it were not for U.S. currency and world tourism, the island probably would sink economically.

Besides medical supplies and clothes, American Jews send and bring in Judaica—religious and school supplies.

There's a joy in bringing in needed items for people who are having a hard time making ends meet. I was proud that in my suitcase, I had medicine for this still materially impoverished Jewish community. I would take the supplies to the Bet Shalom/El Patronato Synagogue and Community Center, Calle 1, between 13th and 15th streets, in the once-upscale Vedado section of Havana.

Driving toward the capital, I noticed that like other Third World countries, road conditions and public transportation are challenging at best. Main roads and center city streets seemed fine, but in outlying neighborhoods, the roads were full of potholes. Traffic was often snarled. Overcrowded buses passed us, the strangest buses I had ever seen: sort of like people-hauler, low flatbed trucks. Positioned on top of the flatbeds is a bus with windows and doors. Two buses are connected to carry more passengers. But the connection of the two sections gives appearance of a hump in the middle, making the long vehicle look like a camel and rightly called *camellos.* They snaked their way along the road. People were packed in, body to body. Many were hanging out of the windows. The buses, the cars, the passing buildings, all looked beat-up. I would see more of the decay of Havana as my visit continued.

Welcome to Cuba! Call it the pearl of the Antilles, the Casablanca of the Caribbean, a tropical paradise. Describe it as exhilarating, lined with seductive beaches melting into a magnificent coastline ringed with deep bays. Add grasslands, gentle slopes, rolling hills, towering mountains, and people who warmly greet visitors. Welcome to Havana, the capital of Cuba, and the largest city in the Caribbean, with 2.1 million residents. Welcome to a city which, although totally run-down, is still a masterpiece of architecture.

As traffic slowed, the delay permitted me to remember my briefings on what to expect on this island, 90 miles south of Key West, Florida. Putting it bluntly: I would discover an impoverished country of about 12 million, living in an area 780 miles long and 119 miles wide.

When Castro took over Cuba in 1959, a tenth of the population went into exile. Of the 12,000 Jews who fled, half settled in the Miami area, with 4,000 going to New York, and the rest emigrating to Israel, Puerto Rico, Venezuela, and Mexico. Eventually, most of the New York contingent moved to South Florida.

About 1,100 Jews remain in Cuba, all but 300 in Havana. Ninety-five percent are intermarried. As we shall see, Cuban Jewry lost an entire generation, a generation that was deprived of Jewish education and religious practices. However, two decades ago it was saved, revived, and given a new lease on life.

Five synagogues now function in Cuba, three in Havana. A religious school, a summer camp, and a kosher butcher shop make up what is turning into a community that offers a Jewish life, to the best of its ability.

Before I reached Bet Shalom/El Patronato, I asked the driver to take a detour of sorts and head to Santos Suarez, once an outlying suburb, where many Jews resided before 1959.

I felt compelled to drive to Santos Suarez in Havana, my introduction to a Cuban neighborhood. My first meeting with Cuban Jews had taken place in 1965 in Brooklyn, New York. As a journalist, I had been given an assignment to write about the Jewish refugees who had fled Cuba.

By the way, regarding the New York Cuban Jewry story that I did in 1965, I would have a lifetime benefit from that interview. After meeting with Cuban Jews, I was scheduled to go to a dance. As it turned out, I met Riva, the love of my life there, and as I am writing this, we've been married forty-six years.

On that rainy, dull Sunday afternoon in Brooklyn, I drove out to the Vanderveer apartments which the Cuban Jewish exiles had quickly dubbed *Santos Tsuris,* from the Yiddish word *tsuris* (trouble). The Vanderveer buildings at best were occupied by low- to middle-income residents. After the luxury of pre-Castro Cuba, where many of the Jews had been in the upper class, the hardworking life of middle-class New Yorkers and adjustment to a new land did have a lot of *tsuris* in it.

Needless to say, like many immigrant groups arriving in the U.S., it was only a matter of time before these newcomers relocated to a better lifestyle and neighborhood.

So here I was in Cuba in 2004, driving through Santos Suarez in Havana. As they say in Brooklyn, "Santos Suarez ain't what it used to be." In the old days in Santos Suarez, before Fidel Castro took over in 1959, the apartments were basically kept in good condition. Most people talked and relaxed and watched television on their terraces, even in the cool nights of fall and winter. During the hot summers, big ceiling fans kept the apartment dwellers cool, according to Betty Heisler-Samuels, writing in *The Last Minyan in Havana*.

Potholes, the curse of every driver in the world, can exact a toll on tires and shocks. Havana must be one of the leading cities where potholes rule supreme. Today, in Santos Suarez, the streets are barely passable. These street ruts are not like the typical winter potholes you sometimes find in Brooklyn or The Bronx, mind you. Here they are actual craters, and you must proceed with caution, block by block. I held my breath for the driver's sake: Save the axles, save the alignment, please! As for the buildings, well, they clearly hadn't seen a coat of paint probably since the Revolution in 1959. The plaster was chipped, the balconies were rusting; the whole area was, as the guidebooks warn you, "a study in decay and decomposition."

This short trip proved what everyone already knew: Even as late as 2011, Cuba has literally not progressed physically since the 1959 Revolution.

Arrival!

While there are two other active synagogues, Bet Shalom/El Patronato is the largest, with 500 members, and is the headquarters of the Jewish community here.

First shock: There are no security guards. The doors were wide open. "No terrorists in Cuba," says a Jewish organization official. Not common in the Jewish diaspora or Israel, where commands ring out: Photo ID, please; open your bag; walk through the security doorway.

The facade of the building, situated on a tree-lined, residential street, features a *Magen David* (Jewish star) right smack in the middle, and an arch covering the front of the structure. The scene gives me the emotional uplift I need. I say to myself: *Am Yisrael Chai* ("The Jewish people live!").

Like thousands of tourists visiting Cuba, I will observe a reborn Jewish community. As the late Dr. Jose Miller, then president of the community, told me in an interview in 2004, "Every Jew in Cuba now is basically linked to the community, either through organizations or small groups."

And although Cuban Jewry exists in a police state, my people can pray openly in a synagogue, learn Hebrew, celebrate Jewish holidays, and yes, despite red tape, even emigrate to Israel, although the anxious wait for departure can take over a year.

However, it wasn't always that way. The first thirty-five years of Fidel and his Communist rulers was not pleasant, and the regime almost succeeded in ending Jewish spiritual and educational life.

Before Castro took power, and even a short while into his new government, he basically covered up his intention to turn Cuba into a Communist state. When the Jews finally realized the regime would introduce Communism, including the nationalization of business and socialization of the economy and property, these middle-class entrepreneurs and land- and factory owners understood they had to depart quickly. And when Cuba became an atheistic state, they realized that this could be the end of Judaism in Cuba.

During the revolutionary government's antireligious campaign, synagogues in Havana were allowed to decay, and two closed down. Jewish life was repressed and virtually nonexistent, cut off from physical contact with the U.S., including communication.

Shortly after Fidel and his guerrillas took over, 90 percent of the Jewish community fled Cuba. They were not persecuted. They were not expelled by force. They did not suffer from anti-Semitism. But since they were involved in trade and business, they fell into the category of enemies of the Revolution.

The tragedy of Cuban Jewry somewhat mirrors the typical Jewish experience in the diaspora. Burmese Jews also fled when that country's army installed a military dictatorship and nationalized the economy. In this case, too, Cuban Jews sensed it was time to depart. Like many, Jews obviously preferred a free country and a free market society.

The Eastern European Jews who left Cuba in the early 1960s had settled on the island in the late 1920s and 1930s. They had faced a tight U.S. immigration policy, so reluctantly settled down in Cuba. Their goal had been to use Cuba as a transit station to depart for the U.S. After Castro took over, they had to flee a country a second time, their property confiscated, notes Robert Levine in his book, *The Jewish Diaspora in Latin America*.

Cuba would never be far from their hearts; after all, it was a tropical paradise, especially for the affluent.

After the Jewish exodus in the early 1960s, the remaining 1,500 to 2,000 Jews bore the brunt of Cuban Communist oppression against all religions. Several synagogues closed down, and Jewish schools ceased functioning. Young Jews avoided going to synagogue for fear of damaging their careers in a government that despised and mocked religion. To get ahead required membership in the Communist Party and precluded the active practice of any religion, except Marxism, of course. Until 1991, Cuban Jewry meant no rabbi, no *mohel*, very few bar or bat mitzvahs. Many had never witnessed a Jewish wedding.

"The only way we knew Jews existed," says Adela Dworin, president of the community, "was when they came to the synagogue once a year to collect Passover food donated by the Canadian Jewish Congress."

"The Jewish community in Cuba is dying," wrote Warren Freedman in the *Southern Jewish Weekly,* in 1976, "not only from a high death rate, a low birth rate, and a high rate of intermarriage, but from lack of contact with other Jewish communities. Cut off from Jewish life, a generation of Jews was lost."

⁓

Everything changed in 1991. During that fateful year, the Union of Soviet Socialist Republics and its totalitarian regime, which for seventy years had suppressed Judaism, collapsed. The Cold War ended, and with it the massive Russian political and financial aid that had propped up Castro. The Soviet Union—Fidel's banker—was history. With the American embargo squeezing the island, Cuba had no choice but to open up a little—not only in allowing some Western investment, but also in permitting tourism and the influx of foreign currency.

At the Fourth Party Congress in 1991, it was decided that members of Cuba's Communist Party were no longer forbidden to belong to a religious community.

And in 1998, Pope John Paul II's visit led to religious institutions being able to function openly. The Cuban constitution was amended, with Cuba officially changing from an atheistic country into a secular one.

Events moved fast in 1991. The late Dr. Jose Miller, president of the Cuban Jewish community, invited the American Jewish Joint Distribution Committee (JDC) to come in and help revive the island's Jewish community.

Dr. William Recant, assistant executive vice president of JDC, recalls that in 1992, he met eight senior Jews in the Patronato synagogue. "Birds flew in and out over the Holy Ark, the roof leaked, and yet, on the wall, was a sign in Hebrew that said 'The Jewish people are alive in Cuba.'"

At that meeting, Dr. Miller told Dr. Recant: "We're a dying community."

A dozen years later, before he passed away, Dr. Miller thanked God, the Jewish community, and the JDC for revitalizing the community, according to Dr. Recant.

Over the last twenty years, that rebirth has included building repair, a new roof, refurbished sanctuaries, shipments of prayer books, the hiring of Jewish instructors, and the opening of a school. Rabbis have visited the community, and tourists have brought in needed medicine, clothes, and Jewish books. The community revived.

Whether Cuban Jewry could have survived without the material, financial, and spiritual aid given over the last twenty years is questionable. Most of the money to support the synagogues, run the school, provide welfare funds, pay for medicines, and cover the costs for Shabbat meals comes from the JDC, which receives its funds from the United Jewish Communities and other groups.

Other organizations also contributed to help Cuban Jewry regain a sense of belonging to the Jewish people, as well as to improve their lives economically and spiritually, including B'nai B'rith, World ORT, Hadassah, Lubavitch of Canada, and federations and synagogues all over the U.S.

Local chapters of B'nai B'rith and Hadassah meet at the Patronato today. Hadassah is composed of doctors, pharmacists, psychologists, dentists, and other health-care practitioners who attend to the health of the Jewish community.

It was 7:00 p.m. on a Friday evening, Sabbath eve in December 2004, and I was standing in the sanctuary of Bet Shalom/El Patronato. Cubans, Americans, Canadians—we were all praying with fervor. Shabbat songs in the service inspired us. At our service a man and two women conducted prayers. As Bet Shalom follows the Conservative Movement of Judaism ritual, men and women sit together on rows of benches in this now rather attractive sanctuary, which features a large aisle down the middle and wood paneling on the wall behind the *bimah* (raised platform).

A fellow congregant tells me about the *Cuban minyan*. In the days following the Revolution, when it was almost impossible to obtain a *minyan,* the congregation counted each *Torah* as a qualifying member in order to begin the prayer service. A *minyan* normally requires ten Jewish men, though in Conservative and Reform synagogues, women are counted.

Riva is asked to light the Shabbat candles. She has done so in many countries, from Russia to Vietnam to Burma, and now Cuba. I know that she is especially moved by the illumination of these Sabbath candles, ushering in the sanctification of the day of rest in this land where Judaism is alive and well.

The Patronato resembles a Jewish Community Center without the accoutrements of an affluent U.S. JCC. The renovated building contains a library, a pharmacy, a large hall that serves as a multipurpose room, a small classroom, and a computer center sponsored by the World ORT organization. Wall decorations feature biblical episodes. Additions are constantly being made. In 2011, a youth center was established by the JDC in the basement of the Patronato, complete with Wii, a pool table, and other recreational items you don't generally find in Cuba.

After the service, we joined the Shabbat meal. The JDC sponsors "a chicken program" which on Friday night serves 400 to 500 dinners in all three synagogues.

We ate slowly, although the people around us devoured their food. You could tell they were hungry. A woman at our table packed up the chicken bones and put them in a take-home bag for soup. No sheepish look, no embarrassment; Cuban reality! Rationing just does not do it.

A man sitting across from us kept eyeing our meals. Not hungry anymore, we had finished eating, and some leftovers remained on our plates. Here again, with no sheepish look, he politely asked if he could have the chicken left on our plates.

"Of course," we said.

Quickly, he scooped the remains of our chicken onto his dish and wolfed it down. This was Cuban reality, too!

Incidentally, a feature of Cuban Jewry is "the most photographed kosher butcher shop in the world," according to Ruth Behar, professor of anthropology at the University of Michigan, and author of *An Island Called Home*. The Jewish community richly benefits from this shop. In hard-pressed Cuba, it is very difficult to find beef; despite meat rationing. Cuban Jews are granted an additional allotment of kosher meat.

Two days later, on a warm December day in 2004, I stood in the Patronato. Several large buses pulled up and discharged the Sunday school children, who come from all over Havana on buses paid for by the JDC. (Today, the school and each of the synagogues own a minivan paid for by North American donors via the JDC.) We are moved at the sight of the young children. The school, which started with ten children in 1991, now has eighty to ninety pupils. As the youngsters filed into the large hall, they were served chocolate milk and cookies. In Cuba, we were told, children over the age of seven do not get milk on their ration cards.

Knowing the history of this beleaguered community, and hearing Cuban Jewish children now sing "*Hatikvah,*" the national anthem of the Jewish state, was emotional for me during this opening Sunday school assembly. My eyes were moist. There before me, standing tall and singing the hopeful words of "*Hatikvah*" (to be a free people in our land), in a Sunday school in Communist Havana, whose government has not had diplomatic relations with Israel for over thirty-five years, are these young people, the future of the Jewish people.

Even though every Cuban has free medical care—certainly an accomplishment of the government—there is still a terrible shortage of pharmaceutical drugs in the country. Stopping into the miniature pharmacy at El Patronato Synagogue, Dr. Miller and Adela Dworin explained that many of the Jews in Cuba, especially elderly pensioners, can now obtain lifesaving prescriptions. The community needs medications for hypertension, heart disease, angina, and cholesterol.

When a person visits Cuba and meets its Jewish community, they usually are moved to do something to help. This is a community still in dire need of the simplest necessities of life, as well as religious objects.

Somehow, we felt compelled to do more. We did not have long to wait to find a project we could undertake once we returned to the U.S. To gain insight into the social and religious situation of Cuban Jewry, we visited the Jewish school. Poverty embraces the young generation, too. This disadvantaged school population—like all of Cuba—needs school supplies, Hebrew books, song sheets, pencils and erasers, notebooks, tapes, and music for *bar mitzvah* prayer chants.

Like many others, my wife, Riva, a teacher, saw the needs. When she returned to her school, Temple Beth El Religious School in Chappaqua, New York, she helped to launch a child-to-child drive for school supplies for the Cuban Jewish school. Even the first graders in Chappaqua were happy to bring in some supplies for the "children of Cuba," as they put it. Shortly thereafter, several dozen cartons of school supplies were sent off to the Jewish community of Cuba.

We had another pleasant surprise in the Patronato: We heard Hebrew folk-dance tunes. A local dance instructor was rehearsing with a dance group made up of young Cuban Jews. They were performing Israeli folk dances just as thousands of American Jewish and Israeli youngsters do in their youth movements and organizations throughout the world. Through dance, these teens learn about Jewish holidays, customs, and traditions. They told us they were practicing for an upcoming Purim celebration.

Naturally, we met up with other visiting Jewish tourists who were also moved to help the community. A Swiss Jew, inspired by the children and the Friday-night service, told Adela and the leadership that he would donate shoes for the ninety students.

Two days later we met an American Jewish doctor whose parents once lived in Cuba. She brought dozens of pairs of eyeglasses for the youngsters.

"We are trying to create a real Jewish Community Center. For us it is very important. We are trying to attract as many Jewish people as possible," William Miller, grandson of the former president, Dr. Jose Miller, recently told the *JWeekly* newspaper in San Francisco.

Walking around the Patronato, I was shown a photo of Fidel, who made an appearance during Hanukkah in 1998. A dozen years later, Fidel's brother, Raul, now president of Cuba, also made a visit to the synagogue for the Hanukkah celebration in 2010.

When Adela invited Fidel to the Jewish Center, he never committed or announced a date for his appearance. But to the astonishment of more than a hundred or so people gathered in the Patronato the first night of Hanukkah in 1998, Castro actually appeared in green fatigues and soldier's boots. He was given the honor of lighting the first candle, and he ate two jelly doughnuts and three latkes with applesauce.

Fidel, being Fidel, offered a two-hour discourse on the parallels between Israelis fighting the Syrians, and of course, the Syrians and the Cubans fighting the Yankee imperialists, before leaving to enthusiastic applause.

Before Fidel (who is now eighty-four) and Raul (now seventy-nine), the country was ruled by dictator Fulgencio Batista, who led a corrupt regime. Batista was good for business, and the economy flourished in the 1950s. Impressive skyscrapers dotted the Havana skyline. Casinos were crowded. Havana had become the Las Vegas of Latin America. Vacationers, including honeymooners from the U.S., flocked to the island, sunning on the beautiful, white sandy beaches during the day and at night, listening to Maurice Chevalier, Lena Horne, and Nat King Cole, some of the celebrities who graced the city's famous nightclubs, according to Leycester Coltman in his book, *The Real Fidel Castro.*

For two years, Fidel and his rebels—known as *barbudos,* the bearded ones—fought in the Sierra Maestra Mountains. They evolved into a formidable guerrilla army, and their insurrection gained strength. In those days, "Castro's powerful personality and persuasive manner enabled him to make both Marxists and democratic politicians believe that he was on their side," notes Coltman.

Batista saw the end in sight and fled on December 31, 1958. On New Year's Day, 1959, Castro's troops entered Havana. The war was over.

After the Revolution, Fidel, then thirty-three, would reveal his true colors as a Marxist and an atheist. And though some in the middle class now say they saw through Fidel, "the overwhelming majority of the Cuban population, of all classes and races, were caught up in the mood of exhilaration and euphoria," that he and his band of rebels had overthrown Batista, notes author Coltman.

Little did they know that Castro would establish the Western Hemisphere's first Communist state. It did not take long for Batista's men to be hauled out to the sports stadium, with the vengeful crowds yelling, "To the wall!" and "Death!" By May, more than five hundred had been shot. Although elections were called, they were not needed by the new regime, according to John Paul Rathbone in his book, *The Sugar King of Havana: The Rise and Fall of Julio Lobo, Cuba's Last Tycoon.*

⌒

Three years after the Revolution, nearly a quarter of a million refugees would flee the country, most arriving in Florida.

Many who stayed in Cuba thought that the dictator would not last. Yet, six decades later, Fidel Castro, undisputed ruler of Cuba, still reigned. However, in 2006, Fidel, who suffered a gastrointestinal illness that almost killed him, handed over the day-to-day rule to his younger brother, Raul Castro, who officially became president in 2008. Later it was revealed by the BBC News that Raul had also become chief of the Communist Party in 2006.

⌒

Speculation continues to surface, that Castro has acknowledged he has Jewish ancestry. The name "Castro" was common among *marranos* (Iberian Jews who converted to Catholicism but secretly practiced Judaism). Marrano, incidentally, is the Spanish pejorative for "crypto Jew," and means "swine and/or pig." The Hebrew word *anusim* (secret Jew) is a more acceptable term.

Castro also said that many of his childhood friends called him *Judio,* because he had not been baptized until the age of seven. Much of the speculation over Fidel's Jewish ancestry deals with his father, Angel, a Spaniard from Galicia whose family may possibly have been converted to Catholicism. It is conceivable, therefore, that Castro's ancestors were Jewish.

We know that Castro "confused the word *Judio* with a similar word, *Jote,* which was the name of a large black bird. He thought it must have been these unpleasant birds which had 'killed Christ.' In any event, he understood that being a 'Jew' was something distinctly unpleasant," wrote Coltman.

⌒

Cuba is a tourist magnet because of the island's natural beauty and the warmth of its people. Wherever I went, I observed a people who smile. Despite their poor conditions, Cubans carry on and manage. You cannot help but be moved by a people who, although they manage on about $20 a month (doctors now make perhaps close to $30), and although they live under a repressive regime, invent ways to make do. The big word here is "barter"—they barter for everything, from a place to live, to medicine, to food, to a car.

It cannot be denied that poverty is everywhere. Sidewalks are cracked, cement peels from building walls, and most structures have not been painted since the Revolution. Large families live in two rooms. Clothes are threadbare.

Time has stood still for so long in Cuba, especially along Old Havana's streets, that I realize I'm walking in the Havana of 1959. Nothing has changed, apart from a few new buildings being constructed, and a few new hotels.

⌒

As I strolled along the cobblestone streets, the infectious Cuban music grabbed me. This small island has had great influence on Latin music as we know it today. Combos on the street corners, in the restaurants, in the cafes, entertain the populace and tourists alike, and make money, too. Cuba has a rich, musical tradition—a medley of African rhythms, as well as melodies and lyricism from Spain that gave birth to what is called Afro-Cuban music. Music is an inherent part of the Cuban heritage. Just stop and listen to the street music and you will be reminded that you are in exotic and mysterious Cuba.

Whether I'm standing on the street corners, or enjoying a show in a Havana nightclub, or having lunch in a restaurant, one particular song haunts me. Long after I return from a visit to the island, whether I'm in Cuzco, Peru, or New York City, or Miami, this particular song sends me into my Cuban mode: "Guantanamera."

Guantanamera
Guajira Guantanamera
Guantanamera
Guajira Guantanamera.

I am a truthful man from this land of palm trees
Before dying I want to share these poems of my soul
My verses are light green
But they are also flaming red.

"Guantanamara" is the best-known Cuban song and the island's most patriotic song. The better known "official" lyrics are based on the first stanza of the first poem of the collection *Versos Sencillos* ("Simple Verses"), by Cuban poet Jose Marti (1853–95). Marti was a Cuban national hero and a symbol of Cuba's bid for independence against Spain in the nineteenth century.

~

My old Chevy—there it is!

Right there on the Paseo del Prado, the eighteenth-century promenade that runs from the seawall to the capitol building, I found what I was seeking: my 1954 Chevrolet, the first car I ever owned. The cars are parked diagonally in front of the capitol, which, by the way, possesses a striking resemblance to our U.S. Capitol in Washington, D.C.

Unfortunately, my former dream car soon turned into a lemon. Six months later, I sold it, thinking I would never see that clunker again. But there it stood in the shadow of the capitol dome in this city of antique cars.

Every tourist to Cuba comments on the motorcar relics. Every guidebook worth its salt says something about these old vehicles. My means of transportation in Havana happened to be a beaten-down Lada, made in the former Soviet Union and exported to former Communist-bloc countries, especially Cuba. Like the city it rambles through, my Lada has aged and, gasping for breath, stalls several times a day. The windows are half down and won't budge. Supposedly, the Russians built it for extreme rugged climates and poor roads. Conventional wisdom has it that the Lada can rack up

300,000 miles. One thing is for sure: Judging by their condition, it seems like the vast majority of automobiles in Havana have definitely put on that much mileage.

No matter. As you drive around Havana, more often than not, you will spy a vehicle with its hood up, its owner's head buried deep under the hood as he tinkers with his 1950s-vintage car.

The Partagas Cigar Factory stands as one of the country's largest and busiest cigar establishments. Stopping there, I was reminded of my late grandfather, Benjamin Frank, for whom I am named. It seems that this very Orthodox man worked in a cigar factory after he brought his family from the Ukraine to Pittsburgh, Pennsylvania. I never knew him, as he died before I was born, but I heard that as a very religious man, he left work early on Friday afternoons to prepare for the Sabbath. We missed the tour to see how a cigar is made, including the level of leaf selection and quality control. Still, I thought of my grandfather as the clerk showed us various brands and sizes. Travelers are not permitted to bring those wonderful Havana cigars back to the U.S. according to the *New York Times.*

Actually, cigars have played a significant role in Cuban and Cuban Jewish history, from the island's discovery. Among the first Europeans to touch Cuban soil was the *crypto-Jew/converso* Luis de Torres. On October 27, 1492, Columbus sighted Cuban land before dusk and dispatched de Torres to the island on an exploratory expedition to find the emperor of China, as well as gold. De Torres, who knew Hebrew, Aramaic, and some Arabic, apparently missed the Mongol, and found instead natives possessing leaves they called "tobacco."

Over the years, more *conversos* landed in Cuba, which became an important strategic outpost of Spain's Empire in the New World. During the Spanish Inquisition, however, those waves of "secret Jews" were hunted down. Jews did not return to Cuba until after the Spanish-American War in 1898. American Jewish veterans of that war were among the first to arrive around the turn of the twentieth century, to be followed by large numbers of Sephardic Jews from Turkey. After World War I, a large wave of Ashkenazi Jews arrived in Cuba.

Whether you walk through the Vedado section, Havana's modern political and cultural center, or drive through Miramar, once the neighborhood of the upper class, you will see the outer decay of the former mansions. I looked at these stately homes on the wide, tree-lined streets and wondered about those former inhabitants who left penniless and had to make their way in new land.

Today, Miramar boasts some upper-end hotels and restaurants. Many have been turned into government offices and embassies. Like most structures in Cuba, these mansions have been battered by hurricanes and humidity. The guide tells us that in some cases, the houses have been occupied by multiple families, and that not once since 1959 have they received any maintenance.

Seeking some relaxation between appointments, we headed to the Old Town, where several of Havana's colonial plazas, or squares, draw visitors. Sitting in a cafe in the Plaza de la Catedral was very refreshing as we absorbed the architecture of the colonial-era structures. The Plaza de la Catedral is within walking distance of La Bodeguita del Medio, a favorite hangout of prize-winning American novelist Ernest Hemingway, whose haunts we would soon visit.

Ernest Hemingway, citizen of the world.

> *You know how it is there early in the morning in Havana with the bums still asleep against the walls? . . . Well, we came across the square from the dock to the Pearl of San Francisco Café. . . .*

Thus, Ernest Hemingway (1899–1961) begins his novel, *To Have and Have Not*. As they say in Havana, "a lot of rain has fallen since then."

> *Hemingway slept here.*
> *Hemingway drank here.*
> *Hemingway fished here.*
> *Hemingway lived here.*
> *Hemingway wrote here.*

No doubt about it; the ghost of Hemingway still hovers over Havana. For twenty-two years, this icon of writers, this 1954 Nobel Prize for Literature winner, romped around the island as if it were his own playground. More important, his Cuban years witnessed the zenith of his writing career.

"I live in Cuba because I love Cuba," he told Robert Manning in an interview, which later appeared in *Atlantic Monthly*.

Hemingway achieved a distinctive writing style, which was characterized by economy and understatement. He certainly influenced twentieth-century fiction. Many of his works are classics of American literature. "The Hemingway Trail," focusing on the mystique of this great writer, is high on my list of sights to see!

Supposedly, Hemingway named his favorite drinks and watering holes when he announced: "My *mojito* in La Bodeguita, my daiquiri in El Floridita!"

So I stopped first at El Floridita, historic and busy restaurant bar in the old part of Havana, located at the end of Calle Obispo. Indeed, this was one of Hemingway's favorite places. Considered one of the top bars in the world, tourists come here to order a double daiquiri. Some stories indicate that Hemingway himself invented the daiquiri.

The Floridita was frequented by many generations of Cuban and foreign intellectuals, artists, and writers, such as John Dos Passos and Graham Greene. The latter wrote *Our Man in Havana*.

Fantasy, of course, but I imagined Hemingway sitting at the bar with his cronies and downing quite a few daiquiris, especially after a long day at the typewriter. I admired the memorabilia, especially that photo of Fidel with the famous writer. In the summer of 1960, Hemingway presented the Cuban ruler with a trophy for winning a sportfishing contest named for Hemingway.

After the Cuban Revolution in early 1959, Hemingway was on good terms with the Cuban government. In the book *Papa Hemingway*, A. E. Hotchner reveals Ernest Hemingway's reaction to Castro taking over: "After Batista any change would almost have to be an improvement."

Later, Hemingway said that "the Castro business" [the Revolution] bothered him. "He [Fidel] doesn't bother me personally. I'm good publicity for them; so maybe they'd never bother me, and [they] let me live on here as always, but I am an American above everything else, and I cannot stay here when other Americans are being kicked out and my country is being vilified." according to Hotchner.

Hemingway left Cuba in 1960, never to return. He committed suicide the following year.

Even half a century later, Hemingway is not forgotten; he remains a cultural hero to the Cuban people.

At the end of the El Floridita bar is a 2003 statue of Ernest Hemingway by José Villa Soberón. The photo of Hemingway awarding Fidel a prize in the fishing contest, in May 1960, adorns the wall behind the statue.

Next, I stopped off at La Bodeguita del Medio at la Calle Empedrado, 207, off Plaza de la Catedral. The rooms are filled with curious objects, including framed photos, and the walls are covered with signatures of famous and unknown customers alike, recounting the island's past. Along with the local food, cigars, music, and *mojitos,* La Bodeguita del Medio offers a glimpse of Cuba's typical atmosphere, touristy as it may be.

The bar was packed, glasses clinking, and the noise and Latin-flavored music kept the customers drinking, talking, and table-hopping. While I usually don't imbibe, I ordered a *mojito* and sipped it while gazing at the roped-off section at the end of the bar, marking a small shrine for "Saint Ernesto," featuring what else, his bar stool. Here he would down his usual *mojito* and chat with the locals. Looking inside, you could see hundreds of writings on the wall, as folks are allowed and encouraged to write their name—that is, if you can find the space to do so. The restaurant serves traditional Cuban dishes and the atmosphere was definitely Bohemian. Amid the partying and raucous laughter, we enjoyed a typical Caribbean dish of boiled rice, and black beans.

My next stop on "The Hemingway Trail" was the Hotel Ambos Mundos, a five-story building located at 153 Calle Obispo. Constructed in 1920, and restored with UNESCO funds, Hemingway moved here in 1939 to work on a manuscript the world would come to know as *For Whom the Bell Tolls.* No wonder he thought of the fifth-floor room on the northeast corner—Room 511, to be exact—as a good place to write; it's as close to the action as you can get in this neighborhood. The Nobel laureate Gabriel Garcia Marquez described it as "a gloomy room, 16 square meters, with a double bed made of ordinary wood, two night tables and a writing table with a chair."

Today, the hotel is something of a shrine for Hemingway admirers.

⌒

Next, the driver took us to a hilltop home outside of and overlooking Havana. This is the most moving site for anyone who considers him- or herself to be a writer, or who respects Hemingway's style and has read his books. How often I have heard, from young and old alike, implied or otherwise: "I'm going to write the great American novel, just like Hemingway."

I walked up the path to the front door of the limestone villa, which is known as The Hemingway Museum at Finca la Vigia (Lookout Farm), in the working-class town of San Francisco de Paula.

Located seven miles from Havana on thirteen acres of banana trees, tropical shrubs, and gardens, Finca la Vigia is where Hemingway finished *For Whom the Bells Toll, A Moveable Feast,* and *The Old Man and the Sea.* The latter is considered his most popular work, for which he was awarded the Pulitzer Prize in 1953.

I told the guard that I am an ardent admirer of Hemingway and a journalist, and after I placed a reasonable tip in his hand, he let me into the room where sits the famous old Royal typewriter on which he wrote *The Old Man and the Sea.* On the rest of the tour, we visited the library, where I saw part of the 9,000-book collection of this writer and avid reader. The books, the animal heads, the bar—all provide the visitor some insight into the man. The house is just as he left it in 1960.

Ah, there it is! The *Pilar,* his custom-made luxury yacht, which he converted into a sort of gunship, using it to search the Cuban coast for lone German U-boats.

Here is the pool where he entertained his guests. He loved to swim in the afternoon and lounge around the pool with drink in hand.

In 1937, Hemingway wrote *To Have and Have Not,* which concerns a broke fishing-boat captain who agrees to carry contraband between Cuba and Florida in order to feed his wife and daughters. Nothing at all like the film, which changed the setting from Key West to Martinique under the Vichy regime and made significant alterations to the plot.

Work is now under way to renovate the termite-ravaged house and repair the damage done to its contents by years of humidity. In 1965, the U.S. National Trust for Historic Preservation placed the estate on a list of endangered sites.

The fishing village of Cojimar is the next stop on the Hemingway Trail. Located nine miles from the Finca farmhouse, this town inspired Hemingway's *The Old Man and the Sea.* I walked along the Old Pier to La Terrazza Restaurant, where the character of Santiago brings in the remains of his epic fish. This is also the hometown of Hemingway's real-life first mate on the *Pilar,* Captain Gregorio Fuentes, who died in January 2002, at the age of 104.

I stared at a memorial bust of Hemingway situated in a gazebo at the village. He will always be the fisherman's fisherman, just as he still is the writer's writer.

With all of Hemingway's faults, and there were many, I was happy that I had traveled the Hemingway Trail. I agree with Gertrude Stein, who so succinctly declares in *The Autobiography of Alice B. Toklas,* "I have a weakness for Hemingway." So does this author.

We stopped at the Melia Cohiba Hotel, a very modern establishment, and a great location overlooking the Malecon, the four-mile-long seafront boulevard that separates the city from the sea. The seawall and promenade are sometimes known as Havana's front porch. From one's room one gets the sweep of the *Malecon* and the nearby neighborhood. The Malecon runs along the northwest coast of Havana for almost four miles, from the mouth of Havana harbor to Vedado past the *Hotel Nacional.*

The Malecon is to Havana what the Eiffel Tower is to Paris or Big Ben is to London or the Shwedagon Pagoda is to Rangoon, Burma.

We walked the Malecon several times. Along the way we could see empty lots where buildings once stood. We passed young couples walking arm in arm or sitting on the seawall and sunbathing. The smell of the ocean is relaxing, a great place to take a break from the hectic pace of sightseeing and interviewing personages for articles.

On one of our hikes we moved along the Malecon from the Old Town to the illustrious Hotel Nacional, which, although it has shed some of its old grandeur, still attracts visitors from all over the world.

Sitting outside on the lawn at the Nacional, on a slight hill above the Malecon and the sea, I realized that I was sitting in the same spot where, in the old days, honeymooning Americans would drink their highballs under the palm trees and try to catch of glimpse of movie stars, such as Frank Sinatra, Ava Gardner, Errol Flynn, and Clark Gable. And yes, even Winston Churchill stayed here, just as he stopped at La Mamounia Hotel in Marrakech, Morocco.

Some say the Nacional is a copy of the Breakers Hotel in Palm Beach. Built in 1930, the popular eight-story establishment remains a landmark and is home to many American tourists. Possessing that grand old-style European atmosphere, the hotel offers some great views of Havana Harbor. Some may have heard stories about Meyer Lansky, known as the "Jewish Godfather," who revamped the Nacional's casino and called it the Parisien. A friend of Batista's, Lansky then built his own hotel, the Riviera.

But the most enjoyable experience we had was taking the little yellow bug taxi known as "Coco," in what we thought would be short trip from the Old Town to the Melia Coheba, our hotel. Coco taxis are the Cuban equivalent of a rickshaw: a three-wheeled, yellow fiberglass, egg-shaped vehicle with two seats glued onto a moped. We took it for the excitement, and to experience a prevalent means of transportation. The only problem with the ride in the Coco on the Malecon was that our miniature taxi broke down several times, and the driver, though pleasant and unruffled, was forced to get out and crank up the old horseless buggy.

⁓

Time for me to visit the other two synagogues that serve the Jewish community.

No rabbi serves the spiritual needs of Cuban Jewry—not even one. The Cuban government simply frowns on outside clergy entering its domain on a permanent basis.

However, Rabbi Shmuel Szteinhendler of Santiago, Chile, is considered the chief rabbi of the Jews of Cuba and makes several visits a year to the island. The rabbi usually leads a delegation of visiting rabbis to teach synagogue members so they themselves can conduct services and in turn instruct others in the community. In addition, young people—usually from Argentina—have worked with Cuban Jewry for more than a decade. So far, the JDC has sent eight couple-representatives who stay two to three years to help the island's Jews expand their knowledge of Judaism.

A few years ago, Nestor Szewach and coworker Mara Steiner represented JDC as community development professionals. Mara headed the religious school, *Machon Tikun Olam*. "It's important to have a good curriculum," she told me, adding that she is setting up a pedagogy center for community teachers. Her main task is to work with these educators at the school. Often, the two professionals conduct services, as well as assist Rabbi Szteinhendler in the conversion program to become Jews. They also plan and coordinate holiday celebrations, run the summer camps, and make sure that the "chicken dinner program" occurs without a hitch.

The new JDC representatives are Ariel Benclowicz and his wife, Johanna. They moved from Buenos Aires to Cuba in 2009 with their one-year-old-daughter. They are graduates of the famed Rabbinical Seminary in Buenos Aires.

Since arriving in Cuba, the two new representatives have also worked with students and young adults who want to participate in the Taglit-Birthright Israel Trips for young people; the "March of the Living," from Auschwitz to Birkenau concentration camp; and the Maccabiah Games, an international Jewish athletic event held in Israel every four years.

Interestingly, back in the 1990s, the Cuban government frowned on allowing Jewish young men and women to join in on the overseas Jewish programs and games because they felt the team members would not return. But the officials finally agreed when the participants promised they would come back to Cuba. They did!

I was standing in front of Adath Israel, located at 52 Calle Acosta and Pictota, talking with several members of the congregation. On the front gate is a Jewish star, and above the entrance door of this Orthodox synagogue is the famous morning service prayer, in Hebrew: *How lovely are your tents, O Jacob, your dwelling places, O Israel.*

In 2005, the upstairs sanctuary was completely renovated, thanks to donations from abroad. Newly installed wood paneling appears in front of the *bimah* and throughout the hall, and new individual chairs rest on newly installed tile floors. The new sanctuary is used for holiday services. As in Orthodox Judaism, women sit in an upstairs gallery section or in a separate area in the sanctuary. A Judaic-designed *mechitzah* (partition) separates the men from the women.

Alberto Zilberstein told me a *minyan* is held here three times a day in the small prayer room downstairs, which is used for services during the week. A *mechitzah* is in place every day.

Zilberstein, former president of Adath Israel, which is located in Old Havana, voiced pride that his daughters were among the first to celebrate their *bat mitzvah* after the Jewish revival in the 1990s. He affirms that the synagogue never closed down, "even though at times we didn't have a *minyan.*"

For thirty years after the Revolution, Alberto did not read or speak Hebrew; he apparently forgot how to do so. After 1991, he relearned the Hebrew language so that he could recite prayers in the language of the Jewish people. He tells me that Adath Israel conducts confirmation services, holiday celebrations, and weddings. This congregation maintains a *mikveh* (ritual bath).

In recent years, Chabad has entered the Cuban scene; for a short time, Chabad and Adath Israel were affiliated, although the Orthodox synagogue apparently broke those ties. Still, during Purim, 2011, a representative from Chabad flew in from Canada to conduct services.

The neighborhood around Adath Israel stands as an example of a city failing to maintain its property. Building facades have cracked walls; cement often falls from the structures to the sidewalk, which is also broken in many spots. Narrow and dirty streets lead to this house of worship, which is in the center of this former immigrant quarter. While in Havana, we met a number of American Orthodox Jews who walk from their hotels to Adath Israel on Friday nights and Saturday mornings. JDC also sponsors the Friday-night chicken dinner at this congregation.

"God has done something for us," said Alberto, referring to what he describes as the "miracle" of the revival of Judaism in Cuba. "The people are doing the rest."

The Sephardic Hebrew Center of Cuba is located at 17 Calle, between E and F Streets in the Vedado section of Havana. Most of the members in this house of worship are descended from families of Sephardic Jews who came to Cuba from Turkey before World War I.

Sometimes photos in a synagogue tell a lot about the nature of the congregation. In this case, when any of the eighty member families come to the synagogue, they see the photo of Theodor Herzl, the founder of political Zionism. I am surprised and pleased to see his picture. Herzl was convinced that the only solution to the Jewish problem would be a Jewish exodus from countries infested with anti-Semitism and a concentration of Jews in their own homeland.

In my interview with Jose Levy, before he emigrated to Israel, he told me he stayed in Cuba after the Revolution because he and his family were members of what he called "the working class."

"We had to fight the government for this building," he said, pointing out that while the construction of the building commenced in 1957, it was not completed until 1960, about two years after the Revolution. At the entrance there is still a plaque with the names of those who donated funds to build the synagogue. Almost all fled to the U.S.

It is difficult to keep some traditions alive, because without a rabbi, "the Jewish community here is almost like living in a house without parents," Levy told an interviewer in an Internet article on Cuba Headline News. Levy left Cuba for Israel in 2006 following his daughter to the Jewish state.

This Sephardic congregation sponsors a number of adult classes. Services are held Friday nights and Saturday mornings. Like other Jewish institutions in Cuba, the Sephardic Hebrew Center has benefited from the aid of the JDC. In March 2011, JDC undertook a presidential mission in Cuba to celebrate twenty years of the organization's return to the island. The group—headed by its chief executive officer, Steve Schwager, and Jerry Spitzer of the JDC, who chaired the mission—dedicated two classrooms at the Sephardic synagogue. The all-purpose classrooms each contain a projector and screen and twenty to thirty chairs, and will certainly help in youth activities.

～

Accurate statistics are very hard to come by regarding *aliyah*. However, it is known that the Jewish Agency for Israel assisted the emigration of about 400 Jews during the period of 1995 to 1999.

In those days, the *aliyah* program was called *"Operation Cigar,"* a name which at the time made a lot of sense. Apparently, Castro did not want to publicize the emigration because it might have looked like he was allowing special arrangements to be made for Cuba's Jews. One story has it that Israeli officials, when referring to Cuban Jewish émigrés, would use the term *cigars* instead of *Jews* to hide the truth about the emigration from the world. To this day, the emigration process goes through the Canadian

Embassy, since Cuba and Israel do not have diplomatic relations. Canada, however, maintains relations with both Israel and Cuba. The Jewish Agency for Israel, it is reported, picks up the tab for flying Jews to Israel. The term *"Operation Cigar"* seems to have floated away.

About 600 to 700 Jews have emigrated to Israel since the late 1990s, although some eventually ended up in Canada or the U.S. In 2009, 58 Jews left Cuba for Israel.

"Most of them were young, but sometimes their parents follow," said Dr. Mayra Levy, the new president of the Sephardic Synagogue, in an interview in 2010 with Liz Harris of the *JWeekly* newspaper in San Francisco. "If you show you have a Jewish life, you can leave," said Dr. Levy. Her son, a thirty-three-year-old computer engineer, emigrated to Israel seven years ago.

"Aliyah is a big problem for us," continued Dr. Levy. "They want to have a better life, so we have to improve their lives here to get them to stay. It's a daunting task. We try to get them better conditions—food, work—but in reality, they want to go. You can't put a chain on them," said Levy in her talk with Ms. Harris.

Some American Jewish observers and authors, such as Rabbi Dana Evan Kaplan, the spiritual leader of Temple B'nai Israel in Albany, Georgia, and adjunct associate professor at Siegal College of Jewish Studies, as well as Ruth Behar, professor of anthropology at the University of Michigan, believe Cuban Jewry is losing members because of departures for Israel.

According to Professor Behar, there are two key factors in a person's decision to leave: poor economic conditions; and the "strong spiritual dimension to the Exodus . . . The Jewish renaissance on the island is real, very real, and it is the force behind many of the departures," she wrote in her book, *An Island Called Home.*

Still, the Jewish population hovers around 1,100 mainly because conversions and a high Jewish birth rate probably make up the difference for those who made *aliyah.* As in the former Soviet Union, some non-Jews begin the process of conversion so they can exit Cuba. Meanwhile, other Jews are intermarrying because they claim the pool of potential Jewish males remains small.

Rabbi Szteinhendler is in charge of the island's conversion program, which covers all the synagogues. He told me that conversion proceedings follow *halakhah,* including *brit milah* (circumcision). Each Bet Din is made up of rabbis who were members of the Rabbinical Assembly (Conservative/Masorti movement). According to Rabbi Szteinhendler, about 200 persons have gone through the process. Undoubtedly, more Cubans will call on the rabbi to join the conversion proceedings.

I left the synagogue and made my way over to the Plaza de la Revolucion. Even if Fidel is not the president anymore, his powerful presence still hovers over Cuba. Some dictators are super orators, and without doubt Fidel is one of those who top the list. He can mesmerize the crowds for hours in this huge square, which at times brought a million persons to hear him rave and rant for hours. Nearby is the Ministry of the Interior with a huge bronze-wire sculpture of the revered Che Guevara, whose pictures and slogans dot the island.

"Our economic war will be with the great power of the North," said Che Guevara, who from the very beginning of Castro's battle to gain power "held more radical and overtly Marxist views than Fidel," notes author Coltman. Che took on the task to ignite Communist guerrilla insurrections in South America and Africa. He was captured and shot by a Bolivian Army detachment in 1967.

Standing in this square, it's impossible for me not to recall the half-century of hostility between the U.S. and Cuba, which began in 1961 just after Castro nationalized U.S. business without compensation and our government broke off diplomatic relations with Havana. Then came the unsuccessful U.S. Bay of Pigs invasion that same year.

When Castro allied Cuba with the USSR and proclaimed it a Communist state, his action made Cuba an enemy of the U.S. In the Cold War, he himself brought about the Cuban Missile Crisis of 1962, which took the U.S. and the Soviet Union to the brink of nuclear war. The USSR had deployed nuclear missiles on the island. The crisis was subsequently resolved when the Soviet Union agreed to remove the missiles. Castro continued to be the *bête noir* of the U.S., stirring up trouble in Africa, including aiding Communist guerrillas in Angola, Ethiopia. He even went so far as to allow 125,000 Cubans, many of them released convicts, to flee to the U.S.

Anti-Israel—but not anti-Jewish or anti-Semitic—seems to be the consensus regarding Fidel. In fact, in 2010, Fidel, in his eighties, seemed to be having "second thoughts" about Jews and Israel. In interviews with Jeffrey Goldberg of *The Atlantic,* he expressed sympathy for persecuted Jews and voiced admiration for Israeli prime minister Benjamin Netanyahu's father, Ben Zion, the world's foremost historian of the Spanish Inquisition. According to Goldberg, Castro repeatedly returned to his excoriation of anti-Semitism, even going so far as to criticize Ahmadinejad of Iran for denying the Holocaust. He urged the Iranian dictator to stop slandering the Jews and said that the Iranian government would better serve the cause of peace by acknowledging the "unique" history of anti-Semitism and trying to understand why Israelis fear for their existence.

These statements probably prompted some analysts to believe that Fidel and Raul Castro are showing more support for Jews in recent months.

In the early days, Fidel was far from an enemy of Israel. In 1961, Jews who emigrated from Cuba to Israel were called *repatriados* (people returning to their native lands), while others fleeing the Revolution were called *gusanos* (anti-revolutionary worms). A decade later, however, Fidel, who sought to lead the nonaligned movement, turned on Israel, supported the PLO, and acted as their principal supporter. He and his government endorsed the United Nations' "Zionism Is Racism Resolution," and sent Cuban advisors to the Syrian army. He broke relations with Israel just before the Yom Kippur War in 1973.

But for now, positive and subtle changes appear to be in store for the Jewish community. Take, for example, the 2010 visit of President Raul Castro to the Patronato to participate in a 2010 Hanukkah ceremony, a first for the new president.

Juan O. Tomayo, writing in the *Miami Herald* in December 2010, saw the visit as "an indication of his communist government's effort to reach out to religious institutions on the island."

And yet tensions between Cuba and the U.S. often overshadow even a president's visit to the Jewish community.

⌒

Tomayo noted that Raul made no mention of Alan Gross, an American Jewish subcontractor for the U.S. government who was jailed in 2009 and later convicted for entering the country as part of a USAID team distributing communications equipment to the island's Jewish community. Gross was sentenced to fifteen years in a Cuban jail.

Secretary of State Hillary Clinton urged Cuba to release Gross on humanitarian grounds, as did the Conference of Presidents of Major American Jewish Organizations, along with his wife, Judy Gross. The Cubans accused Gross of being a spy, tried him, and convicted him of taking part in "a subversive project of the U.S. government that aimed to destroy the revolution through the use of communications systems out of the control of the authorities."

The verdict "is sure to have sweeping repercussions for already sour relations between Washington and Havana," said further the Associated Press on March 13, 2011. Cuban Jewish groups have denied any involvement with Gross.

At the end of March 2011, former president Jimmy Carter made a private trip to the island. He met with the jailed contractor, but did not secure Gross's release.

In the final analysis, Fidel's policies have made Cuba "one of the poorest and most repressive places in our hemisphere," according to a 2010 report of The Jewish Institute for National Security Affairs. In 2003, mass arrests took place and became known as Cuba's Black Spring, which provoked international condemnation. Finally in 2010, after talks with Catholic Church leaders, Raul Castro agreed to free the fifty-two dissidents still behind bars after the crackdown in 2003. The last two dissidents were finally released in March 2011.

Reality: The regime itself has not changed. Early in 2011, Michael Voss of the BBC wrote: "There are no signs of any moves towards political reform or loosening of the one party state."

Thinking about Cuba, I wonder if the old, dedicated Castro veterans who were with him in the mountains, and those who remember the heady days when everything seemed possible, still believe in the Revolution. Do they not witness the poverty which has existed for a half-century? Do they not witness many of their children abandoning the island the first chance they get, seeking a better life elsewhere—whether through a lottery or by other means?

Back in America, I was shocked to hear at the end of 2010 that Fidel Castro had admitted the unthinkable. He told Jeffrey Goldberg of *The Atlantic* and Julia Sweig of the *Council on Foreign Relations,* "The Cuban model doesn't even work for us anymore."

That year Cuba launched a program of major economic changes designed to reduce the State's overwhelming role in the economy and to promote private enterprise. Raul Castro, the new Cuban president, announced that a million state workers would be laid off. He encouraged them to find new jobs in the practically non-existant private sector. He warned that a withering economic crisis is pushing Cuba to the edge of a precipice.

About 85 percent of all Cubans with jobs are employed by the State, and earn about $20 per month in exchange for free access to services like health and education and a ration of subsidized goods.

Hoping to triple the country's private sector, the government has issued 250,000 licenses allowing people to run their own businesses. Under the new rules, Cubans will be permitted to employ people other than relatives. They will be able to rent out rooms to tourists, work as self-employed gardeners, iron clothes and shine shoes. The ration card, which provides ten days' worth of food per month at dirt-cheap prices, will be "eliminated in an orderly fashion as part of the campaign to cut back massive government subsidies," the *Miami Herald* reported on November 9, 2010.

Still, the Castro regime is capable of slamming shut the system whenever it desires. While controls were relaxed in the 1990s, some economic reforms later were rolled back, with Fidel Castro denouncing what he called the "new rich."

Cuba is not about to revert to capitalism. Yet a new class of entrepreneurs and small business owners may start to emerge. Already a few new private storefronts are opening: a barber here, a hairdresser there, a few jewelry stands, some new cafes and food stores. Resourceful Cubans are setting up these small enterprises on balconies and front porches.

Conceivably, private restaurants (known as *paladares*) might expand. I recalled that the driver on our Hemingway tour took us to one. We devoured a very tasty fish lunch, which was brought to us as we relaxed on a veranda surrounded by palm trees and tropical flowers. Maybe someday, I thought, Cuban citizens, not just tourists, will partake of the good life, too.

At the same time, change came regarding the lifting of restrictions on travel to Cuba. In 2011, the Obama administration modified and eased the restraints so there could be more contact between people in both countries. This action by the Obama administration paved the way for synagogues and federations to organize more missions to Cuba, and by the summer of 2011, the number of Jewish federations traveling to Cuba had increased two or three times which meant the community was receiving more aid.

The modifications fell into the category of religious, educational, and academic purposes. A letter from a religious organization is still needed to travel to Cuba, according to Mayra Alonso of Marazul Charters, located in North Bergen, New Jersey.

But the decades-old trade embargo against the island's Communist government will stand.

"Why are we still maintaining a trade embargo against Cuba?" I was often asked this question by American tourists in Cuba and in the U.S. For five decades, the battle lines have been drawn. Those who oppose lifting the trade embargo against Cuba say that to do otherwise means aiding the regime and allowing it to reap the harvest of a free fall of billions of dollars for itself. They also oppose lifting the embargo until Castro embraces human rights and democracy.

Those who want to lift the ban say the embargo has done nothing to bring down Castro and force him to adopt more-inclusive democratic policies. In fact, they argue that the U.S. position may have given Castro a tangible enemy to point to, thus keeping the masses in line. They point out that in spite of the embargo, Castro's Cuba has survived for twenty years after its longtime Soviet benefactor collapsed.

In the last analysis, I believe the Jewish community is better off today than even a decade ago when it comes to their personal being. The medicine, the clothes, the supplies, and the donations help the community to overcome the harshness of life in Cuba and to meet the challenges of a strangled economy. Now because of the increased influx and volume of needed aid, JDC is trying to coordinate equal distribution of the supplies not only to

Havana synagogues but houses of worship and communities outside the capital, according to Dr. William Recant.

Some observers say the Jewish community is "thriving," and in many ways, it is. This is a Jewish community that has been rescued by world events (the fall of Communism in 1991), and of course, by fellow Jews from abroad, the Jewish organizations from the U.S. and Canada, the federations and welfare groups, as well as the Cuban Jews who live in Miami—many of whom help their brothers and sisters in that nearby Caribbean island. Let us not forget the teachers, professionals, and rabbis who have contributed their knowledge and skills in educating these wonderful people who have a hunger for Jewish life and a love for the Jewish state.

After I returned to the U.S., my friend Ellen Lavin, who was on a Federation mission, told me that upon landing in Havana, she was picked out by an inspector who took her passport and said, "Follow me." The customs official asked her a few questions, and quickly checked her purse.

"What's the purpose of your trip to Cuba?" he asked.

"I am here in Cuba as part of a humanitarian mission to the Jewish synagogue in Havana," she answered."

"Oh! Nice," replied the inspector as he handed back her passport. "My friend is married to a Jewish lady. Good people over there," he said, and waved her on through customs.

ISRAEL

Coming Home

*You yourselves have seen what I did to Egypt, and how I bore you on wings
of eagles, and brought you to Myself.*

—*Exodus 19:4*

I was eighteen years old and I knew I was in trouble. I figured I would be
robbed of the items I had carefully tucked away in my new rucksack.

The year was 1952. I wasn't cramped into a foxhole in Korea where
the U.S. was battling the North Koreans and Chinese, nor was I tied up
as a hostage in Lebanon or Jordan. I had disembarked from an old, former
U.S. cargo ship, now a dilapidated Israeli freighter known as the SS *Negba*.

On this chilly fall night, only four years after the founding of the State
of Israel, I found myself in a pitch-black, one-room tin hut surrounded by
hundreds of one-room tin huts located in a huge tin hut city known as a
ma'abara (transit camp) at the top of the ancient city of Tiberias, overlooking beautiful, blue Lake Kinneret, also known as the biblical Sea of Galilee.

Even though I hoped I was protected by the likes of Rabbi Akiva and
the *Rambam* (Maimonides), both of whom were buried in this holy city, I
was worried. The presents and goods in my rucksack weren't mine; they
were given to me by friends back home for their relatives in Israel.

How had I come to land in this ghetto-like area, which resembled
a European DP (Displaced Persons) camp, inhabited by my own people?
Why was I frightened?

I hadn't come to Israel by myself. I was part of a group of thirty members of the Labor Zionist Youth Movement, Habonim. We had come to

the Jewish state as part of that organization's "Youth Workshop in Israel," located at Kibbutz Kfar Blum in the Upper Galilee.

As Isaiah had promised, and repeated time and time again by the Biblical prophesies of Isaiah and other prophets, the "Ingathering of the Exiles" was taking place. The Jewish people were coming home to the land of Israel on the wings of an eagle, which in some cases just happened to be twin-engine passenger planes flying the newcomers from Yemen to the Jewish state.

In the early 1950s, more than 130,000 Iraqi Jews had arrived, bringing the number of persons living in the camps to more than 220,000. More than 80 percent of the residents consisted of refugees from across Muslim lands in the Middle East and North Africa.

For some reason, our kibbutz leaders did not tell us until the last minute that we would have a week's free time to visit relatives or friends. As I had no family in Israel, I was planning to visit some friends' family, and was bringing them gifts. We had immediately been forced to scramble, knowing that in Israel in those days, bus and train lines normally shut down by early evening, and cars and trucks were few and far between at night.

My destination was the sleepy town of Afula, located in the middle of the fertile *Emek Yisrael* (the valley of Israel). Conventional wisdom in Israel describes it as a boring, dusty place, far from desirable, and whose inhabitants are closed-minded and all dress and act the same. I later found it to be a town that was content with itself, with many warm and friendly people.

Looking back on it today, from a historical perspective, those early years of Israel's existence remain a wonderful time in the annals of the Jewish people. After 2,000 years in the diaspora, my people had returned to a Zion restored.

They came by ship and by plane, and the Jewish state was engulfed in a massive effort to absorb thousands of immigrants, many from Europe, but mostly from North Africa, the Middle East, and Asia. This effort had resulted in massive austerity programs, known as *tzena*. This *tzena* is not connected in any way with the the popular song "Tzena, Tzena" They are pronounced the same but spelled differently. Believe me, *tzena* was rationing at its worst. After all, as children growing up in America during World War II, we'd had it easy; we barely knew what it meant to be denied food.

In Israel, however, you couldn't even buy a chocolate bar in a store. Your only opportunity came when old men would stand in doorways and try to sell you black-market chocolate. Once, for instance, when I visited some friends in Rishon Le Zion, a small container of cottage cheese was passed to me. I thought it was just for me until I was told (nicely, of course) that it was for the whole table.

At dinner in Kibbutz Kfar Blum, I witnessed a telling scene in that cooperative's dining hall, where tables were set up cafeteria-style. A serving wagon went up and down the aisles with dinner platters. The server would hand the diner a plate with a meal on it. On the plate that evening was herring. I was sitting next to a veteran member of the kibbutz. When the server handed him his portion, the veteran *kibbutznik* answered, "I only eat herring twice a day. I'll take *bimkom* (the other choice)." Even with austerity, people get tired of eating herring every day, the kibbutz member explained to me. He got a platter of cheese as the other choice.

That evening in Tiberias, I realized I only had a slight chance to get to Afula before sunset. I set out anyway with the words of a popular, optimistic Israeli expression: "It will be good"—which is the opposite of one of their old expressions, "No choice." Both expressions were popular during the 1948 War of Independence, when the odds were overwhelmingly in favor of the Arabs.

As students, we tried to save our money and hitchhiked whenever possible. This meant being able to jump onto the back of a truck or climb up into what they called a "tender" (similar to our pickup truck). Everyone hitched rides, then—students, civilians, and soldiers.

Needless to say, I had missed the bus connection to Afula and had only gotten as far as Tiberias, where I once again tried to hitchhike. I got a ride to the top of the hill on the Tiberias road, direction Afula, where I planted my feet in front of a *kiosk* (refreshment stand).

A group of men were standing around, drinking soda and smoking cigarettes—and there I was, on the edge of the road, still hoping to get a *tremp* which is what Israelis call hitchhiking.

A truck approached but it didn't stop. Another one didn't stop, and then a few more. I guessed that just like in the U.S. not everyone stops to pick up hitchhikers. Meanwhile, I soon became aware of the stares from the men in the kiosk. They were looking at me, an easily recognized American, wearing a new khaki shirt, new khaki pants, and new boots. Being an American in those days, like today, was definitely not a disadvantage in Israel, despite the foreign-policy twists and turns of both countries.

In the early 1950s, you didn't have to be in Israel for more than a day when you'd hear "Watch out for Moroccans—they'll pull a knife on you," or "Stay away from those Iraqis; why, they'll steal everything you've got." Stereotypes! I heard them all the time.

Yet the ominous warnings caused some uneasiness, as I stood on the road waiting for a ride. The uneasiness was caused also because I had heard that the crime rate among North African Jews had risen during that time. It's hard to imagine it would have been otherwise, especially when a family was crowded four or more to a room, with a monthly income of less than $20. The large room in those tin huts that I could see from the road, was not connected to either water or electric systems, so there was no running water, no showers. Running water was available only from central faucets, but it had to be boiled before drinking. These were the new homes of Jews from the Maghreb.

So, still waiting, it came as a surprise that evening when a man came up to me and said, "You can stay with us!" He told me his name was Aziz. "You can sleep in my sister's hut; she's away. Stay over and get up early in the morning," the man continued. "The trucks from the kibbutzim will be moving then and you'll get a ride."

I agreed and thanked him and walked into the *ma'abara* with him to his sister's hut.

That night, despite his kindness, I held the rucksack that contained the packages so close to my body that I could feel the edges of the gift boxes piercing my skin. With my hands wrapped so tightly around the backpack, it would have taken a gorilla to wrest it away.

Not only did my anxiety keep me awake, but it was also difficult to sleep with the somewhat-Oriental melodic sounds penetrating the thin walls of the tin hut. Needless to say, I did not sleep well.

When Aziz woke me up the next morning, it was still dark. By the time I got to the road, however, the morning light was illuminating the narrow two-lane highway.

Aziz bade me farewell and I thanked him.

"All Jews are brothers," he said. A good lesson, which I have tried to remember all my life, not always with success, I must admit. The first truck came by. I yelled. I used the Israeli way to get a ride: hand outstretched, moving it up and down, indicating *Stop*, not the American way of holding my thumb up, as if asking "Hey, going my way?"

"Stop, stop, stop," I pleaded.

The truck stopped. "Climb up!" he yelled.

I understood enough Hebrew to answer "Afula! Thanks!"

When I got back to Kfar Blum after our brief vacation, I told my friends about my experience in the *ma'abara* and the fact that I slept over in one of those huts.

For the entire year, whenever my friends and I passed the *ma'abara* in Tiberias, we would yell out, "There's *Benny's Ma'abara!*" In my teenage years in the youth group, I (the author) was called "Benny!"

⌒

After being forcibly exiled from their land, the people kept faith with it throughout their Dispersion and never ceased to pray and hope for their return to it and for the restoration in it of their political freedom.
—*Declaration of the Establishment of the State of Israel*

⌒

The first Hebrew word I heard in Israel was *savlanut* (patience). When we arrived on the rickety old *Negba,* we had docked in Haifa port. Standing at the top of the gangplank was this short, uniformed keeper of the peace, a policeman, who entreated the passengers, jostling for position to get off, saying *Savlanut . . . savlanut.*

To be honest, the command to be patient was the wrong advice for yours truly, along with the several hundred other bored, seasick, and weary passengers. None of us, I am sure, possessed this quality at just that moment. Jews had heard enough promises of "Just wait," or, as Aneurin Bevan, foreign minister of Great Britain, had said (and I paraphrase): Jews should take their turn in the queue.

Definitely the wrong word for this writer. I never had patience, don't now, and probably never will. Maybe that's why I became a reporter—so I could always be on the move and chasing a story. But I digress.

As I have observed, neither the Zionist movement or World Jewry, or the State of Israel or its citizens—especially after World War II and the Holocaust—will ever—endure pain or difficulty with calmness.

~

The State of Israel will be open for Jewish immigration and for the Ingathering of the Exiles.

—Declaration of the Establishment of the State of Israel

~

We appeal to the Jewish people throughout the diaspora to rally round the Jews of Eretz-Israel in the task of immigration and up-building and to stand by them in the great struggle for the realization of the age-old dream—the redemption of Israel.

—Declaration of the Establishment of the State of Israel

~

Between May 1948 and December 1951, Israel absorbed some 700,000 Jewish immigrants—or slightly more than its total Jewish population at the dawn of statehood. And they kept on coming! Between 1948 and 1970, the total was about 1.4 million Jews; their absorption, an impossible task for most countries, was an incredible burden for a small country without resources.

I knew that the one million forgotten Jews from North Africa were arriving. What made the absorption process difficult for the newcomers was the fact that the Israelis and the European Jews who resided in Palestine at the time of Jewish statehood had "had almost no contact with those [Jews] living in the Arab world since about the sixteenth century," according to Andre N. Chouraqui, author of *Between East and West: A History of the Jews of North Africa.*

"The Jews of Europe and America, for their part, found it difficult to accept the idea that these people of darker hue, imbued with Arabic culture and customs, were in fact Jews and their brothers," Chouraqui continued, adding that they "tended, consciously or not, to look down on the new arrivals from the Moslem countries. . . ."

More than a half-century later, my colleague, author and journalist Raphael Rothstein, echoed the voice of many when he wrote in the

National Jewish News, in 2007, on the situation in Israel during the 1950s and '60s, when thousands of Moroccan Jews arrived and "were subjected to prejudice and insult."

Rothstein wrote: "We knew nothing of Moroccan Jewry. We had no appreciation of its rich history and traditions, its communities and its deep and abiding Jewishness. . . . This was sad, pitiable. And it is a shameful thing. But *ila fat mat* [what's past is dead], and today the children of these Moroccan Jews flourish in Israel, and there is knowledge and understanding of what was built here [in Morocco] over the centuries."

Most of the newcomers in those days came through Haifa port only to be settled in the abandoned Arab neighborhoods of the big towns, or in depopulated small towns. When the housing ran out, huge transit camps known as *ma'abarot* were erected. The new immigrants, known as *olim,* found themselves stuck in the corrugated-iron shacks with no electricity, drains, or running water. Sharing sanitation facilities was the norm; in one community it was reported that there were 350 people to each shower, and in another, 56 people to each toilet.

As the noted Israeli writer Amos Oz put it:

> *Accountants from Iraq, goldsmiths from Yemen, tradesmen and shopkeepers from Morocco, and watchmakers from Bucharest were crowded into these huts and employed for a pittance on government schemes of rock clearing and reforesting in the Jerusalem hills.*

Other communities, such as Iraqi Jews and Yemenites, arrived as an entire community. The Jews of the Maghreb split into two groups: the urban, educated, French-speaking Jews emigrated to France, while the rural poor headed to Israel.

Maghreb Jews were penniless when they came to Israel, and were unsuited to the rigors and demands of life in the new state. At the same time, as author Benny Morris points out in his book, *1948: A History of the First Arab-Israeli War,* "the Arab states derived massive economic benefit from the confiscations of property that accompanied the exodus . . ."

In an April 30, 2010, article in the *Jerusalem Post* entitled *"The Nabka of Morocco's Jews,"* Lela Gilbert reminds us that "most of the Jews of the Maghreb lost everything but the clothes they wore."

While the Arab refugee problem—created by the Arab-initiated attack on Israel—is constantly raised in international circles today, few recognize the nearly 1 million Jews who were expelled or given little choice but to leave Arab lands. Their plight has never been recognized by the Arab world.

Recently, all ten Jewish communities displaced from Arab countries appeared to be pleased with a law passed by the Knesset in 2010, which mandated that any Israeli government entering into peace talks use those talks to advance a compensation claim for those who suffered in leaving Arab lands.

Traveling through Israel several times in the early part of the twenty-first century, I kept an eye out to ascertain how some of the groups that I had visited in other lands were managing in their new homeland. What I saw was that every immigration wave has made "a safe landing." There are difficulties, of course. Moving in itself is stressful, even within the same country, let alone to a foreign land with a different language, customs, and culture. Obstacles have been overcome, and while there are poor and disadvantaged people in Israel, a safety net exists—not as high as some would like it, but it's there.

Part of Israel's recent economic success remains its ability to "absorb immigrants," noted Saul Singer, coauthor with Dan Senor of *Start-Up Nation: The Story of Israel's Economic Miracle,* in an interview with David Horovitz, in the *Jerusalem Post,* May 6–12, 2011.

"This is the most pro-immigrant country on Earth," declared Singer. "Here we have politicians campaigning for more immigrants. We have an Absorption Ministry! Sure, we complain about how it works. But other countries are coming here to learn from us about how we absorb immigrants. We've turned a potential problem into an asset."

Indeed they have. Most would agree that by the second decade of the twenty-first century, absorption has been successful in that most young Israelis often don't know and rarely care where anyone's parents or grandparents came from.

As Singer put it: "Most everyone here is either an immigrant, the child of immigrants, or the grandchildren of immigrants; it takes determination to be an immigrant, and that means a willingness to take a risk."

⌒

Seeing Israel yourself is one thing. Seeing Israel through the eyes of a twelve-year-old is another, especially when the child is your grandson.

What is described as the ultimate journey begins when Randy, my wife, and I board El Al flight 28, to the Jewish state. Security is tight. How tight? They ask our grandson the name of his rabbi at his day school. He knows it!

⌒

It's early morning, forty-five years after my encounter in the Tiberias *ma'abara*. The first tour of the day is in Independence Hall at Beit Dizengoff, 16 Rothschild Street, the former home of Meir Dizengoff, mayor of Tel Aviv, whom we met in Odessa in chapter 1. The Dizengoffs purchased the land in 1909 and moved in a year later, part of a plan to establish a new Jewish neighborhood in what was to become Tel Aviv. The museum houses exhibits on the signing and history of Tel Aviv.

With the exception of my wife and grandson Randy, the main room is filled with college students—members of *Taglit-Birthright Israel,* which over the years has sent 50,000 young adults, mostly college students, on trips to Israel.

On that historic day, May 14, 1948, the hall was hastily prepared using chairs from nearby cafes to provide the seating for more than 300 invitees. As people in the neighborhood got wind of what was happening, they gathered in front of the building and heard David Ben-Gurion, soon-to-be Israel's first prime minister, deliver the historic declaration over a loudspeaker.

At Independence Hall with grandson Randy that August 2009 morning, the museum's spokesperson held up a picture of a bearded man. "Do you know who this is?" she asked. The college students are non-plussed. There was silence in the room. My wife and I kept quiet.

We gently nudged our grandson Randy, age twelve. "Theodor Herzl," he said.

This is not to criticize *Taglit-Birthright Israel,* for it's likely that many of these students' parents may also not recognize the picture of the founder of modern Zionism, even though this is the man who radically changed the course of Jewish history.

After being in Israel for ten days or so, young people now in this historic hall can analyze events for themselves. Surely, they will always remember this trip, and they will remember Herzl. During the ceremony they hear that about fifty years after Herzl declared "*If you will it, it is no dream,*" the Zionist dream became reality. Israel was born. Herzl was correct. He was, after all, the Zionist movement's organizer and prophet.

At eight o'clock on the morning of May 14, the British lowered the Union Jack in Jerusalem; their mandate over Palestine ended. By mid-afternoon full-scale fighting had erupted throughout the country. The next day, Israel was being invaded by five Arab nations plus Palestinian regulars.

I observed that underneath a picture of Herzl in the main hall, the chairs were arranged as they had been the day Israel became independent.

Sitting in the audience with these young people, I was transported back in time. I listened to that shrill but excited recorded voice of David Ben-Gurion, prime minister, as he read the Israel Declaration of Independence at about 4:00 p.m. that Friday afternoon in May. Members of the Vaad Leumi (Jewish National Council) and leaders of the Jewish community were in attendance. The Jewish population listened on the radio, except for those in Jerusalem, which had no electricity. When Ben-Gurion finished, Rabbi Maimon Fischman recited the *Shehecheyanu* blessing and the Declaration was signed.

The Israel Philharmonic was in the hall. They played *"Hatikvah,"* Israel's national anthem. The audience on the record joined in, and we did as well. The music and the voices of those men and women reverberate with pride, honor, and a sense of accomplishment. Israel was born.

An Israeli guide talked to the *Taglit-Birthright* young men and women. He gave a dramatic speech—"from his gut," as he put it. He told the young people that in any country of the world, wherever and whenever Jews are in trouble, whenever they are being threatened, attacked, or persecuted, they have a home, an address: "The Land of Israel."

Some readers of this book will remember where they were on that day in May 1948, the rebirth of Israel. My friends tell me that large numbers of American Jews danced the *hora* (the Jewish national dance) in Times Square. As for this writer, well, I and my youth movement friends danced around the flagpole at Taylor Allderdice High School in Pittsburgh, Pennsylvania. Afterward, we went to an Israeli friend's house and listened to the news from the new nation on shortwave, only to hear that Israel had been attacked by the armies of five Arab nations. For the moment, our joy was tempered.

Sixty-three years later, the flagpole was still there. So is the State of Israel. After the emotional encounter in this cramped, modest building where Israel's statehood was proclaimed, my wife and I took Randy to a neighborhood restaurant for *falafel, hummus, tahini, baba ghanoush, pita,* Israeli chopped salad, and a cup of tea.

Then we walked around the neighborhood and observed some of the 1930s Bauhaus buildings that helped earn Tel Aviv a UNESCO World Heritage site designation. We wandered along Rothschild Boulevard and spotted coffee shops, sushi stands, and street performers.

That night, we headed to the old Tel Aviv port, which has been reclaimed and turned into a place where you can cool off and relax amid boutiques, sporting goods stores, ice cream and frozen yogurt parlors, and outdoor restaurants. Above all, it's a place where you can find a spot on a bench and watch the world go by.

Sitting there and observing the old sea breakers, my thoughts returned to the old days when Jews coming to Israel used this small port.

The port of Tel Aviv was built in the 1930s as a result of the 1936–39 Arab riots and was a major accomplishment, an actual harbor built by Jews in place of Jaffa Port, which was then controlled by the Arabs. Basically barred from Jaffa, the Jews had no choice but to build this harbor. With Israeli independence came the first Israeli ship carrying immigrants to Israel. I could imagine some of those first arrivals doing just what S. Y. Agnon, Israeli Nobel Laureate, described in his novel, *Only Yesterday,* "A Jew arrives in the Land of Israel, leaps off the ship and kisses her soil, in the joy of weeping and weeping for joy."

⁓

"Israel is fun," Randy wrote on a postcard halfway through our trip. He especially enjoyed the beach and town of Netanya. What youngster would not enjoy riding a horse at "The Ranch," in Havatzelet Hasharon, just north of Netanya (www.the-ranch.co.il). Saddling up, he moved out onto rolling sand dunes along the beckoning blue Mediterranean. He also loved racing around in go-karts at GO Karting Poleg (www.gokarting.co.il)—going around and around the indoor track is popular with kids and adults alike.

⁓

Our base was an apartment in cosmopolitan Netanya on the coastal plain which runs between the Lebanese border and Gaza. According to Martin Fletcher in his book, *Walking Israel: A Personal Search for the Soul of a Nation,* "seventy percent of Israel's people, Jews and Arabs, live within ten miles of the beach, along the coastal plain, in relative harmony."

To overcome jet lag after we'd first arrived, we had rested for a day and later surfed, swam, and basked in the sun. One of the city's highlights is the sea-view elevator, designed in response to the 40-meter gap between City Center Netanya and the beach. It provides a twenty-second-long comfortable descent from various viewpoints down to the beach.

Our niece, Jeanette, also twelve, and her parents will travel with us. The children immediately take to Netanya, with its large French and Russian population, its *croissants* and *borscht,* and its Saturday-night carnival-time atmosphere in the city's festive *Kikar Atzmaut* (Independence Square). The neighborhood boasts pizza parlors, entertainers, cafes, and stall after stall filled with costume jewelry and crafts. "A lot to see," Randy said, as he picked out a new *Magen David* that he ended up wearing during the entire trip.

I met a young couple, both speech therapists, on the beach in Netanya. During our conversation, I asked about Israel's economy.

"Couldn't be better," they replied. As we talked, the two who were on vacation, took pictures of the scenery, the beach and the beautiful blue of the Mediterranean. "It's great to get away, even for a couple of days. Netanya is so different from Jerusalem," they declared. Even though it is a small country, Israelis find that there is a great scenic variety between the hills of the Galilee and the sands of the Negev.

Both speech therapists whom I met that day in Netanya were working full-time. The couple was correct regarding Israel's economy. In 2010, the country's economic growth was better than expected, expanding by approximately 4.5 percent.

Back in the U.S. one night, watching TV, I was startled to hear Israel's prime minister Benjamin Netanyahu, aka "Bibi," tell the American audience that Israel is a "prosperous country with 5.5 percent GDP," and to top it off, he continued, the Jewish state had discovered a trove of natural gas—not bad for a nation of nearly 7.5 million people. The growth is continuing, including a steep rise in high-tech exports, according to the April 18, 2011, issue of *Haaretz*. The Central Bureau of Statistics reported that during the first quarter of 2011, the Israeli Gross Domestic Product rose by 4.7 in annual terms compared to the last quarter of 2010.

In the last decade, Israel, existing in a very dangerous neighborhood and bereft of natural resources, "has nonetheless managed to outstrip every nation on earth in terms of high-tech innovation," wrote David Horovitz in his interview with Saul Singer, coauthor with Dan Senor in their book, *Start-Up Nation: The Story of Israel's Economic Miracle.*

"Truly amazing. Israel has the largest number of 'start-ups' per year of any country, outside the U.S. Not per capita. The largest number. Period. We have about 500 a year, and all of Europe has 600 to 700. Our 7.5 million people compared to that whole continent's 700 million people," noted Singer. In addition, "more Israeli companies are listed on the NASDAQ exchange than all companies from the entire European continent," according to *Start-Up Nation.*

The fact that nearly everyone serves in the military helps to build an economy and new businesses. Soldiers and officers learn how to adapt and do things outside of the box in order to accomplish a mission. Israel's start-ups are successful because of military thinking. It's all about risk-taking. Sounds like capitalism, eh?

I have learned more about the Israeli company, Better Place, described by *Time* magazine as "the most sophisticated electric-car enterprise in the world." Meaningful, especially when it is predicted that within this decade, the top-selling car in the world will be the electric car.

Israel expects to end global oil dependency by 2020 and to make their country a global center for alternative-energy technology.

⌒

As one of Israel's foremost seaside resorts, with hotels and guesthouses, tourism is Netanya's main business. At Israel's birth, Netanya's population was 8,500. Today, it is the ninth-largest city in Israel, with a population of about 190,000, expected to reach 350,000 by 2020.

Travel writer David Laskin, writing in the *New York Times* on September 29, 2010, called Netanya a "rather drab but beautifully situated 1970s-era beach town north of Tel Aviv with a weird mix of French and Russian clientele."

I found the mix of French and Russians quite exciting, challenging, and cosmopolitan. During the hot summer afternoons, our condo building on Danker Street remained quiet, as did the town. In this hot part of the day, people here take a break until late afternoon.

In the mornings, we woke up to the blue Mediterranean. Our balcony not only overlooked the street below, but the beach as well, so that I felt I was on the upper deck of a cruise ship. Paragliders floated by our window.

Slightly less than 20 miles from Tel Aviv and 35 miles south of Haifa, Netanya celebrated its eighty-second birthday in 2011 with poetry readings, dance company presentations, concerts, and theater productions, including a presentation of *Women's Minyan* by Naomi Ragen.

Walking to the *Kikar* (Independence Square) on Saturday nights, you hear a lot of Hebrew, French, Russian, some English. The people of Netanya, that sweating, summertime humanity of Israelis, French, Ethiopian, and Russian Jews, in packed restaurants, cafes, and pizza parlors, makes one feel at home.

These are happy, fun-loving people, yet also serious and competitive, always looking over their shoulders at possible danger, some even sensing the possibility of another war in the future.

～

Russian Jews? What better place to meet them than in Netanya, where most of the stores have Russian-language signs, announcements, and price lists. Russian is heard everywhere—yes, everywhere—which reminded me of the old days, especially the story about the *Sem Sorok train,* the 7:40 a.m. train from Moscow to Vienna.

When Jews first left the former Soviet Union, beginning in the 1970s, as well as later from its successor, Russia, they came home by plane, by boat, and by rail. One such conveyance was a train that ran from Moscow to Vienna and moved right through the heart of the *shtetls* of Eastern Europe, where, before the Holocaust, Jews lived, worked, and prayed. Now the twentieth-century Jews of Russia were traveling through that heartland to the Jewish homeland.

Some people gave that line's train an odd nickname: *Sem Sorok,* after a happy, fast-moving, Russian song that was based on an old, nineteenth-century Bendery-Odessa line that brought Jews to work in Odessa and arrived at that city's railway station at 7:40 a.m. The train's railroad cars were made up in the Russian capital, the former home of the czars and Stalin, and the passengers disembarked in Vienna, the former home of the Habsburgs, and the center of Nazism before World War II. So much Jewish history recorded in those two cities.

Each day, the human cargo on the *Sem Sorok,* as on the other trains, planes, and boats, would enhance the State of Israel with more new immigrants. Eventually, about 1 million Russian Jews settled in Israel.

"It was an exodus and a flood of Jews who were completely cut off from the rest of world Jewry, robbed of any knowledge of Jewish history, Jewish language, and culture," remembered Mrs. Eleonora Shifrin-Poltinnikova of Jerusalem. Along with being a translator, journalist, and an *aliyah* and absorption activist, she has also served for twenty-three years as a volunteer area coordinator for Keren Klita, a volunteer organization that supports and helps immigrants from the former Soviet Union.

Many had no time to sit and ponder their going to Israel. Some people were "dragged by the stream." In fact, Mrs. Shifrin-Poltinnikova stresses, it was often the wife who encouraged the couple's departure.

They were "awful times" in Russia, those years after 1989, so the cry went up among Russian Jews: "As long as it's possible, let's get out of this dreadful country." They did. They knew there was no way back, and that this was the only land for them and their children, said Mrs. Shifrin-Poltinnikova.

And so they came home to Israel, "a hard country to live in," she opined. "In Israel you have to know why you came to this land."

While the Absorption Department could only do so much, Keren Klita helped with things like how to apply for and get a job. Back home, Russian Jews were taught to be modest. In Israel, that would get you nowhere in an interview. Advice was given to newcomers on how to deal with medical problems, language problems, social problems—all the difficulties that new immigrants face, even to the extent of how to get a hearing aid. The group provided every family with linens, blankets, pillows, kitchenware, heaters, and children's books.

The Absorption Department often sent new immigrants to Keren Klita to learn how to shop in the supermarket, how to negotiate a lease, how to buy an apartment. The new arrivals, however, only knew Russian. Not knowing Hebrew or English often held some professionals back from getting a job, so much so that it created psychological barriers to their adjustment.

One attribute that the Russian professionals, technicians, doctors, and people of the arts shared was the ability to work hard. In Russia, under the Communists, it was never a question of money or salary; it was pride in doing your job well, the only way for a Jew to get promoted. "This pride in performing a high quality of work" accompanied Soviet Jews to Israel, Mrs. Shifrin-Poltinnikova said.

Russian Jews in Israel are the largest Russian community outside of Russia, and their absorption has basically been successful. Two decades after they left the former Soviet Union, their contributions to the State of Israel in the arts, sciences, and technology are beyond measure. But in the beginning, this writer noticed a few difficulties among the new immigrants, such as marital and drinking problems and even buying Santa Claus figurines at the end of the secular year.

Rabbi Jonathan Porath, an author and lecturer who spent fifteen years in Russia working for the JDC, says "The Russians who came were part and parcel of overall Russian culture no less than American Jews are Americans. They do what is natural for them, and do not see it as contradictory to living in Israel, particularly when their large numbers of over a million Russian-speakers in Israel gives them cultural backup." He added that Russian Jews "are undoubtedly and increasingly become integrated into Israeli life."

Rabbi Porath remembers launching an absorption project in his neighborhood in the Jerusalem section of Neve Orot in Ramot. Many Russians usually arrived with nothing, he recalled, mostly because many said that "their bags were lost en route." He recollected one evening when he was told that twenty to thirty Russian families had arrived and were entering their new apartments nearby, which were ready, but completely empty. The newcomers were going to sleep on their suitcases. So Rabbi Porath and his neighbors borrowed a truck, and in a few hours, they had collected some beds and mattresses from the area for the new arrivals.

"Welcoming new immigrants was my way of repaying those who helped me when I arrived as an immigrant," said the rabbi.

Many of today's IDF front-line combat troop units are made up of Russians, I was told. As the rabbi notes, "When your kids are in the army, you know you're an Israeli." Like all Israelis, Russians have also paid with their lives to defend Israel. Scenes of the captured Russian-Israeli soldier who was murdered and beaten to death in Ramallah, capital of the Palestine Authority, were broadcast in 2000 on Arab and international television, along with images of the young Russians who died in the suicide bombing in 2001 in the disco on the boardwalk in Tel Aviv.

Netanya remains a special place for Mrs. Shifrin-Poltinnikova. On June 22, 1989, a ceremony took place in that city to mark the dedication of a new street in her father's name. Dr. Izhak Ben-Khanan (Poltinnikov) was a physician and a scientist, a veteran of World War II, and an *aliyah* activist who died on July 1, 1986, in Israel. His wife and a daughter died in Russia after eight years of prolonged hunger strikes; they had tried to force the government to give them exit visas, and the Soviets had refused.

Netanya has come a long way since its founding in 1929 as a *moshava* by forty young people of the Bnei Binyamin Association. Once it was a center of diamond polishing, especially in the 1940s when diamond merchants from German-occupied Belgium arrived in the country. The diamond industry eventually moved to Tel Aviv. Netanya did not sit on its laurels, however, it reinvented itself as a tourist town.

Like most towns in Israel, it has suffered its share of heinous Arab terrorist attacks, including a suicide bombing on the town's Park Hotel in 2002 that took 22 lives and wounded 140 at a Passover *seder*.

Netanya is named after U.S. Jewish philanthropist, Nathan Straus (1848–1931), son of Lazarus Straus. Nathan and hs brother, Isidor, became co-owners of R. H. Macy & Co. in 1896.

In Netanya stands the Wingate Institute, the National Sports Institute of Israel, which was named after British-born Major General Orde Wingate (1903–44). In the 1930s, Wingate trained members of Haganah, the pre-Israel self-defense units now known as the IDF (Israel Defense Forces). The Wingate Institute, located on 120 acres of landscaped grounds, prepares Israel's Olympic athletes as well as the country's sports instructors and teachers. Free tours are offered (www.wingate.org.il).

Randy's and Jeanette's eyes lit up as we watched the athletes practice, especially the skilled Israeli Olympic female volleyball team.

"I'd hate to be on the other side of the net when they slam-dunk a shot," I said to myself.

Wingate was born in India into a nonconformist family. He served in Palestine during the 1936–39 Arab uprising, and fought the Arab terrorist campaign, particularly the attacks on the Iraq Haifa pipeline for which he was awarded the DSO. As noted in chapter 5, he was a popular supporter of the Jewish cause; indeed, he gained the confidence of the leaders and soldiers of Haganah. They referred to him as *Hayedid* ("the friend"). He helped Haganah form special night squads and used unorthodox but highly successful tactics in countering and preventing Arab attacks. In fact, the Israel War of Independence was mostly fought at night, a lesson learned by Haganah from Wingate.

In March, 1944, Wingate operating from bases in India helped train Allied brigades, referred to as Chindits, to penetrate behind Japanese lines in Burma. On board a U.S. air force bomber, he flew to assess several established Chindit bases in Burma. But the aircraft crashed in northeast India and he and the American crew were killed. Originally buried at the crash site, his remains and those of the other victims were transferred in 1947 to the British Military Cemetery in India. But in 1950, all the remains of those on board the flight were reinterred at Arlington National Cemetery in keeping with the custom of repatriating remains in mass graves to the country of origin of the majority of the personnel.

A children's village on the slopes of Mount Carmel is named *Yemin Orde,* in his honor, as is Wingate Square in Jerusalem, and a forest planted by the Jewish National Fund on the slopes of Mount Gilboa. His wife Lorna, although a Christian, was a leader of *Youth Aliyah* in Britain.

Over the next ten days—with necessary breaks, as you just can't tour every day with kids—we made it to Yad Vashem, the Tank Museum, Mini-Israel, Masada, the Dead Sea, Haifa's Carmel Center, Tel Aviv port, Weizmann Institute, Safed, and the place I really wanted to show my grandson—Tiberias. *Benny's Ma'abara,* where I slept overnight in 1952.

Somehow I have an affinity for towns and cities that others think are ugly. My travel maxim remains: If you enjoy a city and have a good time there, then it must be beautiful. "Don't judge a book by its cover" can also be a travel motto.

Tiberias, population 41,000, is not known for its glamour. However, in the last decade it has become a tourist center, home to several luxury hotels, cafes, first-class restaurants, hot springs, and beautiful boat rides on the Sea of Galilee (Lake Kinneret).

"Come here for fun and sun," declare the town's promotional brochures, which enhance the city as a lakeside resort. Most tourists come here to see what is one of the most breathtaking lakes in Israel, the Sea of Galilee, or Lake Kinneret—*Yam Kinneret* in Hebrew, because it's shaped like a *kinnor,* or harp. From Tiberias, I can see across to the Golan Heights, thriving with vineyards and farms and still part of Israel.

Located high above beautiful Lake Kinneret, Tiberias sits on the lake's western shore, approximately 9 miles from the northern tip of the Kinneret, and approximately 6 miles from the lake's southern tip.

I asked someone where the *ma'abara* (transit camp) was located. I don't dare say it was once called *Benny's*—(my nickname back in the 1950s)—*Ma'abara.* "There," says an older man, pointing into the distance, a man who looks like he does not want to recall sad things.

"Where was it, exactly?" I asked another. Someone remembered that it was way up on the hill. But now, in place of the *ma'abara,* middle-class houses dot the area known as "Tiberias elite." The houses are already showing their age, the white paint fading away under the glare of the hot summer sun.

One thing is for sure: The *ma'abara* may be gone, but the view has been here for thousands of years. It's the same view of the city that I saw that day over fifty years ago when I stood atop the hill on the old road to Afula. Breathtaking!

As capital of the region, Tiberias moves full speed ahead; it's a busy place, with tourists constantly pouring into this metro area, making it difficult to even find a parking space on the narrow downtown streets, which have parking meters but few garages.

The idyllic landscape surrounding the lake dates back 5,000 years, and witnessed the birth and spread of Christianity. It is particularly important to Christians "because it was here that the major part of the ministry of Jesus, as it has been recorded, was spent," according to John Bowker in *Aerial Atlas of the Holy Land*.

Tourists saunter along the boardwalk that passes by myriad seafood restaurants. One of the best is Decks Restaurant, which features delicious barbecue, whether it's grilled chicken, St. Peter's fish, or steak. This establishment, one of the most enjoyable first-class restaurants in Israel, sits on a long deck that juts out over the lake. The waves lap against the covered pier. The food is barbecued over citrus wood, olive wood, and American hickory imported from Georgia. Lamb is a specialty in this restaurant that will long be remembered for its magical atmosphere.

By all means take a romantic boat ride, day or night, and enjoy the beautiful setting. You can either watch the water-skiers and windsurfers or join in the fun.

In the War of Independence, Tiberias, with its 4,000 Jewish residents, became the first town of mixed population in the country to become all Jewish. The battle for the city was over in forty-eight hours, according to Benny Morris in *1948: A History of the First Arab-Israeli War*. The Arab notables, "perhaps on their own initiative, perhaps heeding British advice, decided on an evacuation of the population," wrote Morris.

Tiberias is considered one of four holy Jewish cities. Here is buried Rabbi Akiva, "one of the most outstanding *tannaim,* probably the foremost scholar of his age," according to *Encyclopaedia Judaica*. Later in his career, Akiva was imprisoned by the Romans for openly teaching the Torah in defiance of their edict. He gave enthusiastic support to the second war against the Romans, hailing the leader, Bar Kochba. He defied Emperor Hadrian's edict against teaching Torah. At the age of about ninety, he was condemned to death and executed by the Romans in Caesarea. According to Jewish sources, the torture consisted of tearing his skin off with iron combs. With his dying breath, he pronounced the last word of the Shema prayer: *echad (one)*.

Tiberias was founded as a Jewish city sometime around 20 CE by Herod Antipas, son of Herod the Great, who made it the capital of his realm in Galilee. The city was named in honor of the Roman emperor, Tiberius.

"From Moses to Moses, there were none like Moses." In Tiberias, Randy and I stood at the tomb of the *Rambam,* from the acronym, Rabbi Moshe ben Maimon, reading these words on his tombstone *"From Moses to Moses, there were none like Moses."* The first Moses was the prophet Moses who spoke to God on Mount Sinai; the second was the Rambam, Moses Maimonides. I visited what purports to be his residence in Fez, Morocco. As a physician, he journeyed to Eretz Israel, then to Alexandria, and then to Fostat, the old city of Cairo.

"As a *halakhist* and philosopher, Maimonides was the leading intellectual figure of medieval Judaism," says *The New Encyclopedia of Judaism,* adding, "his major *halakhic* work, *Mishneh Torah (The Second Torah)* is universally accepted as one of the most important compendia of Jewish law of all ages." The issues raised in his major philosophic work, *The Guide for the Perplexed,* "set the tone for Jewish philosophic discussion and controversy for hundreds of years."

Maimonides died on December 13, 1204, in Fostat. His remains were taken to Tiberias for burial and many pilgrims visit his grave. We joined the visitors in saying a prayer at his tomb.

Lake Kinneret merges with the Jordan River, and three of the most famous kibbutzim are located here: Degania Aleph, Degania Bet, and Kinneret. All three kibbutzim were attacked in the War of Independence. Degania Aleph still displays the Syrian tank it captured during that war.

Degania was founded in 1909 on the banks of the river Jordan, south of the Sea of Galilee. The Arabs called the area *Umm Jouni,* and the settlers Hebraized the name to Degania, according to Murray Weingarten in his book, *Life in a Kibbutz.* "Their idea," wrote Weingarten, was "to set up a communal settlement which would be an outpost of Zionist colonization in Palestine."

No question—the kibbutzim played a dominant role in settling the country. They went where no one else would tread. Although their members made up only about 4 percent of the population, they held prominent places in the military and politics.

Before we left Tiberias and headed back to Tel Aviv, Randy planted a tree in the Jewish National Fund (JNF) forest at the religious Kibbutz Lavi, near Tiberias, in memory of his other grandmother, Sharon. Then we headed south down Route 6, an express, toll-highway, three lanes each side which runs from south of Haifa to near Be'er Sheva.

Certain sounds come to mind when I think of Tel Aviv as it was back in the 1950s: First, there was the voice of the bus driver announcing the final stop, with a loud, guttural "Tel Aviv, Tel Aviv!" The drivers were usually tall, dark, and handsome, with handlebar mustaches, and they wore khaki shorts and shirts and sandals. No one, from teachers to business executives to the mayor, wore a tie in those days, which was called a *dag maluach* in Hebrew (a herring). Then there was the sound of the street vendors with their pleading sales pitch: *garinim, botnim* (seeds, nuts), *garinim, botnim*. Yes, Tel Aviv: Just saying that city's name conjures up the magic of that city, with its favorite haunts and shouts.

If you were a teenager who had lived on an austerity diet during the 1950s, good, old-fashioned ice cream fulfilled a deep desire. The Brooklyn Ice Cream Bar, on Allenby Street, was a favorite haunt: American-made ice cream, tables and chairs out on the sidewalk. A woman from Brooklyn ran it, and we spoke English to her. Kalman Goldner, of Givatayim, one of the foremost tour guides in Israel, recalls that her ice cream was something quite different for Israelis.

Tel Aviv ranks high among the world's best cities for art, music, and culture. Whether you crave night life or golden beaches, it's all here. "Hedonistic," as some put it, especially Sheinkin Street, which today is very "in" for small restaurants, cafes, and bars.

A trip highlight for this writer, but especially for Randy, was the Memorial Site and Armed Corps Museum in Latrun, otherwise known as the Tank Museum (www.yadlashiryon.com). This Taggart fort still shows scars (bullet and shell holes in the walls) of the tough battles fought over it during the War of Independence, when the IDF could not take Latrun.

Fortunately, the Israelis found an alternative supply route to West Jerusalem. They called it the Burma Road, and it followed a series of dirt paths which the Israelis discovered, according to Benny Morris in *1948: The First Arab-Israeli War.* Jordan held Latrun until the Six-Day War.

Fitting that the Tank Museum was placed on this very spot in honor of the Israelis who fell in battle at Latrun.

Randy and Jeanette eagerly climbed up onto every tank displayed in the courtyard: Shermans, Centurions, and Israel's own Merkava. I didn't have to ask how they felt about this site; you could see it on their faces and hear it in their language: "Cool!"

⌒

"If I forget thee, O Jerusalem, let my right hand forget its cunning."

Psalms, Chapter 137

⌒

"Today I went to Jerusalem and saw the holiest place in Jewish history," Randy wrote in his journal about the trip to the *Kotel*, the Western Wall. "So much history ... holiness ... praying ... touching the Wall," Randy told me with an awesome look on his face as we walked around the square. He took pictures with Israeli soldiers; they all look so proud.

Randy has visited the Holocaust Museum in Washington, D.C. After spending two hours at Yad Vashem (www.yadvashem.org), we entered the Hall of Names. He searched but couldn't find his great-great-grandparents' names. "I'll work on it from home," he said.

At Yad Vashem, we met Rabbi Yisrael Meir Lau, the former Ashkenazi chief rabbi, who that day was honoring the late Feodor Mikhailichenko as "Righteous Among the Nations." The man saved the rabbi's life, and Mikhailichenko's daughters are present to accept a medal. We take a photo of Rabbi Lau and Randy.

The City of Jerusalem has remained the spiritual capital of the Jewish people throughout the ages. Jews have always resided in Jerusalem, even if only a few. This sacred city has always been the focus of the Jewish faith, and Jews have always prayed for the city within walls built by the Ottoman sultan Suleiman.

When I was in Israel in the early 1950s, the Arab Legion held the Old City. Jerusalem was divided. We could spot the Jordanian soldiers because they wore their red *kafiyas* as they positioned themselves atop the walls of the Old City. In front of them was the barbed wire in no-man's-land which divided the city for nineteen years, until the Six-Day War when Jordan attacked Israel. Today Jerusalem is united, one city, the capital of Israel.

Actually, *Ynetnews Travel* reported that Jerusalem ranks among the top ten cities in the world according to a recent massive online poll conducted by the travel site, TripAdvisor. The capital was described as having "profound cultural and historical significance."

Next, we visited a must-see on any tour: the *Chain of Generations* program and its striking glass sculptures, artistic illuminations, and video presentations (www.thekotel.org). We began a forty-minute walk through exhibits recalling generations of Jewish history. Here we experienced the continuous chain of generations beginning with the story of Abraham and Sarah, and we learned about the centrality of Jerusalem. Then we went on the informative tour through the Western Wall tunnel which parallels the entire length of the Temple Mount.

Randy was moved, he said, "because there is so much history behind that Wall."

Before the tour, following custom, we kissed the wall. It was cold, but its stones have nourished the Jewish heart for centuries. We prayed and inserted our notes into the ancient crevices.

The Western Wall extends 1,601 feet, of which some 197 feet constitutes what today is commonly known as the *Kotel*. According to most opinions, the Wall is a retaining wall for the Temple Mount.

"Prayers at the Western Wall should never be taken lightly," says Jay Levinson in his book, *Jewish Journeys in Jerusalem: A Tourist's Guide*. "The wall should never become just another tourist site," he declares.

In the tunnel, one can see the variety of stones used to build the Western Wall. The tunnel's exit brings the visitor to the Via Dolorosa, north of the temple.

⌒

Mahane Yehuda on Agrippas Street is a city retail produce market that turns into an experience during which one can observe and find a seemingly endless supply of fresh fish, fruits, and vegetables; baked goods, nuts, and candy; and delicacies such as smoked and pickled fish and falafel. Vendors let you taste their goods. It's an experience—a place to buy something to eat from a piece of fruit to an entire meal, and to enjoy the hustle and bustle of the market which has served Jerusalemites since the Ottoman Empire before World War I.

From the market, I usually go to the nearby *Ima Restaurant,* 189 Agrippas Street, where I partake of Middle Eastern cuisine: salads, *hummus, baba ghanoush,* as well as main courses of *kibbeh,* stuffed grape leaves, and stuffed peppers. Not only do I have a delicious meal but I also end up chatting with foreign journalists, usually from *Haaretz* and BBC.

⌒

Young people are aware of danger, too.

"Are there Arabs over there?" Randy asked during our long drives, sometimes near the border.

"Yes, there are," we answered, but we comforted him with the reassurance that Israel has good security, and the fact that all Arabs are *not* terrorists. It's not righteous to hate an entire people. That point was made—without words—when a friendly Arab taxi driver in Jerusalem dropped us off to pick up our car at a parking lot. He added, after we asked directions, "Follow me," going out of his way to guide us out of Jerusalem.

Jerusalem rivals Tel Aviv in shopping, too. We head to Mamilla Street in the capital where Randy found a temporary resting place in the Nike store. Mamilla is home to one of Israel's outstanding pedestrian malls, full of fashionable boutiques, cafes, and sports stores. It reminds me of rue du Faubourg Saint-Honoré in Paris or sections of Fifth or Madison avenues in New York City.

Until 1967, Jerusalem was divided, with the walled city of Jerusalem in Jordanian hands. Considered part of Jordan and garrisoned by soldiers of Jordan's British-founded Arab Legion, the Old City and the Western Wall were cut off from the Jews, who lived in the modern part of the city.

I recalled that a few years before I first visited Israel, when I was still in high school in Pittsburgh, I worked in the post office. During a break I went next door to a pub to watch Edward R. Murrow discussing Jerusalem and mentioning the "Wailing Wall," which prompted a few guys at the end of the counter to say that the Jews "have been wailing ever since." I am not sure they would say that today; then again, they might.

Certainly a landmark of the capital of Israel is the King David Hotel. I walked from this hotel the first time I visited the Wall, on July 2, 1967. It was an auspicious occasion, to say the least; I felt I was blessed to touch the Wall of my people.

They say that the streets of a city contain memories. If so, King David Street is very special to residents and visitors alike. Standing tall at No. 23, in all its majesty, is the King David Hotel, now celebrating its seventy-fifth year. The name is fitting; after all, King David chose Jerusalem as the capital of Israel in about 1000 BCE.

The hotel's location is superb. Across the street is the towering YMCA. It's only a twenty-minute walk to the Old City and the Jaffa Gate, and another ten minutes or so will bring one to the Western Wall. One can stroll to nearby fine restaurants and shopping. Another of the hotel's neighbors on King David Street is Hebrew Union College, at No. 13. Physically, the hotel stands on the crest of a hill that overlooks the Old City. A wonderful view fixes one's eyes on the Tower of David, the walls of Jerusalem, and the Old City. Some of the rooms on the side of the building that faces the Old City have balconies. If you are lucky enough to snare one of these rooms, you can let your historical imagination run wild. You won't have to say "If I forget thee, O Jerusalem"—at least from a non-spiritual point of view. The King David opened in 1931 and has never lost its majesty. It remains Israel's flagship hotel and has guarded its reputation ever since.

In 1946–47, the *Yishuv* (Jewish residents in Palestine before the State of Israel) entered upon a long struggle against the British. So-called illegal boats carrying the survivors of the Holocaust continued to arrive on the shores of Palestine. The British stopped them from entering the Jewish homeland. Cracking down on Jewish resistance, the English pulled off "Black Saturday" on June 29, 1946, when members of the Jewish Agency Executive were arrested. The men of London searched the kibbutzim to take away arms needed by the Jews to defend themselves against the Arabs. Besides looking for guns and ammunition, they were also trying to do extensive damage to the will of the Jews.

Tensions reached new heights when on July 22, 1946, the Irgun Zvai Leumi blew up the British Army headquarters, the Secretariat of the Palestine Government in the King David Hotel. The British disregarded the warning that gave them a half-hour to evacuate the building. Ninety-one persons were killed and forty-five injured, including government officials, civilians, Britons, Jews, and Arabs. Kol Yisrael, Haganah's radio station, denounced "the heavy toll of lives caused by the dissidents' operation."

Today one can barely notice the seam in the southwestern corner of the hotel, to the right of the front entrance. This was the entire wing that housed British government and military offices, which had to be rebuilt. The two top floors were added later.

~

Heading north, we felt we had to chill out a bit, so we stopped at Carmel Forest Spa Resort near Haifa, considered by many to be the best spa in the country. Even U.S. senators know where to go in Israel to unwind after a long flight, a lot of touring, meetings, speeches, and discussions. Take Senator Joseph Lieberman of Connecticut, a staunch supporter of Israel, and his wife, Hadassah, whom we met here.

"We're on vacation," said Mrs. Lieberman as the couple moved about this luxurious spa with its two swimming pools, authentic Turkish bath, wet and dry saunas, a sophisticated fitness room, and tennis courts. Nestled high up in the Carmel forest, the spa's motto is "A vacation for mind, body and soul. Relaxing, pampering and rejuvenating." We stress the word *pampering*.

The health and fitness craze of the 1990s has developed into the spa trend of the twenty-first century here in Israel, too. Carmel Forest Spa Resort offers many health-oriented programs in a vacation setting, with everything from bodybuilding equipment to nutritional philosophy. What makes this spa unique for both Israelis and Americans is the fact that in such a small country, it is truly away from everything. The setting is beautiful—truly a place where you can "chill out."

Unlike many such institutions, Carmel Forest Spa offers two-day stays instead of a week. Israelis live with a lot of tension, and it's harder for them to get an entire week off from work (and if they do, they usually go abroad). Many American tourists end their hectic tours in Israel at the spa to rest and take advantage of the ninety-plus health and beauty treatments offered. And the staff speaks English, too.

The daily schedule has much to offer. The first day here, we were able to choose from a range of activities, including an advanced fitness walk; a class for swimming improvement; a stretching lesson; body shaping or aqua aerobics in the indoor swimming pool; or a belly-dancing workshop. On the second day, we could choose from beginning yoga; back-pain prevention exercises; a lecture on nutrition and health; *tai chi; chi kong;* and meditation. At night we could attend a lecture or peek into the world of card reading. Needless to say, we took advantage of many of the options. The spa is only fifty minutes from Tel Aviv and twenty minutes from Haifa center (www.isrotel.co.il).

⁓

Driving up north in the Lower Galilee, I told Randy that I had lived for a year in the Huleh Valley up north, where there was nothing but malaria-infested swamps. The *halutzim* (pioneers) drained them and established kibbutzim in the area called the Upper Galilee.

It all comes back to me at this point—memories of an earlier trip when I went back to Kibbutz Kfar Blum, my home in 1952. Once, this kibbutz was known as Kibbutz Anglo-Balti, composed of settlers from the U.S. and the Baltic countries. Later it was named after a Jewish prime minister of France, Leon Blum.

To this day, I can remember most of the names of the kibbutzim near Kfar Blum, Upper Galilee, where I had lived for a year: Amir, Shamir, Maayan Baruch, Dan, Dafne, Lahavot Habashan, and, of course, Gonen, in the lower foothills of the Golan Heights. In the early 1950s, I watched that kibbutz being established in the Galilee. I witnessed the trucks driving in, the prefabs and tents being set up, and young people arriving to establish their home.

I hadn't been back to Kibbutz Kfar Blum in the Upper Galilee for fifty years, and did I ever get the shock of my life when I returned. In the middle of the dining room stood a computer-terminal cash register manned by a woman who was punching out the price of food items for members and their guests and debiting the purchase from the kibbutz member's account. The presence of such a machine certainly contradicted all the ideals of the kibbutz. How could they do such a thing? The kibbutz, after all was socialist and egalitarian!

In his classic book, *Life in a Kibbutz,* Murray Weingarten wrote: "No money was to be used within the community; the group as a whole was to assume responsibility for agricultural production and provide for all the community services and all the individual needs of the membership. There was to be no private property. No hired labor was to be employed. . . . All profit, if there was any profit, was to be ploughed back into the future of the settlement and of the Zionist cause."

Michael Livni, now of Kibbutz Lotan, explains that the world has changed, and Israel has had to change along with it. Newcomers are now absorbed by urban cities such as Karmiel, Be'er Sheva and Kiryat Shmona. "The kibbutz was no longer as necessary for securing borders and unsettled areas," he wrote.

The challenge of absorbing mass immigration played a big part in the weakening of the institution. Even as early as 1952, the government implored these agricultural collectives to employ hired help—also a negative, according to kibbutz ideology. I myself watched every day as groups of immigrants from Arab countries came to Kfar Blum to work in the fields and were paid wages; "hired help" they were called.

Livni insists that the kibbutzim were no longer guided by the principles of their original vision. Most have been privatized, even renting out or selling some of their homes.

Another shock, of course, came when I purchased some goods at a small *makolet* (supermarket), where members and guests bought necessities. No such institution in the old days. Then, everyone ate free in a kibbutz. The conventional wisdom was that a guest could stay three days, but after that, you'd have to work to live up to the ideals of the kibbutz.

In the 1980s Israel moved from a democratic socialist economy to a free market one. With that came new conservative governments that did not subsidize the kibbutz movement. Moreover, Israel began to transform itself into an industrial, high-tech-based economy. This weakened the kibbutz movement. As a result, most kibbutzim adapted and privatized. Kibbutz Ein Harod exported high-tech equipment to Europe. Kibbutz Beit Hashita built a packing factory for olives and pickles and shipped them to U.S. supermarkets.

Another way to bring in much-needed revenue for kibbutzim was to build guesthouses. Location, location, location also applies to these guesthouses, which are actually hotels. Pastoral Kfar Blum happens to offer one of the best; the hotel likes to describe itself as "four-star with five-star service." Its 130 spacious rooms and 10 suites are well up to American and European standards. The man who brought this successful hotel to fruition was the late Saadia Gelb, author of *The Chase Is the Game: The Journeys of an American-Israeli Pioneer.* Gelb, raised in America, emigrated with his family to Israel in 1947. Although trained as a rabbi, he worked as a tractor driver, fisherman, youth leader, and hotel manager. The hotel opened on January 8, 1963, with five rooms.

American tourists certainly feel at home here in the garden setting. At day's end, I watched them get out of their tour buses, vans, and rental cars. Weary from a day's sightseeing, hiking, and swimming in local pools or sections of the biblical Jordan river, they now see a different Israel, where it is calm—where one can view the everlasting Mount Hermon and hear the melodic birds of the Huleh Valley, a birders' paradise, or have a coffee in a local town cafe.

Despite all the noise, the kibbutz movement—now numbering about 275 kibbutzim, with about 125,000 members—will not fade into oblivion. Not if Michael Livni and Alex Cicelsky and the sixty souls of Kibbutz Lotan have their way. Located in the desert, about 40 miles north of Eilat, this cooperative kibbutz is the most unusual one this writer has seen in half a century of traversing the Jewish state. Established by the youth division of the Reform Movement of Judaism, Kibbutz Lotan is a congregation of the Israel Movement for Progressive Judaism (www.kibbutzlotan.com).

Pulling up to the entrance either by car, taxi, or regional bus, the place does not resemble the well-to-do entryways of the more-established kibbutzim up north. But looks can be deceiving. A different kind of "richness" mingles here with the desert wind. Walking along the sidewalks, strolling in the eco park and migratory bird reserve, visiting the synagogue and talking to young people from all over the world, one inhales spirituality and a deep desire to spread the message of *Tikkun olam* (repairing the world).

I watched these *halutzim* (pioneers) as they recycled organic waste, reused solid waste, and built houses with tires, clay mud, and straw bales. For those seeking a different type of vacation or work period, Kibbutz Lotan is a good suggestion. Visitors can take an in-depth tour to learn about the Kibbutz Lotan community and environmental development work that takes place here in the south of Israel, including hands-on workshops organic gardening and natural building, which means building with recycled materials.

With pride, Livni took me on a guided natural history tour around the kibbutz to gain insight into the unique flora, fauna, geology, archaeology, and modern history of the region. I ate kosher food in the stark dining hall, visited the synagogue, watched birders sitting at Lotan's migratory bird reserve and its ringing stations. I talked to young people from all over the world who wanted to do something about being "green."

I met interns who are part of the Green Apprenticeship Permaculture Design Program, which works with Friends of the Earth (Israeli, Palestinian, and Jordanian youth education). The people of Lotan say that they are fulfilling the biblical ideal to till the earth and preserve it.

"We always considered ourselves [to be] creating and living as a Liberal Jewish Zionist Community," says Cicelsky, a founder of the nearly thirty-year-old desert kibbutz. "But it's tough to live here a long time. It takes a certain determination," says Livni, who in his golden years left another kibbutz to seek new challenges and work in Lotan where daily he can view the red-tinted mountains of Edom to the east and deep canyons westward.

Cicelsky notes that over the years, "Many felt isolated ... from the populated Israeli 'north,' and left and went home. But they encountered some or all of our ideals, and many have taken what they have learned and experienced with them. They joined or created communities of many flavors in Israel and the world." Today, tourists can taste those different flavors.

While Lotan's facilities are not five-star luxury-hotel, the kibbutz does contain country lodging suited for individuals, families, and youth groups. The "management" says that three stars will do for their more than twenty air-conditioned guest rooms with kitchenettes, bathrooms, and a central kosher kitchen. Guests can take their meals with the community in the kosher dining room for the full kibbutz experience. The Watsu Center, Magic Mud Building, bird reserve, and the Center for Creative Ecology are all part of the kibbutz, which produces delicious yogurts and cheeses made from their goats' milk.

On location is a solar-powered tea house that serves light meals during the day and is available for catering gourmet kosher dairy meals. This establishment also houses a store with artwork, Judaica, pottery, and jewelry made by community members and local artists.

"*Tikkun olam* is to live in the Negev desert, a tremendous challenge . . . especially when considering environmental impact," notes Cicelsky. "We strive to make Jewish communal living creative, vibrant, and relevant." Indeed! In fact, there is a waiting list of people interested in moving to Lotan.

"I think what is most interesting and unique about Lotan is that it allows visitors an opportunity to experience a community that is attempting to deal with modern issues of religion, consumerism, resource use, and education in a creative and holistic way," adds Cicelsky.

And where are future Israelis going to live? Today the Negev represents 66 percent of the land and only 14 percent of the population. Without shade and water, the Negev would perish and revert to the desert. Indeed, I quickly became conscious of the desert. It's calm and quiet here compared to up north. Here in the desert one can feel the history of Israel. I remember that 10,000 people once lived in the nearby Masada area. Determination has always been the watchword of Livni and all Israelis.

Regarding security involved in visiting Israel, everyone makes their own calculations. But security is tight. Still, we decided that we wouldn't go to malls or crowded restaurants, or ride on buses. However, within hours of our arrival, we did all three. Livni reveals that when he lived in Jerusalem, he rode Bus No. 18, a popular target of terrorists. Foolhardy, some say, while others declare that this is how a nation builds inner strength and character.

Leaving the kibbutz, we rode with Sasson Sasson, owner of a taxi service. Every nation has its country mice and city mice. Sasson espouses the country. This entrepreneur shepherds tourists around Eilat in his new, immaculately kept Mercedes. Like Israel's first prime minister, David Ben-Gurion, who compared Tel Aviv to Sodom and Gomorrah, Sasson disparages the big metropolis. After his retirement from government, Ben-Gurion settled on a kibbutz in the Negev to set an example. Sasson tells me he's afraid "of being mugged in Tel Aviv." I explained that cities go through cycles. "Reminds me of New York in the 1970s," I told him. "It's a phase. The Big Apple is much better now."

But Sasson may be correct: Crime is up in Israel. An executive in Tel Aviv told me that roving gangs reconnoiter office buildings and grab computers. Sadly, he lost his laptop to thieves while on a bathroom break.

Highly recommended to me was a jeep safari. Sitting around a small campfire, baking fresh pita bread, smearing it with thick chocolate, and washing it all down with hot mint tea was a desert experience that I will never forget.

Israel has its own drug problem—so much so that some families look for every possible opportunity to provide experiences that will strengthen their child's resistance to drugs. Sometimes this occurs in the strangest places.

On our trek through the desert at Eilat as part of our safari, our deeply tanned, hardened, sharp-tongued guide, a veteran of several of Israel's wars, talked to us around the small fire. For the life of me, I don't recall how it came up, but the guide divulged that he had been hooked on drugs, but has been clean for many years. Why he would disclose that is beyond me, but the Israeli parents in the group loved it; they pushed him to elaborate on his story.

"Don't try it," he told the audience as the sun went down over the darkening mountains. "Don't be tempted," he added as the light of the campfire reflected on the steep walls of the cliffs and the parents' worried faces. "Don't experiment," he said, as a final warning. With that, our safari ended.

I hold the picture in my hand, a color copy. Don't know what happened to the original. We are all thin, young, on the go. Our lives are ahead of us.

It's the 1950s. Our Habonim workshop group has just walked through the desert from near Be'er Sheva to the Dead Sea.

Masada is situated on an isolated rock plateau on the eastern fringe of the Judean Desert, near the western shores of the Dead Sea south of Ein Gedi. Rock by rock, we climbed Masada, a symbol of Jewish resistance. Behind us was the salty Dead Sea. I remember the exhilaration, walking with a rifle on my shoulder. Self-defense in Israel, always. Going up Masada, we hoped that we were as tough as the Israelis who were on the hike with us. The incline cable car was nonexistent.

A place of pilgrimage, the story of the epic siege of the fortress in 66 CE began when a group of Jewish zealots who started the revolt against the Romans seized Masada from them. Leader El'azar Ben Yair waited out the war at Masada and held it after the fall of Jerusalem in 70 CE. Three years later, 15,000 Roman legionnaires challenged less than 1,000 Jewish defenders. When the Romans entered Masada, they discovered the bodies of the defenders laid out in rows, repudiating defeat and refusing slavery. The men had first killed their own families and then themselves, drawing lots for a final ten to carry out the act, the last one elected killing the other nine before committing suicide.

In those youth movement days, we sang, "Masada will not fall," which can also mean, Israel will never fall. We viewed those that held out until the bitter end as heroes. Did not Ben Yair say it was better to take their own lives and the lives of their families than to live in shame and humiliation as Roman slaves?

Years later I returned with Randy, only this time we went up by cable car. Call it scheduling error, human error, driving error—but we didn't arrive until mid-afternoon, the worst possible time to visit this last bastion of Jewish freedom fighters. Fortunately, we brought water with us and drank it frequently; we also had hats and good walking shoes. Still, yours truly got doused with a bucket of water by an ever-watchful park warden. It was 120 degrees Fahrenheit.

The view from the plateau, about 1,300 feet above sea level, is unbelievable: desert and desolation, and yet someday, it may yet bloom again.

Ein Gedi is an ancient site. In the early days of history, even before the destruction of the Second Temple, life existed on plantations. Even in those days, fruit and black mud were mixed, creating cosmetics. Today a whole beauty industry thrives in Israel.

For hundreds of years, nothing lived here. Now, a kibbutz, youth hostel, and a field school of the National Parks Authority are located here. I admire the flora and fauna, the nature preserve, and the desert farming of the kibbutz, which produces various types of fruits and vegetables. Down the main road are spas and wonderful hotels, just waiting for guests to come and relax and enjoy the refreshing healing that results from the Dead Sea minerals. We try a 6:00 a.m. dip in the Dead Sea, which is now approximately 1,400 feet below sea level, making these beaches the lowest dry points on Earth.

⌒

Eilat is the only city in Israel where three countries converge: Egypt in the south and Jordan in the northeast (Akaba) meet up with Israel here. Egypt and Jordan are open and relatively easy to cross into, as long as you have correct documentation.

Eilat lives up to its travel posters. That's why they come by the tens and twenties and hundreds, each winter day, those tall Swedish, Norwegian, Finnish, Danish tourists, young Europeans seeking the warm sun of Israel's resort getaway, this glitzy playground of sun worshippers who bathe in the deep, purple-blue of the Red Sea.

Although always busy and a bit brash, Eilat flaunts itself as a happy vacationland, with sandy beaches, pear-shaped pools, and romantic lounges. "It's definitely a place to hang out," says tour guide Mike BenAvi. "It's always been a place for those who like to hike, scuba-dive, and snorkel—even snorkeling with dolphins."

When winter arrives in Europe, a mass migration of storks descends on the Holy Land. This area is a birder's paradise, positioned as the land bridge between Asia and Africa, making it one of the world's most important bird migratory routes.

As in Netanya, the French bring a cosmopolitan flair to Eilat. So many Parisians have been buying condos here that real estate agents are now distributing handouts and brochures in French. You don't have to be a rocket scientist to spot a small wave of French immigrants settling in Israel. Fed up with anti-Semitism and being called "Jew" on crowded Paris buses, French Jews are buying condos in Eilat, too.

Many Jews are leaving France, a woman told me in the breakfast hall at the Dan Eilat Hotel. The woman emigrated from North Africa during the decades of the mass Jewish exodus of the 1950s and 1960s. Then, her compatriots left without possessions from the *mellahs* of Casablanca, Fez, and Marrakech, where I have visited. Now these aristocratic-looking Jews are Israeli professionals, promenading along the boardwalk fronting the five-star hotels, walking into fine restaurants, or reclining on the chaise lounges in Eilat just as they would relax in St. Tropez or Juan-les-Pins on the Mediterranean.

The woman's sons became dentists in the French Republic. Her eyes and facial expression convey what a tragedy it would be if these French Jews had to leave a part of France a second time because of fear and anti-Semitism.

⁓

Another group that comes in large numbers once a year to Eilat are Indian Jews living in Israel and represented by the Central Organization of Indian Jews, founded in 1986 and composed of *Bene Israel*.

After discussing in earlier chapters how Russian and Moroccan Jews were faring in Israel, I was eager to learn about the Indian Jews who made *aliyah* a half-century ago. According to Noah Massil, president of the organization (formerly of Mumbai, now Jerusalem), *Bene Israel* in the Jewish state number about 50,000; Cochinis, 5,000; and Baghdadi Jews, 1,000.

"We tried to form an umbrella organization of all three communities, but failed," Massil said, reflecting on divisions of the three groups back in India. As noted in chapter 6, there are divisions and stress between these three Jewish groups in India. The *Baghdadis* are not friendly toward the *Bene Israel,* or, in the words of Massil, "The *Baghdadis* thought they were 'more Jewish' than [the *Bene Israel*]."

When founded, the main goal of the organization was "to help Indian immigrants get their rights," explained Massil, a social worker who arrived in Israel in 1970. The group maintains contact with twenty-nine branches, which meet and conduct activities.

The early years of *Bene Israel*'s absorption into Israel were marked by disputes with the rabbinate, especially dealing with whether the *Bene Israel* were, in effect, Jewish, according to *halakhah.*

"A lot of noise" was made by the Indian community, who made it clear, explained Massil, that they are Jews in every matter according to *halakhah.* They pointed to the fact that Jewish Agency for Israel representatives came to India before the *Bene Israel* emigrated, and confirmed this fact. The dispute continued for many years until it was eventually settled by the chief rabbinate. Henceforth, *Bene Israel* were recognized as Jewish.

When the first wave of Indian Jews arrived in Israel, "[T]hey did experience a singling out as Indian," wrote Maina Singh, author of *Being Israeli: Migration, Ethnicity and Gender in the Jewish Homeland.* "Some of them have stories of the initial years when they faced a color bias," she told an interviewer. However, Massil maintains that Indian Jews did not face undue problems because of this bias.

Back in India, Jews had white-collar jobs. In Israel, many settled in agricultural communities in the Negev. The Cochin Jews, for example, often had professional careers as physicians and bankers. "They spoke English well," wrote author Nathan Katz, adding, "When they came to Israel in the 1960s or 1970s, they had access to reasonable positions in Israeli society." The Cochin Jews did not face rabbinical questioning over their status as Jews.

Speaking about Cochin Jews, Katz noted that many old traditions were forgotten, although recently there has been a "resurgence of songs" in the Malayan language, with older women teaching younger ones. A Cochin women's singing group performs throughout Israel.

Indian Jews in Israel come to Eilat every year in January to celebrate *Hoduyada,* a grand cultural get-together. The group turns the celebration into a joyful weekend for this festival of Indian song and dance. Occasionally, musical artists from India perform. "Family and friends come together; it's a happening," explained Massil.

Another holiday celebrated by the community is Maharashtra Day on May 1. *Bene Israel* celebrates the occasion that honors the Indian province with Marathi dramas, songs, dance, and Indian meals. Performers fly in from Maharashtra, the state where Mumbai is located. The Indian ambassador usually attends.

In the difficult austerity years, from 1950 to 1960, very few families returned to India. Today, some go back for business or to find a spouse, just as Jews living in India travel to Israel for a spouse. As many as 20,000 Indian Jews in Israel apply each year for Indian tourist visas to visit friends and family.

India and Israel established diplomatic relations in 1992, notes Massil, who has tried to present India's views—so much so that Israeli friends have called him the ambassador of India to Israel. Massil said he left India for Israel because of his Zionism and his love for the Land of Israel. India for him is his motherland, which he never forgets, and he respects it, "as we never suffered anti-Semitism [there] as [do many Jews] in European countries."

India's *Bene Israel* Jews began arriving in Israel in the 1950s, most coming from Maharashtra. Even though Indian Jews speak Hebrew, they felt a need to revive and communicate in Marathi, the language spoken in Maharashtra. So in 1985, Massil founded the literary quarterly *Mai Boli,* which contains essays and poems in that language.

Even though they have adjusted to Israeli society, one can see that Indian Jews are still attached to India in cultural ways. One of the activities sponsored by the organization is the celebration of India's Independence Day every year on August 14. At that program Israeli-born Indian children perform Indian dances and songs.

Today, Indian Jews are located throughout Israel, though the largest numbers live in Ashdod and Haifa, each with four or five synagogues. Their integration seems complete, especially when one is told that the Indian people marry Jews from other groups. Massil pointed to his own four children who married Israelis: one was Moroccan; one, Romanian; one, Russian; and one of Syrian-Turkish background.

Glitzy Eilat flaunts itself as a happy vacationland that offers the best in underwater sports. Then there's the natural beauty of the coral reefs, the quiet of the Red Sea, and the peaceful desert surrounding the city that forces you to relax. If you want a bit more excitement, you can walk along the North Beach sea promenade. People-watch and stop at the kiosks along the way. Dine at delicious fish restaurants and munch at snack bars.

At the end of the boardwalk is a shopping mall packed with tourists, travelers, and soldiers on leave. The beach is right there for a quick dip.

Eilat, with its approximately 75,000 inhabitants, is a relatively new city. It was once considered the dead end of the world. The city's past stretches back to biblical times. *Eilat* is the modern spelling for the biblical town of Elath, which is first mentioned in Exodus when the Israelites wandered the desert. Sometimes, it is identified with biblical *Ezion-Geber,* which was situated at the head of the Gulf of Aqaba. Here, King Solomon based his Red Sea merchant fleet. Some even go so far as to say that the Israelites stopped at Eilat during the Exodus from Egypt into the Promised Land. Later, Uzziah (Azariah), king of Judah (785 to 733 BCE), rebuilt Eilat, restoring it as the port of Judah on the Red Sea.

A Jewish community probably existed here until the middle of the tenth century, and possibly until the Crusader period. By the fourteenth century, the town was almost completely destroyed, and only under Turkish rule was an attempt made to develop it.

Modern Eilat stands on the site of a one-time wasteland, which bore the Arabic name, *Umm Rashrash.* Captured by Israeli forces on March 10, 1949, in *Operation Uvdah,* it was the last military move in the War of Israeli Independence. A makeshift flag, a white sheet with a Star of David inked on it, was raised by the IDF over the abandoned police station.

In December 1948, a kibbutz was set up, and in the next few years a few buildings were erected. By 1956, a thousand residents called Eilat their home. The rest is history.

Visiting Eilat, you will see that it is surrounded by desert formations, wide spaces with amazing geological shapes and ancient archaeological sites, as well as beautifully colored cliffs one can enjoy either by driving or hiking through them. I observed the range of shades from sandy beige to rich red and dusky black on the mountains. Yes, those red-tinted mountains of Edom and deep canyons are a must-see.

⟋

With its holy sites and Mediterranean beaches, Israel has long been a tourist magnet. Not only have I encouraged Russian, Moroccan, and Indian Jews whom I have met in the diaspora to come to Israel, but I also try to get everyone I know to visit Israel. From a historical, spiritual, adventurous, or just plain fun point of view, this is a welcoming and invigorating country.

Fifty-five years after my first trip to Israel, the dramatic alterations—the skyscrapers, the four-lane express highways, the cloverleafs, the high-speed trains—have not changed the basic premise: This is a great place to live or to visit, to enjoy a vacation from which you will come away inspired and reflective on what a nation can achieve.

I agree with Martin Fletcher, special correspondent for NBC News, who in his new book, *Walking Israel: A Personal Search for the Soul of a Nation,* commented:

> This quirky, surprising complex, difficult, and disturbing country is actually a great place.... For all the attention focused on this tiny land, and all the effort spent on fixing its problems, Israel has to be the most analyzed yet least understood country in the world.... I'm convinced that Israel and its people have long gotten a raw deal in the world's eyes.

Despite the negativism toward Israel, more than 3.4 million visitors toured Israel in 2010. Who came in second place after U.S. tourists? Russia! About a half-million Russians visited the Jewish state in 2010.

On our last day in Israel, as we rested on the beach in Netanya before our nonstop flight home that night, Randy asked, "*Sabi,* maybe you can get me a surfboard?"

"But Randy, it's too big to lug on the plane," I said.

"No problem. Get it now, and we'll store it. When I come back, I'll have it."

I have no doubt he'll be back.

So will I.

Selected Bibliography

Behar, Ruth. *An Island Called Home: Returning to Jewish Cuba*. New Brunswick, NJ: Rutgers University Press, 2007.

Ben-Sasson, H.H., ed. *A History of the Jewish People*. Cambridge, MA: Harvard University Press, 1976.

Cernea, Ruth Fredman. *Almost Englishmen: Baghdadi Jews in British Burma*. New York, NY: Lexington Books, 2007.

Chouraqui, Andre N. *Between East and West: A History of the Jews of North Africa*. New York, NY: Atheneum, 1973.

Coltman, Leycester. *The Real Fidel Castro*. New Haven, CT and London, UK: Yale University Press, 2003.

Connelly, Karen. *Burmese Lessons: A True Love Story*. New York, NY: Doubleday, 2009.

Cowen, Ida. *Jews in Remote Corners of the World*. Englewood Cliffs, NJ: Prentice Hall, Inc, 1971.

Cox, Christopher R. *Chasing the Dragon: Into the Heart of the Golden Triangle*. New York, NY: Henry Holt and Company, 1996.

Crawford, Peter. *Nomads of the Wind: A Natural History of Polynesia*. London, UK: BBC Books, 1993.

Fall, Bernard B. *Hell in a Very Small Place: The Siege of Dien Bien Phu*. Cambridge, MA: Da Capo Press, 1966.

Fernandes, Edna. *The Last Jews of Kerala: The Two Thousand Year History of India's Forgotten Jewish Community*. New York, NY: Skyhorse Publishing, 2008.

Fletcher, Martin. *Walking Israel: A Personal Search for the Soul of a Nation*. New York, NY: St. Martin's Press, 2010.

Frank, Ben G. *A Travel Guide to Jewish Europe*. Third Edition. Gretna, LA: Pelican Publishing Company, 2001.

_____. *A Travel Guide to Jewish Russia & Ukraine*. Gretna, LA: Pelican Publishing Company, 2000.

_____. *A Travel Guide to the Jewish Caribbean & South America*. Gretna, LA: Pelican Publishing Company, 2005.

Frazier, Ian. *Travels in Siberia*. New York, NY: Farrar, Straus and Giroux, 2010.

Heisler-Samuels, Betty. *The Last Minyan in Havana*. Aventura, FL: Chutzpah Publishing, 2000.

Israel, Benjamin J. *The Jews of India*. New Delhi: Mosaic Books, 2004.

Karnow, Stanley. *Vietnam: A History*. New York, NY: The Viking Press, 1983.

Katz, Nathan and Ellen S. Goldberg. *The Last Jews of Cochin: Jewish Identity in Hindu India*. Columbia, SC: University of South Carolina Press, 1993.

Katz, Nathan. *Who Are the Jews of India?* Berkeley, CA: University of California Press, 2000.

Kay, Robert. *Hidden Tahiti and French Polynesia: Including Moorea, Bora Bora, and the Society, Austral, Gambier, Tuamotu, and Marquesas Islands*. Sixth Edition. Berkeley, CA: Ulysses Press, 2008.

Lak, Daniel. *India Express: The Future of the New Superpower*. Hampshire, UK: Palgrave Macmillan, 2008.

Laskier, Michael M. *North African Jewry in the Twentieth Century: The Jews of Morocco, Tunisia, and Algeria*. New York, NY: New York University Press, 1994.

Levinson, Jay. *Jewish Community of Cuba: The Golden Age 1906–1958*. Nashville, TN: Westview Publishing Co., Inc. 2006.

Meier, Andrew. *Black Earth: A Journey Through Russia After the Fall*. New York, NY and London, UK: W.W. Norton & Company, 2003.

Morris, Benny. *1948: A History of the First Arab-Israeli War.* New Haven, CT: Yale University Press, 2008.

Nordhoff, Charles and James Norman Hall. *The Bounty Trilogy,* comprising the Three Volumes, *Mutiny on the Bounty, Men Against The Sea,* and *Pitcairns Island.* Boston, MA and Toronto, CAN: An Atlantic Monthly Press Book, Little, Brown and Company, 1936.

Oz, Amos. *A Tale of Love and Darkness.* New York, NY: Harcourt, Inc., 2003.

Reich, Bernard. *A Brief History of Israel.* New York, NY: Facts on File, Inc., 2005.

Sachar, Howard M. *A History of Israel: From the Rise of Zionism to Our Time.* New York, NY: Alfred A. Knopf, Inc., 1996.

Senor, Dan and Saul Singer. *Start-Up Nation: The Story of Israel's Economic Miracle.* New York, NY and Boston, MA: A Council on Foreign Relations Book, 12, Hachette Book Group, 2009.

Sheinin, David and Lois Baer Barr, eds. *The Jewish Diaspora in Latin America: New Studies on History and Literature.* New York, NY and London, UK: Garland Publishing, Inc., 1996.

Steinberg, David I. *Burma/Myanmar: What Everyone Needs to Know.* Oxford, UK: Oxford University Press, 2010.

Sweig, Julia E. *Inside the Cuban Revolution: Fidel Castro and the Urban Underground.* Cambridge, MA: Harvard University Press, 2002.

Thant, Myint-U. *The River of Lost Footsteps: A Personal History of Burma.* New York, NY: Farrar, Straus and Giroux, 2009.

Volkov, Solomon, *St. Petersburg: A Cultural History.* New York, NY: Free Press, 1995.

Wintle, Justin, *Perfect Hostage: A Life of Aung San Suu Kyi, Burma's Prisoner of Conscience.* New York, NY: Skyhorse Publishing, 2007.

About the Author

Ben G. Frank, author, journalist, is considered one of this country's most distinguished travel writers and commentators on Jewish communities around the world.

With the publication of *The Scattered Tribe: Traveling the Diaspora from Cuba to India to Tahiti & Beyond,* he breaks new ground in reporting on far-flung exotic Jewish outposts. He is the author of *A Travel Guide to Jewish Europe,* 3rd edition, *A Travel Guide to Jewish Russia and Ukraine,* and *A Travel Guide to the Jewish Caribbean and South America.*

A former newspaper reporter with the *New Haven Register* and *Elizabeth Daily Journal,* he has published articles in *Hadassah Magazine, Reform Judaism Magazine, National Jewish Monthly of B'nai B'rith, Jewish Frontier, Jewish Telegraphic Agency, Jewish Press, Jewish Exponent, Jewish Week,* as well as *The New Haven Register, Inside Chappaqua Magazine,* and *Inside Magazine,* Philadelphia, PA.

His books have been cited and reviewed in the *New York Times,* the *Chicago Tribune, Associated Press, Pittsburgh Press,* the *Miami Herald,* and *Journal News,* White Plains, N.Y.

Frank has given talks at Jewish Book Fairs, synagogues and temples. His many lectures include, "Tolerance and Identity: Jews in Early New York, 1654–1825," at the Museum of the City of New York, as well as a talk at the 92nd Street Y. He has appeared on hundreds of radio and TV talk-shows.

He is a B.A., *cum laude* graduate of the University of Pittsburgh and an M.A. graduate of the Center of Israel and Jewish Studies, Columbia University. He has been active in such professional organizations as the National Academy of Television Arts and Sciences, the Overseas Press Club, the American Jewish Public Relations Society and the Pacific Area Travel Association.

Frank is president of The Frank Promotion Corp., a public relations firm, specializing in radio-TV talk-shows.

He lives with his wife Riva in Palm Beach County, Florida. The couple have two sons, Martin and Monte, and four grandchildren.